Connecticut Walk Book

Wesleyan University Press
Middletown CT 06459
www.wesleyan.edu/wespress
© 2017 Connecticut Forest & Park Association;
distributed by Wesleyan University Press
All rights reserved
Manufactured in the United States of America
Typeset in Sina

The Connecticut Forest & Park Association protects
forests, parks, walking trails, and open spaces for future
generations by connecting people to the land.

Library of Congress Cataloging-in-Publication Data
available upon request

5   4   3   2

Contents

Acknowledgments

The twentieth edition of the Connecticut Walk Book is a collaborative effort of many passionate and committed trail folk.

Editors: Clare Cain and Wayne Fogg.

Editorial assistance provided by: Colin Carroll, Eric Hammerling, Digger Stolz, and Lindsay Suhr.

Additional support from the CFPA staff has been invaluable: Elizabeth Fossett, Martin Gosselin, James W. Little, Kara Murphy, and Terri Peters.

CFPA would like to thank the following dedicated individuals who helped make this book possible: Peter Dorpalen, Ralph Fink, James Giana, Tim Johnson, David Leff, Anita Montanile, Lynn Mulligan, Tom Mulligan, Jeffrey O'Donnell, Louise Perrine, David Reik, Liane Stevens, and Christine Woodside. Additionally, special thanks to all of CFPA's incredible volunteer trail managers who provided important feedback and fact-checking for the book.

Cartography assistance provided by Jeff Bolton and the Farmington River Watershed Association.

Special thanks to Wesleyan University Press for their guidance and professional assistance.

This edition would not have been possible without financial support from our sponsors. Thank you for believing in the *Connecticut Walk Book*.

Last but not least, there are three special groups that we always make sure to acknowledge because of their importance to the continuity and maintenance of the trails: state, municipal, and private landowners provide the land base that hosts the trails; CFPA trail volunteers dedicate over 20,000 hours each year to work with CFPA staff to maintain the trails; and members and supporters of CFPA like you help fund the work we undertake on the trails each and every year.

Introduction

Where shall we walk today? This book was compiled to help you find that answer. Connecticut, with its rugged hills, glacial streams and lakes, and traprock ridges running up and down the Connecticut River valley, provides excellent hiking country. Although the state is densely populated, there is a surprising amount of attractive and accessible wild land. Go out for a few miles from any of the larger cities and you can soon be on a forest trail. You can drive to a distant part of the state, put in a day of good hiking, and be back in your own bed at night.

The Connecticut Forest & Park Association (CFPA) is pleased to place the twentieth edition of the *Connecticut Walk Book* in your hands, and welcome you to a community of hikers interested in the enjoyment and conservation of Connecticut's more than 825 miles of Blue-Blazed Hiking Trails. We wish the reader many happy hours afoot in the Connecticut hills.

About CFPA

Your purchase of this *Connecticut Walk Book* helps to support the Connecticut Forest & Park Association (CFPA)—the first private, nonprofit member-based organization established in Connecticut, and the founder and maintainer of over 825 miles of Blue-Blazed Hiking Trails. If you're not already a CFPA member or volunteer, please join and support our ongoing efforts. If you are already a member or volunteer, you are awesome and we thank you!

In 1929, CFPA's Trails Committee proposed a radical idea—establish and maintain hundreds of miles of walking trails by a workforce of volunteers organized and trained by CFPA. Now, ninety years later, this radical idea is still being carried forward by volunteers, members, partners, CFPA staff, and many landowners who have joined forces over time to maintain, improve, and expand the "Blue Trails."

CFPA's mission is to connect people to the land in order to protect forests, parks, and trails for current and future generations to enjoy. CFPA implements its mission through four primary activities: 1) protection of forests, parks, and trails to ensure access to important recreation lands and working forests; 2) environmental education for people of all ages to build appreciation for Connecticut's outdoors; 3) advocacy for strong environmental laws and public policies; and, of course, 4) trail stewardship to ensure the Blue-Blazed Hiking Trails continue to be the best-maintained trail network in Connecticut.

Visit CFPA online at www.ctwoodlands.org or contact our office at 860-346-TREE to learn more about our ongoing work. Hopefully your experience on the Blue-Blazed Hiking Trails will inspire you to get involved!

What Are the Blue-Blazed Hiking Trails?

The "Blue Trails" as they are often called, are hiking trails maintained by CFPA or one of its major partners. The main trails are marked with vertical rectangles painted blue known as "blazes" that identify the path. Initiated in 1929 by CFPA's Trails Committee, the trails were conceived to generate interest in land protection and open spaces. The idea was to connect people to the land via hiking trails and experience the natural beauty of the state. These trails have also been designated as official Connecticut State Greenways and are actively maintained and managed for the hiking public.

How to Use the Blue-Blazed Hiking Trails

The Blue-Blazed Hiking Trails were constructed with landowner permission and are intended for foot travel. In most state parks the Blue Trails are restricted to hiking use only. Where the trails cross private lands, hiking is usually the only allowed activity. There are sections of trail where hiking use is shared with other activities. In all other instances, use of the Blue-Blazed Hiking Trails by motorized vehicles, bicycles, horses, or other four-footed animals (except leashed dogs) is not permitted without the express authorization of the property owner. CFPA maintains a detailed policy on the use of the Blue-Blazed Hiking Trails. A copy of this policy may be requested by contacting CFPA. When in doubt, use your feet, and please follow all posted signage at trailheads.

About this Book

The information contained in this edition of the *Connecticut Walk Book* is the result of hundreds of hours of work by many dedicated individuals. Though the team took great care, they were only privileged to use the information available at the time the *Walk Book* was compiled. Due to maintenance work, relocations, and changes in natural features, the trails are constantly changing as well. For more information about current trail conditions, closures, and relocations, visit www.ctwoodlands.org.

How to Use this Book

At the end of this introduction, you will find a statewide reference map displaying the general location of all the Blue-Blazed Hiking Trails. Below you will find more information about the maps and mileage tables you will find in this book. This information is intended to be used in conjunction with our online interactive trails map. The online information is maintained regularly and is our most up-to-date data. There you can get Google Maps directions to trailhead parking and learn about trail closures or relocations.

You can throw this book in your backpack and take it with you on your hike. To lighten your load, make a copy of just the trail chapter you need (secured inside a ziplock bag to protect it from the elements), or take a picture of the maps and mileage tables you'll want to reference with your smartphone.

Trail Maps

Each of the major trails has one or more trail maps depicting its location, length, and the surrounding area. These maps are compiled with data from a variety of sources including the Connecticut Department of Energy and Environmental Protection (DEEP), the Department of

Emergency Services, property data from towns, ownership and trail data from partners, elevation data from the national database, and trail data collected by CFPA personnel. Because the information is derived from different sources, there are bound to be both inconsistencies and inaccuracies. In all cases, we have done our very best to reflect the actual conditions on the ground. If you find an inconsistency or inaccuracy when you are out on the trail, please contact CFPA to let us know.

Refer to the Master Legend for an explanation of the elements depicted on the trail maps. The legend will be integral to your hike planning and your understanding of the symbols on the map.

Mileage Tables

Mileage tables are included for our longer trails. Because these tables typically refer to specific points on the corresponding maps, we suggest that maps and mileage tables be used in conjunction with one another. Using these items will not only help you avoid getting lost or disoriented, but also will help you get more out of your hike. Mileage tables are oriented from south to north or east to west, depending on the particular trail. Please note that not all items indicated on the mileage table are represented on the maps, and vice versa.

Local Trails

Occasionally, other area trails or trail systems are depicted on the maps. This is for reference purposes only. We do not recommend using our maps as the definitive guide for hiking the local trails. Instead, we encourage you to visit the website of the managing organization to download or purchase its trail maps to be used in conjunction with this book; this will provide you with the full spectrum of hiking opportunities in your area of interest. We cannot attest to the accuracy of local trail data but have included it to offer other points of reference on the landscape.

Parking

Two types of parking are noted on the maps—parking lots and road shoulder parking. Parking in all areas, whether displayed in this book or not, is at your own risk. CFPA is not responsible for any damage or loss to vehicles or contents. At parking lots, please follow all posted signs regarding trailhead closures. Parking locations and availability are subject to change with the seasons, weather, and changes in land ownership. For the most up-to-date parking information, visit CFPA's interactive trails map at www.ctwoodlands.org.

Overnight Sites

There are a number of lean-tos and campsites on the Blue-Blazed Hiking Trails. CFPA does not manage most of these sites. Please plan any overnight hikes accordingly and contact the state or relevant landowner for the appropriate permits.

Private Property

Throughout the Blue-Blazed Hiking Trail System, trails travel across public, state, and private lands. Without the generosity of private landowners, these great hiking trails would not exist. Please respect all posted signs, keep pets leashed, and remain on the trail, even if private property is not immediately indicated. As guests on this land, all hikers need to be especially considerate. Carelessness by one inconsiderate trail user could cause a trail to be closed to the public.

Planning Your Hike

The Blue-Blazed Hiking Trails are generally well marked and great pride is taken in their maintenance. The following information is meant to help you take the proper precautions so that you have a safe and enjoyable hike.

Make a Plan

Use thoughtful preparation to decide where you want to go and what you hope to see. The maps and mileage tables in this book will help you plot your route. Create an itinerary before you go and leave it, along with an expected return time, with someone you trust. Pay attention to sunset and plan to return to the trailhead before dark.

Go with a Group

If you are new to hiking, consider a "guided" hike, led by CFPA volunteers, or another group hike, before heading out on your own. There are many hiking groups and clubs around the state. Connecticut Trails Day, the first weekend in June, is a great time to participate in a group hike and visit a new trail.

What's the Weather?

The weather in Connecticut varies throughout the diverse regions of the state. Check forecasts while planning your trip and before leaving. Bring appropriate clothing in case the weather changes during your hike, and do not be afraid to turn back.

What's on Your Feet and in Your Pack?

Keep your feet happy. Sturdy shoes will provide traction and help prevent injury. Wool or synthetic socks will help keep your feet dry and prevent blisters.

Pack the essentials:

- trail map
- matches/lighter
- compass
- first-aid kit
- whistle
- extra clothing (hat, mittens, and rain/wind gear)
- extra food and water
- pocket knife
- cell phone (fully charged)

Hunting Season: Orange You Glad You Wore Orange?

The prime hiking seasons in Connecticut—spring and fall—coincide with hunting seasons. Many of the Blue-Blazed Hiking Trails cross hunting areas in state forests and wildlife management areas. Yearly hunting schedules are available on the Connecticut Department of Energy and

Environmental Protection (DEEP) website. To reduce the rare incidence of hunting accidents, hikers should take the following precautions:

- Wear blaze-orange during hunting season.
- Do not wander off marked trails.
- Keep your dog leashed, equip it with an orange vest and/or attach a bell to its collar.
- Be especially mindful during prime hunting times—a half hour before sunrise and a half hour after sunset.

On the Trail

Once you are out on the trail, here are a few more things to keep in mind.

Which Way Do I Go?

Follow the blazes—the Blue-Blazed Hiking Trails are marked for daylight travel, using a system of painted "blazes" on trees, posts, and rocks. Each blaze is a rectangle of paint visible in a prominent place along the trail. The majority of the trail system is blazed in CFPA blue (similar to sky blue), but some trails within the system may be blazed with blue and an alternate color such as green, orange, yellow, red, or white. If you have walked a few minutes without seeing a blaze, retrace your steps until you locate one. Occasionally, a trail will be rerouted around hazards, land features, or private property. When your map or guidebook indicates one route but the blazes show another, follow the blazes.

Tread Lightly!

You are in the outdoors to enjoy the wild places that the trail takes you to. Please follow these basic principles to ensure the trail is in good condition for those who visit after you:

- Stay on the established trail; don't wander or shortcut.
- Pack out what you pack in. Pick up litter as you go.
- Leave what you find; don't take vegetation, rocks or other natural artifacts.

How to Read Trail Blazes

Trails in Connecticut that are maintained by Connecticut Forest and Park Association (CFPA) volunteers are marked with blazes. The standard blaze is two inches wide and six inches high, and painted on tree trunks as shown in the following diagrams. The color of the blaze on CFPA's major trails, such as the New England Trail, is light blue. Other trails, such as side, bypass, or access trails, are marked with  the standard light blue and another color to indicate a connecting or side trail. Trails maintained by CFPA in state parks may be painted a variety of colors.

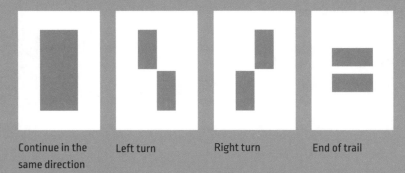

Continue in the same direction

Left turn

Right turn

End of trail

• Respect wildlife. Don't approach or disturb wild animals.
• Be considerate of other trail users.

Keep an Eye Out for Trail Hazards

There are all kinds of hazards in the woods. You can minimize your risks on the trail by being prepared, knowledgeable, and alert. Keep the following in mind as you hike:

- The trails will occasionally follow steep ridges and cliffs as well as traverse streams and unstable terrain. Pay special attention to your footing, especially during wet and inclement weather.
- During and after your hike, check your skin and scalp for ticks, which can carry Lyme disease.
- Be cautious of poison ivy, poison sumac, bees, and other wildlife on the trail.
- Consider a shorter hike, or postpone your outing entirely if the weather is extreme.
- Hiking can be a lot of work. Take frequent breaks to recharge your "batteries." Make sure to drink lots of water to adequately replenish yourself.

Help Make the Trails Even Better

CFPA staff, landowner trail hosts, and volunteers are constantly working together to maintain and improve the trails. You can play a role by alerting us if you come upon a trail problem or notice any prohibited use. For updated trail notices, to report trail problems, and to learn about upcoming hikes and trail activities, visit www.ctwoodlands.org.

You Can Volunteer to Help the Trails

CFPA volunteers dedicate over 20,000 hours each year to maintain over 825 miles of trails. If you have the time to assist ongoing efforts to steward your favorite trails, you can attend a work party, become a trail monitor, or even become one of our outstanding trail managers. More information on how to volunteer is available at our website.

The Blue Trails Challenge

The Blue Trails Challenge invites you to discover the Blue-Blazed Hiking Trail System and do something good for your body and mind. Hike any of the trails in the system and accumulate miles and memories as you go. There's no time limit; you can complete a challenge category in a single season or across your hiking lifetime. Challenge categories include: 200-miler (t-shirt), 400-miler (water bottle), and 800-miler (fleece vest).

If you're new to the trails, the Blue Trails Challenge is a chance to discover the many health benefits of hiking. And if you're already a hiker, it's another way to keep active and explore new trails outside your immediate region or in different seasons. Visit our website for our online mileage form and for additional program specifics.

CFPA Membership —Take the Next Step!

This *Walk Book* was put together by the dedicated staff and volunteers of the Connecticut Forest & Park Association (CFPA), and we ask you to please join CFPA today! The strength of our ongoing work to protect and maintain trails rests in the citizens who make up our membership. CFPA is a private, nonprofit membership organization and membership is open to all. New members are always welcome. As a member, you support CFPA's efforts in public policy, environmental education, land conservation and, of course, the Blue-Blazed Hiking Trails. All members receive a subscription to *Connecticut Woodlands* magazine, our annual *Conservation Agenda*, our annual Trails Day events booklet, and invitations to a variety of special programs and events throughout the year. Please visit www.ctwoodlands.org to join. Your support is appreciated greatly, and CFPA welcomes you to join us!

Connecticut Walk Book

Alain and May White Nature Trails, John Muir Trail, and Walcott Trail

The Alain and May White Nature Trails in Sunnybrook State Park link to the John Muir Trail in Paugnut State Forest, and the Walcott Trail in Burr Pond State Park. Together this system of interconnected trails meanders for 11.5 miles over rolling, forested terrain.

Alain and May White Nature Trails

LENGTH 4.0 miles   BLAZE COLOR Varied

The trail system in Sunnybrook State Park consists of two main trails: the Testone Boulder Loop and the Fadoir Spring Trail. The varied but gentle landscape provides ideal conditions for family hikes that can be enjoyed by all ages. A bronze plaque affixed to a boulder in the Sunnybrook State Park parking lot dedicates the trails to naturalist Jerome "Jay" Bacca of Torrington. Jay and his wife Lorrie developed the trails in the early 1980s in memory of Alain C. White and his sister May White. Together the Whites established the 4,200-acre White Memorial Foundation in nearby Litchfield and Morris, and donated substantial lands to early state forests and parks in western Connecticut. Alain White was president of CFPA from 1923 to 1928.

Testone Boulder Loop

LENGTH 1.8 miles   BLAZE COLOR Blue

The Testone Boulder Loop forms the perimeter of the Alain and May White Nature Trails. It goes through a floodplain and open forest of conifers and mixed hardwoods and passes a large glacial erratic. The trail connects to several shorter side trails featuring interesting wetlands and ponds that provide rich habitat for a variety of birds, plants, and animals.

Fadoir Spring Trail

LENGTH 0.9 miles   BLAZE COLOR Yellow

This trail forms a short loop to explore wetlands and ponds. It passes two side trails and is linked by a connector trail to the more challenging Testone Boulder Loop, providing options for longer hikes of varying difficulty.

Madden Wetlands Trail

LENGTH 0.3 miles   BLAZE COLOR White

The Madden Wetlands Trail begins and ends on the Fadoir Spring Trail. It follows an old millrace to its source at Madden Pond, leads past a mammoth freestanding boulder, and travels through open woods. The trail is named in honor of naturalist, writer, and educator William Madden (1914–1986).

Beaver Pond Loop

LENGTH 0.4 miles   BLAZE COLOR Red

The Beaver Pond Loop is characterized by the gnawed trees and beaver lodges that hikers will see along the trail.

Fyler Pond Trail

LENGTH 0.5 miles   BLAZE COLOR Orange

The Fyler Pond Trail travels through mixed hardwoods and features scenic Fyler Pond, as well as significant rock outcroppings. Hikers can use the trail to link to the Testone Boulder Trail. Formerly a peat bog, Fyler Pond was dug out with a steam shovel in the 1900s.

John Muir Trail

LENGTH 2.1 miles   BLAZE COLOR Blue

The John Muir Trail, located in Paugnut State Forest, ascends through forest to a terrain of ledges and boulders. A short side trail takes hikers to the summit of Walnut Mountain.

SIDE TRAILS

Muir/Walcott Connector

LENGTH 0.5 miles   **BLAZE COLOR** Blue/White

This connector trail provides a direct link between the John Muir Trail and the Walcott Trail, offering the opportunity for a continuous long-distance hike from Sunnybrook State Park to Burr Pond State Park. A good portion of the connector coincides with the closed section of Starks Road, which is the boundary between Paugnut State Forest to the south and Burr Pond State Park to the north.

Buttrick Trail

LENGTH 1.3 miles   **BLAZE COLOR** Blue/Red

Named for former CFPA secretary-forester and Civilian Conservation Corps supervisor Philip Buttrick, the Buttrick Trail offers a connector to the John Muir Trail from the Harris Drive parking lot of the Sue Grossman Still River Greenway that runs along Winsted Road. The Buttrick Trail also extends to connect with the unpaved segment of Guerdat Road in Paugnut State Forest.

> ▮ *Hunting is permitted in state forests intersected by this trail. Please use caution and wear orange during hunting season.*

Walcott Trail

LENGTH 2.5 miles   **BLAZE COLOR** Blue

The Walcott Trail circles Burr Pond in Burr Pond State Park and is linked to the John Muir Trail via the blue-white blazed Muir/Walcott Connector at the southern end of the pond. The area around Burr Pond abounds in hardwoods and hemlock with an understory of laurel and young striped maples, and is studded with gigantic glacial boulders. The trail features Burr Mountain Brook, laurel-lined trail sections, and wonderful picnic spots.

The trail is named in honor of Senator Frederic C. Walcott (1869–1949). In 1909, Walcott started what is now known as the Great Mountain

New footbridge constructed by volunteers on the Saugatuck Trail.
Photo courtesy Robert Andrews.

Forest with fellow Yale University graduate, Starling W. Childs. In 1913, Walcott and Childs convinced the newly formed State Park Commission to purchase 15,000 acres of "woods, lakes and mountains for the purpose of reclaiming deforested land and preserving game."

Walcott became the president of the Connecticut Board of Fisheries and Game (1923–1928), chairman of the Connecticut Water Commission (1925–1928), and was then elected to the U.S. Senate, where he served from 1929 to 1935.

Under President Franklin Delano Roosevelt, Senator Walcott served as the chairman of the Senate Committee on the Conservation of Wildlife Resources and supported the newly formed Civilian Conservation Corps. On May 24, 1933, a CCC camp named in Walcott's honor was located in the Paugnut State Forest (at what is now known as Burr Pond State Park). Camp Walcott is where Philip L. Buttrick (former board secretary of CFPA) was stationed; Buttrick was the forester that designed and built the loop trail around Burr Pond.

For more information on visiting Burr Pond State Park, visit the Connecticut Department of Energy and Environmental Protection (DEEP) website.

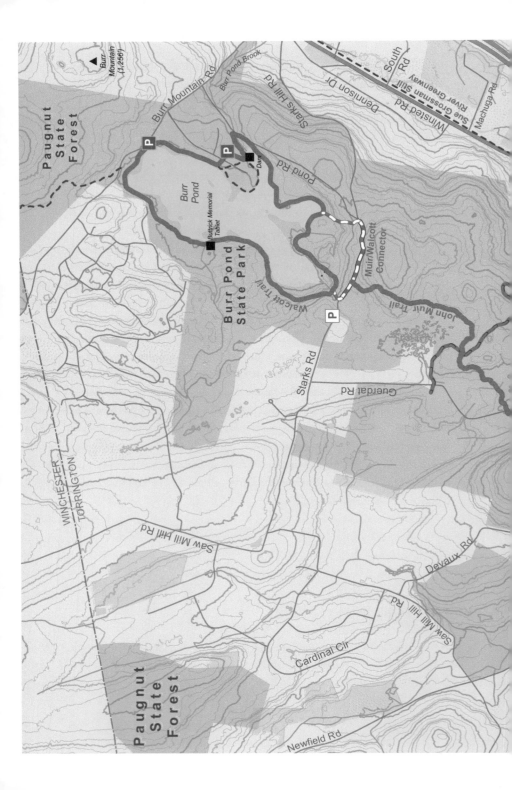

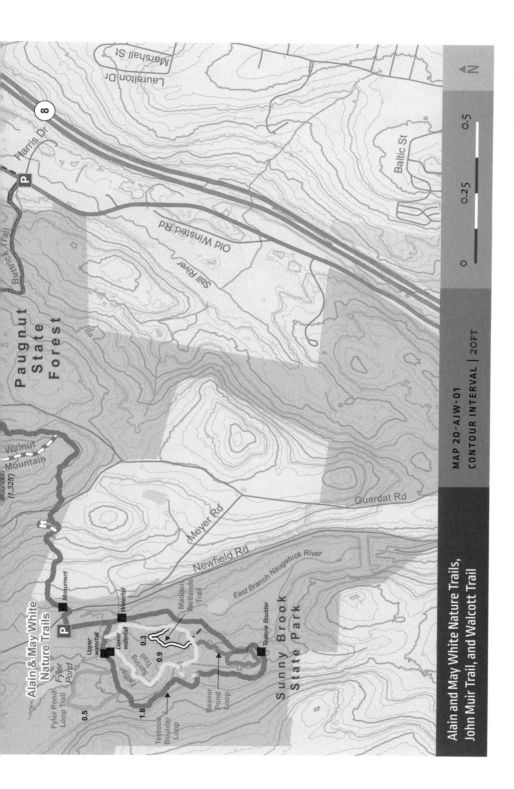

Alain and May White Nature Trails,
John Muir Trail, and Walcott Trail

MAP 20-AJW-01
CONTOUR INTERVAL | 20FT

Alain & May White
Nature Trails

Paugnut
State
Forest

Walnut
Mountain
(1,325)

Sunny Brook
State Park

Fyler Pond
Loop Trail

Fyler
Pond

Upper
waterfall

Lower
waterfall

Spring
Trail

Padlor

Testone
Boulder
Loop

Beaver
Pond Loop

Madden
Wetlands
Trail

Testone Boulder

Monument

Waterfall

Buttrick Trail

Harris Dr

Old Winsted Rd

Still River

Meyer Rd

Newfield Rd

Guerdat Rd

East Branch Naugatuck River

Laurelton Dr

Marshall St

Baltic St

8

P

P

P

N

0   0.25   0.5

0.5

0.3

0.9

1.8

American Legion and Peoples State Forest Trails

LENGTH 14 miles   BLAZE COLOR Varied

American Legion State Forest and Peoples State Forest are situated on opposite sides of the Farmington River's West Branch in Barkhamsted. A 14-mile network of hiking trails provides opportunities for exploration of the forests' rugged terrain with rocky cliffs, spectacular waterfalls, and breathtaking views of the Farmington River Valley. The trails lead past several historic and cultural sites, including old mills, a soapstone quarry, and a former Indian settlement known as the Barkhamsted Lighthouse.

The Austin F. Hawes Memorial Campground (open from mid-April to Columbus Day) in American Legion State Forest offers thirty campsites near the river.

American Legion State Forest Trails

Henry Buck Trail

LENGTH 1.8 miles   BLAZE COLOR Blue

This loop trail was designed and built by Henry R. Buck, vice president of the Connecticut Forest & Park Association from 1928 to 1930. It passes through a mature forest that is approaching old-growth stage. In late April and early May, dozens of native wildflower species grow in abundance along the first half-mile of trail.

Turkey Vulture Ledge Trail

LENGTH 0.4 miles   BLAZE COLOR Blue

This trail features a short ascent to heights where turkey vultures and other raptors can be seen soaring on the thermal updrafts that rise from the river far below. A short climb with little elevation gain, it's an easy outing for hikers of every experience level.

Peoples State Forest Trails

Agnes Bowen Trail

LENGTH 2.7 miles   BLAZE COLOR Blue/Orange

The Agnes Bowen Trail begins at the Peoples Forest Nature Museum and intersects the Charles Pack and Robert Ross trails. The trail was named for a former secretary of the Barkhamsted Chamber of Commerce. Agnes Bowen, a local artist and writer, guided state representatives on a tour of the forest in 1923 that resulted in the decision to establish Peoples State Forest on its original 400 acres.

Elliott Bronson Trail

LENGTH 2.2 miles   BLAZE COLOR Blue/Red

The Elliott Bronson Trail extends across the southern portion of the forest and climbs steeply over Ragged Mountain.

Walt Landgraf Trail

LENGTH 0.2 miles   BLAZE COLOR Red

This trail honors Walt Landgraf, historian, curator of the Peoples Forest Nature Museum, and longtime CFPA trail manager. The Landgraf Trail is a short spur off the Bronson Trail that leads to a former Native American soapstone quarry.

Barkhamsted Lighthouse Interpretive Trail

LENGTH 0.1 miles   BLAZE COLOR Yellow

The name "Barkhamsted Lighthouse" comes from those traveling along the then stagecoach road to Riverton. When travelers saw the lights in the woods on the hill, that was their signal that Riverton was only another mile or so away. This short trail leads to the remains of the old settlement. The trail has a few interpretive signs that chronicle the history of James Caugham, Molly Barber, and other resident "outcasts" on the hill.

Anything look out of the ordinary? Storm damage blocking the trail? Report trail conditions on our website so we can make the trails better for everyone.

Nature Trail

LENGTH 0.2 miles   **BLAZE COLOR** Blue

This short trail links the Agnes Bowen and Elliott Bronson Trails.

Charles Pack Trail

LENGTH 2.2 miles   **BLAZE COLOR** Blue/Yellow

The Charles Pack Trail follows mostly flat terrain, traveling through an old farm site on the back side of Beaver Swamp.

Robert Ross Trail

LENGTH 2.4 miles   **BLAZE COLOR** Blue

The Robert Ross Trail leaves from East River Road and the Peoples Forest Nature Museum and features steep cliffs overlooking the Farmington River.

Jessie Gerard Trail

LENGTH 1.7 miles   **BLAZE COLOR** Blue/Yellow

The Jessie Gerard Trail starts from East River Road at the remains of an old settlement known as Barkhamsted Lighthouse. A series of switchbacks eases the dramatic 300-foot elevation gain to Chaugham Lookout, with breathtaking views of the Farmington River Valley and the village of Riverton and to Massachusetts in the far northern distance.

Falls Cut-Off Trail

LENGTH 0.3 miles   BLAZE COLOR Blue/Red

The Falls Cut-Off Trail features a series of 299 stone steps that climb beside a seasonal waterfall. During the winter, beautiful ice formations can be seen along this section. The trail itself is often dangerously wet or icy, and ice falling from the rocks above can be treacherous as well.

▮ *Greenwoods Road, the primary road through Peoples State Forest, and Legion Road are closed from first snow until about May 1.*

▮ *Hunting is permitted in state forests intersected by this trail. Please use caution and wear orange during hunting season.*

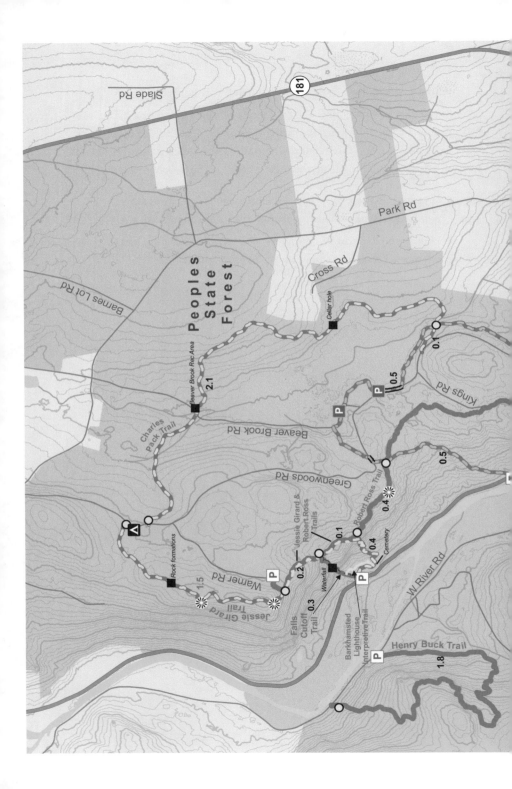

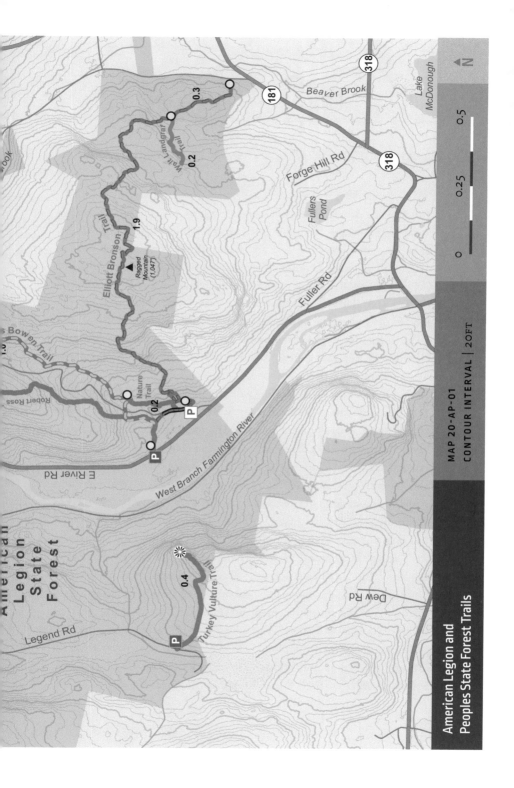

American Legion and
Peoples State Forest Trails

MAP 20-AP-01
CONTOUR INTERVAL | 20 FT

0   0.25   0.5

N

Appalachian Trail

LENGTH 56.6 miles (New York–
Connecticut border to Sage's
Ravine in Massachusetts)

BLAZE COLOR White

The Appalachian Trail (AT) in Connecticut is part of the fabled through-route from Springer Mountain in Georgia to Mount Katahdin in Maine, a distance of approximately 2,200 miles. The trail was the first in the nation to be named a National Scenic Trail, so designated by an act of Congress in 1968. Most of the original route in Connecticut was blazed by Ned K. Anderson, CFPA chair of the Housatonic Valley section from 1929 to 1932, when the AT was one of the early Blue-Blazed Hiking Trails. Today the entire length of the trail is blazed white, with most side trails blazed blue. The trail is maintained by the Connecticut chapter of the Appalachian Mountain Club.

The Connecticut section of the AT extends from Sherman at the New York state line to the brook crossing at Sage's Ravine, just north of the Massachusetts state line at Salisbury. The trail goes up the Housatonic River Valley and twice crosses the river. The region is noted for its forested landscape, rugged rocky hills, open valleys, ravines, waterfalls, and magnificent vistas. Wildflowers abound in spring and summer, and year-round sightings of deer, turkey, and fox are not uncommon. From the mid-eighteenth century until the early twentieth century, the area was home to a thriving iron industry. The foundries and blast furnaces were heated by charcoal to the extreme temperatures required to melt raw iron ore into molten crude, or pig iron. The charcoal was produced by itinerant colliers who chopped wood cut from the forested hills, stacked it into huge mounds, and burned and smoked it over several weeks. Remains of these hearth sites (flat circular areas) can be seen along the trail.

Several designated camping areas are available on or near the trail. Camping is allowed only at these designated locations. Camp and cook fires are prohibited along the AT throughout Connecticut. Additional information and detailed trail descriptions are available in the *Appalachian Trail Guide to Massachusetts-Connecticut*, published by the Appalachian Trail Conservancy.

▌ *Trail mileage on these maps and this mileage table differ significantly from other information currently in print.*

SIDE TRAILS

Pine Knob Loop Trail (see Map 20-AT-04)

LENGTH 2.3 miles   **BLAZE COLOR** Blue

The Pine Knob Loop Trail is located in Housatonic Meadows State Park and Housatonic State Forest on the west side of the Housatonic River, north of Cornwall Bridge. A short and challenging trail, it coincides with the Appalachian Trail for a portion of its length. Hikers will enjoy beautiful vistas over the river valley. The trail is accessible from the state park's campground and group camping area via unmarked trails.

15

Universal Access Loop (see Map 20-AT-06)

LENGTH 0.4 miles   **BLAZE COLOR** Blue

This loop trail is handicap accessible and offers a nice, flat loop through the woods. When used in conjunction with the AT, walkers will enjoy beautiful views along the Housatonic River.

Limestone Springs Trail (see Map 20-AT-06)

LENGTH 1.2 miles   **BLAZE COLOR** Blue

From the AT near Rand's View, this trail descends steeply to the Limestone Springs Lean-to, and continues to the woods at the end of Sugar Hill Road.

Lion's Head Trail (see Map 20-AT-07)

LENGTH 0.4 miles   **BLAZE COLOR** Blue

The Lion's Head Trail leads from the end of Bunker Hill Road (please respect private property) to the AT. Follow the AT an additional 0.2 miles to the summit of Lion's Head.

Undermountain Trail (see Map 20-AT-07)

LENGTH 2.0 miles   **BLAZE COLOR** Blue

The Undermountain Trail is challenging and can be used to access the AT and some of the highest peaks in the state. The Paradise Lane Trail can be accessed off the Undermountain Trail at 1.1 miles from the Route 41 parking area.

Paradise Lane (see Map 20-AT-07)

LENGTH 1.9 miles   **BLAZE COLOR** Blue

Pass a blue-blazed side trail which leads to the Paradise Lane group camping area. In another 50 yards, find the intersection of the Undermountain Trail and Paradise Lane (both have blue blazes), then turn onto Paradise Lane to continue your ascent up the mountain on a narrow forest path beneath the shoulder of Bear Mountain. The hiker will encounter a black spruce bog and a small pond. During late fall and winter, views of the steep north side of Bear Mountain are possible. Paradise Lane joins the Appalachian Trail 0.3 miles south of Sages Ravine Brook.

16

Mileage Table

APPALACHIAN TRAIL

0.0	Hoyt Rd (P)
0.3	Spur to Rte 55 Parking (50 ft, P)
0.6	Ct Rte 55
2.0	Summit, Tenmile Hill (999 ft)
2.1	Jct Herrick Trail (blue)
3.0	Spur to Tenmile River Lean-to (blue, 400 ft)
3.1	Spur to Tenmile River Campsite (190 ft)
3.2	Tenmile River bridge
4.0	Jct Bulls Bridge Rd Connector (0.3 mi, P)
4.4	Bulls Bridge Rd / Begin roadwalk—Schaghticoke Rd
4.7	End roadwalk—Schaghticoke Rd
9.0	Spur to Schaghticoke Mountain Campsite
12.3	Spur to Mount Algo Lean-to (blue, 340 ft)
12.7	Ct Rte 341 (P)
15.9	Skiff Mountain Rd
16.8	Calebs Peak / View
17.5	View
17.6	St. John's Ledges
18.2	Begin roadwalk—River Rd (P)
19.3	End roadwalk—River Rd (P)
20.7	South jct Spur to Stewart Hollow Brook Lean-to (360 ft)
20.8	North jct Spur to Stewart Hollow Brook Lean-to (360 ft)
21.2	Spur to Stony Brook Campsite (0.1 mi)

PARADISE LANE

BRIDGE CLOSURE DETOUR

UNDERMOUNTAIN TRAIL

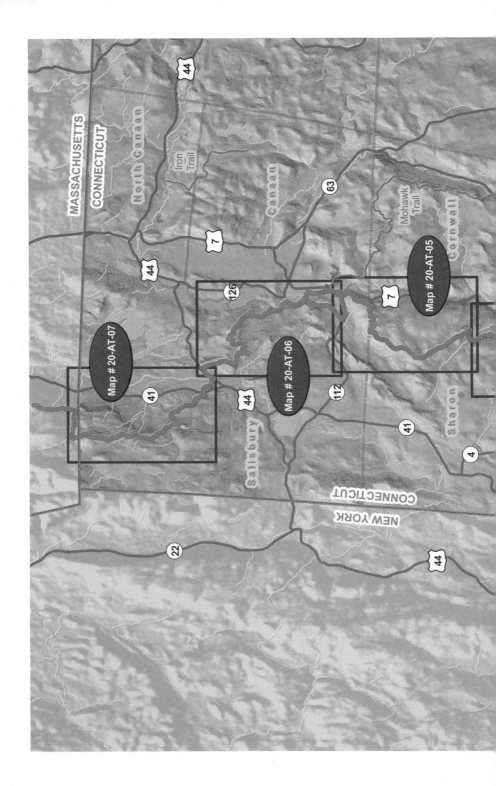

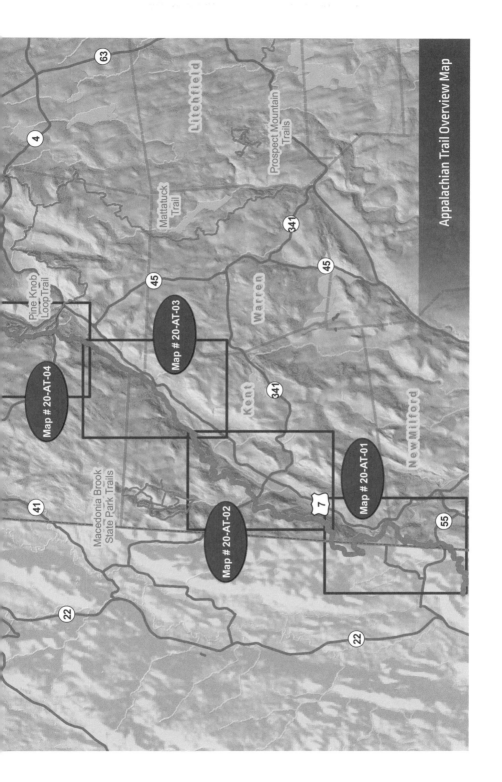

Appalachian Trail Overview Map

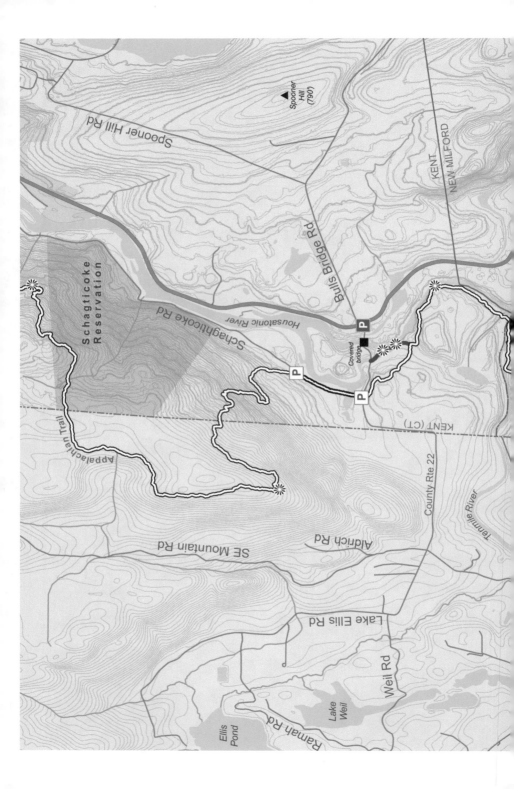

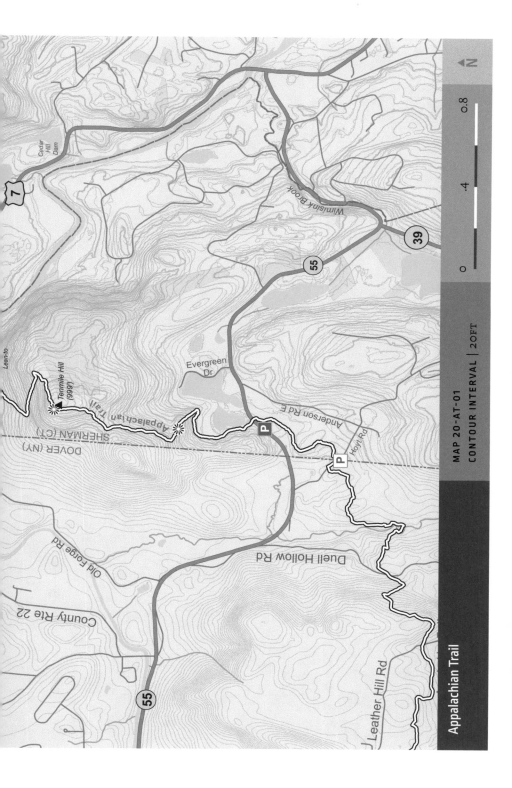

Appalachian Trail

MAP 20-AT-01
CONTOUR INTERVAL | 20FT

N

0   .4   0.8

7

Cedar
Hill
Dam

Winisink Brook

55

39

Lean-to

Tenmile Hill
(999')

Appalachian Trail

SHERMAN (CT)
DOVER (NY)

Evergreen
Dr.

Anderson Rd E

P

P

Hoyt Rd

Old Forge Rd

County Rte 22

55

Duell Hollow Rd

Leather Hill Rd

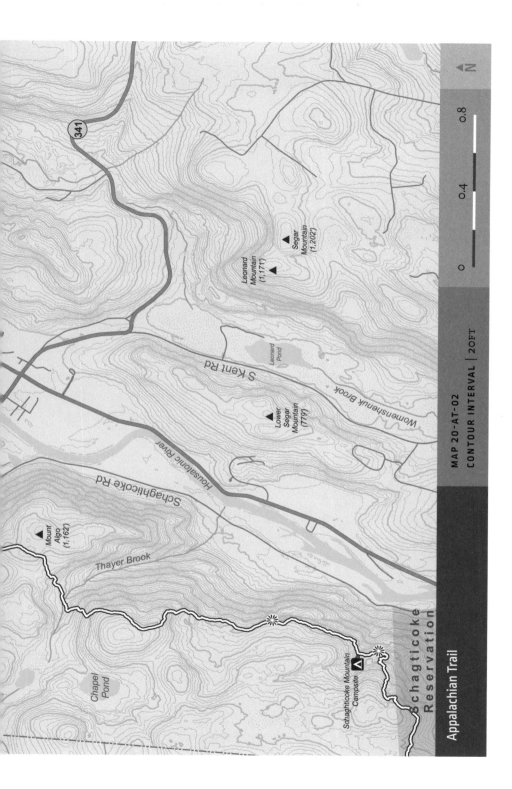

341

Leonard
Mountain
(1,171')

Segar
Mountain
(1,202')

S Kent Rd

Leonard
Pond

Womenshenuk Brook

Lower
Segar
Mountain
(779')

Schaghticoke Rd

Housatonic River

Mount
Algo
(1,162')

Thayer Brook

Chapel
Pond

Schaghticoke Mountain
Campsite

Schaghticoke
Reservation

Appalachian Trail

MAP 20-AT-02
CONTOUR INTERVAL | 20FT

0   0.4   0.8

N

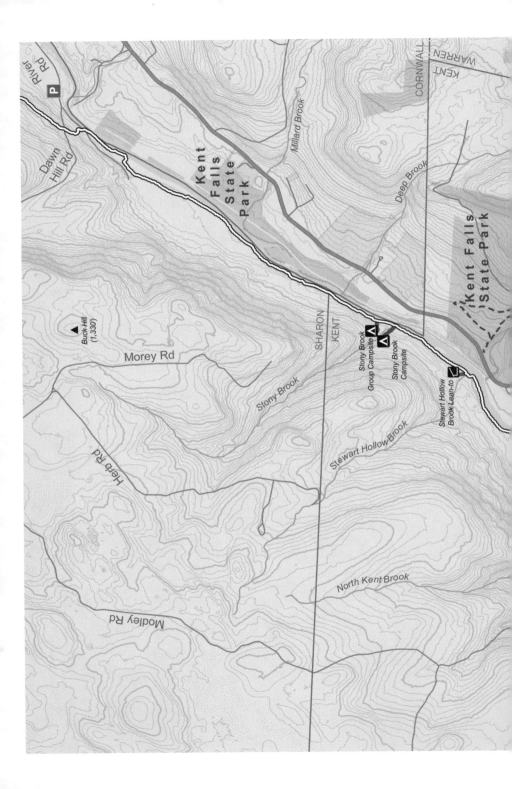

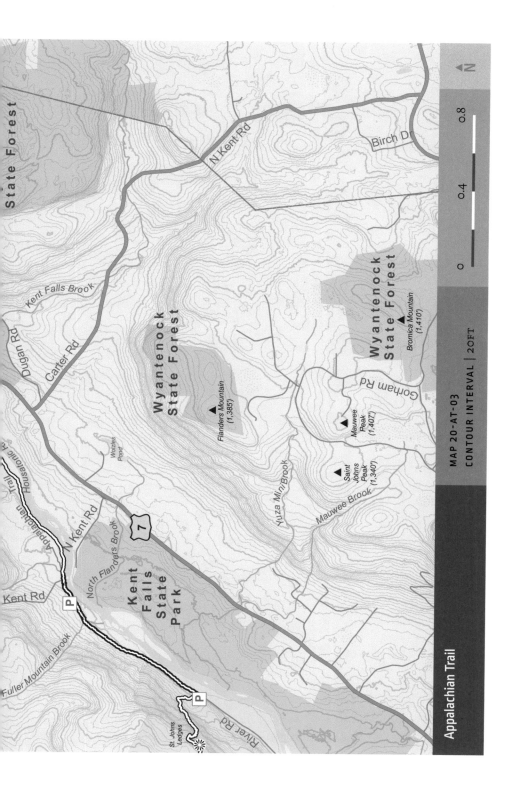

State Forest

Wyantenock State Forest

Wyantenock State Forest

Flanders Mountain (1,385)

Bromica Mountain (1,410)

Mauwee Peak (1,407)

Saint Johns Peak (1,340)

Gorham Rd

Kent Falls Brook

Dugan Rd

Carter Rd

Wolzies Pond

Yuza Mini Brook

Mauwee Brook

N Kent Rd

Birch Dr

Appalachian Trail

Housatonic R

N Kent Rd

North Flanders Brook

Kent Rd

Kent Falls State Park

Fuller Mountain Brook

St. Johns Ledges

River Rd

7

P

P

N

0   0.4   0.8

MAP 20-AT-03
CONTOUR INTERVAL | 20FT

Appalachian Trail

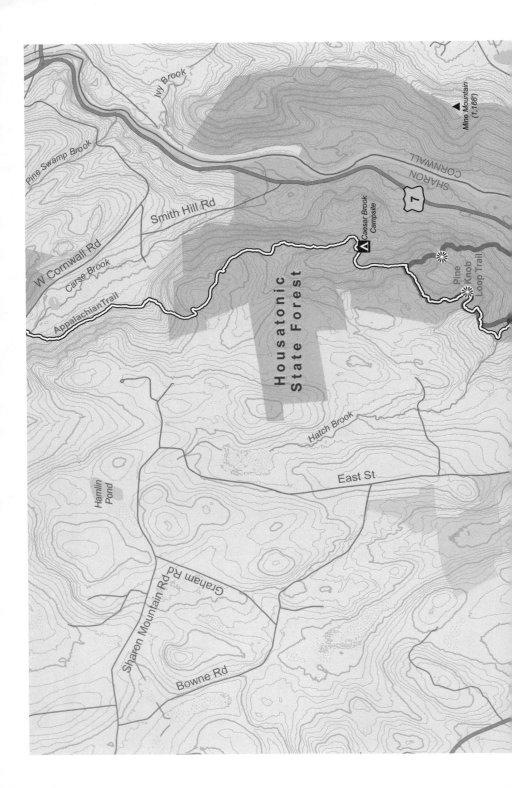

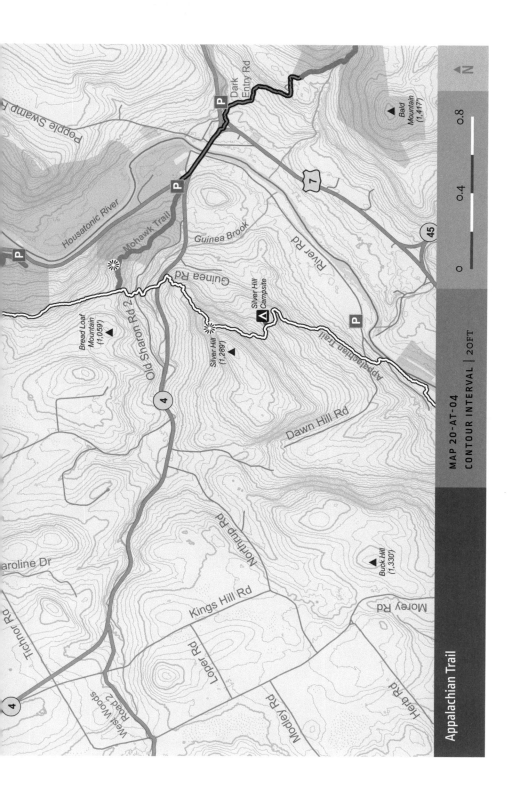

MAP 20-AT-04
CONTOUR INTERVAL | 20FT

Appalachian Trail

N

0   0.4   0.8

Bald
Mountain
(1,417')

7

45

Dark
Entry Rd

P

P

Housatonic River

Poppie Swamp R

Mohawk Trail

Guinea Brook

Guinea Rd

River Rd

Silver Hill
Campsite

Bread Loaf
Mountain
(1,059')

Old Sharon Rd 2

Silver Hill
(1,289')

4

Appalachian Trail

P

Dawn Hill Rd

Caroline Dr

Northrup Rd

Buck Hill
(1,330')

Tichnor Rd

Kings Hill Rd

Morey Rd

West Woods
Road 2

Loper Rd

Modley Rd

Herb Rd

4

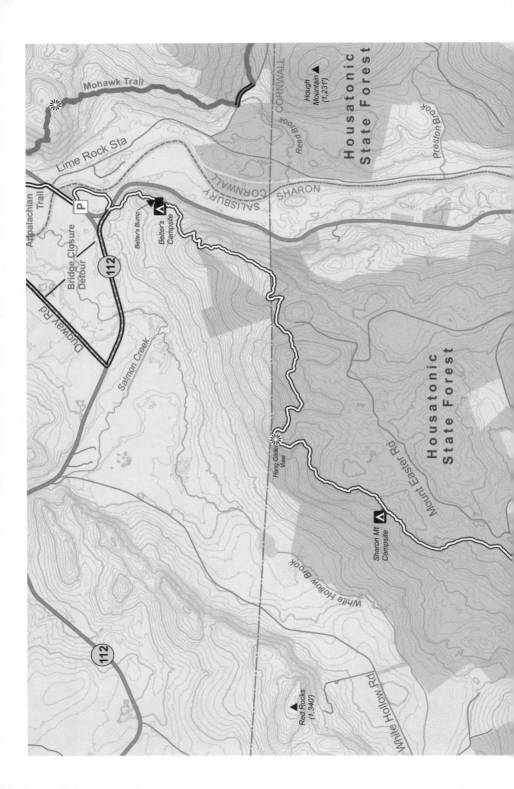

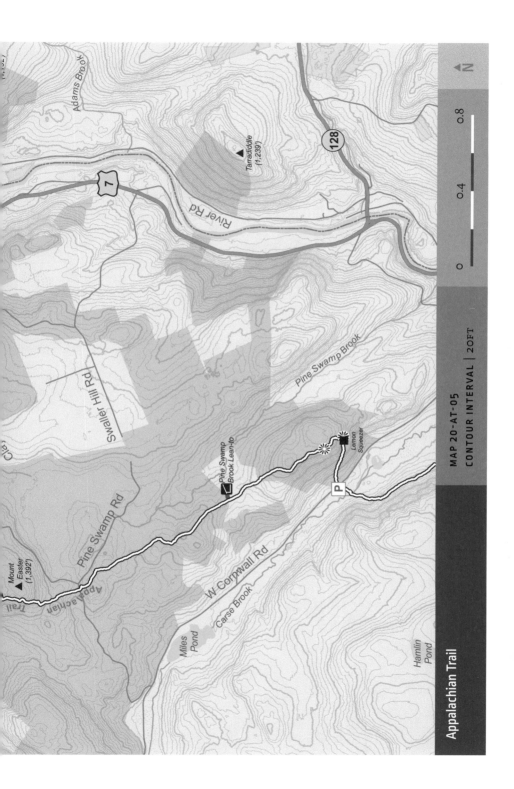

Adams Brook

7

River Rd

Tarradiddle
(1,239')

128

Pine Swamp Brook

Swaller Hill Rd

C... Rd

Pine Swamp Rd

Pine Swamp
Brook Lean-to

Lemon
Squeezer

P

Mount
Easter
(1,392')

Appalachian
Trail

Trail

W. Cornwall Rd

Carse Brook

Miles
Pond

Hamlin
Pond

N

0   0.4   0.8

MAP 20-AT-05
CONTOUR INTERVAL | 20FT

Appalachian Trail

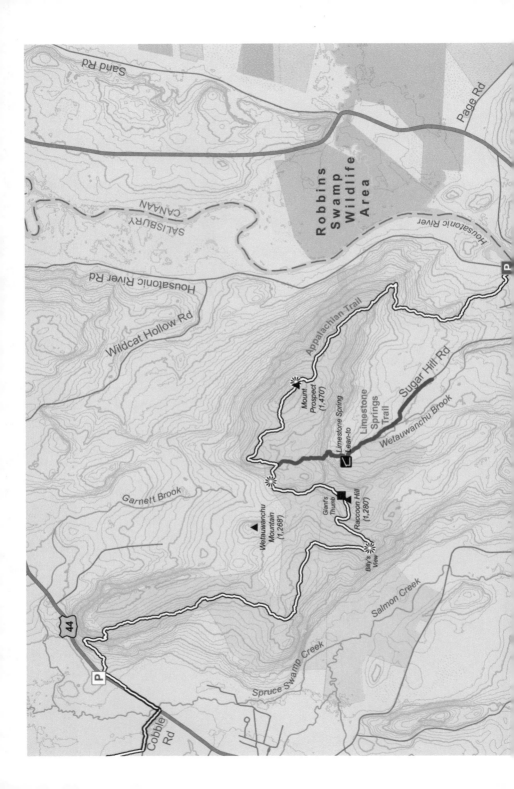

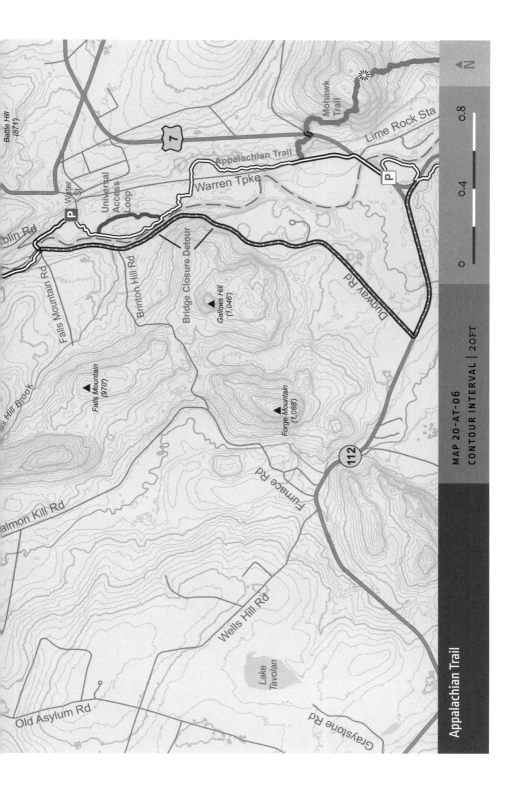

Appalachian Trail

MAP 20-AT-06
CONTOUR INTERVAL | 20FT

N

0   0.4   0.8

Battle Hill
(871')

7

Water St

Universal
Access
Loop

Appalachian Trail

Warren Tpke

Mohawk
Trail

Lime Rock Sta

P

P

blin Rd

Falls Mountain Rd

Brinton Hill Rd

Bridge Closure Detour

Dugway Rd

Gallows Hill
(1,046')

Falls Mountain
(970')

Forge Mountain
(1,088')

s Hill Brook

almon Kill Rd

Furnace Rd

112

Wells Hill Rd

Lake
Tavolan

Old Asylum Rd

Graystone Rd

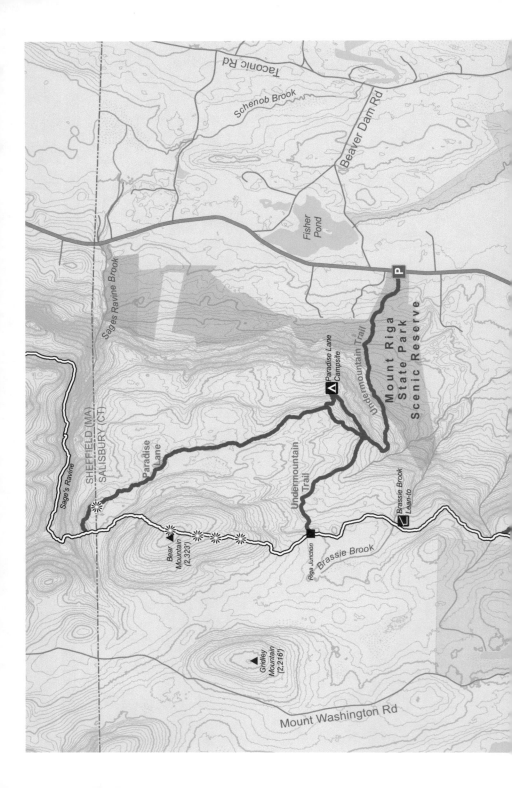

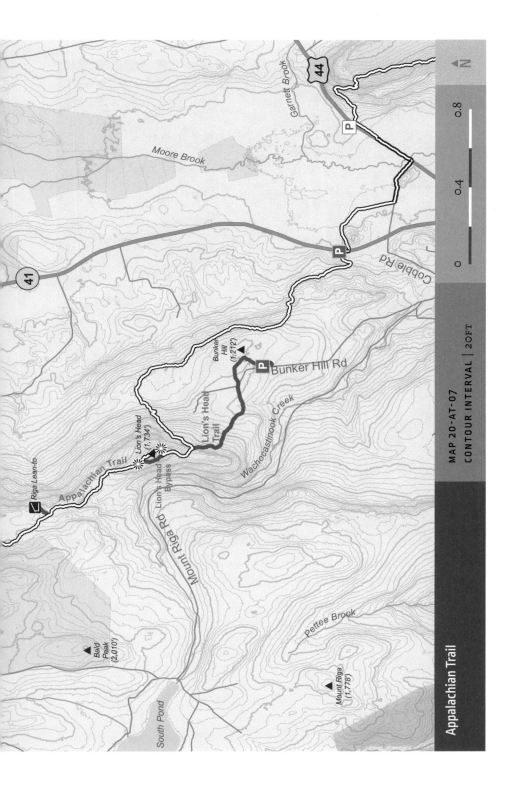

Garnett Brook

44

Moore Brook

41

P

Cobble Rd

P

Bunker Hill Rd

Bunker
Hill
(1,212')

Lion's Head
Trail

Wachocastinook Creek

Lion's Head
(1,734')

Lion's Head
Bypass

Appalachian Trail

Riga Lean-to

Mount Riga Rd

Pettee Brook

Bald
Peak
(2,010')

South Pond

Mount Riga
(1,778')

N

0   0.4   0.8

There's so much to learn about our Connecticut forests from ground level on the trail. Photo courtesy CFPA.

Aspetuck Trail

LENGTH 6.9 miles   **BLAZE COLOR** Blue

Located within the Aspetuck River Valley area of Fairfield County, the Aspetuck Trail intersects the towns of Newtown, Redding, and Easton. This woodland trail travels through the Centennial Watershed State Forest and connects to the trail system in Collis P. Huntington State Park. Notable features include the Aspetuck River, scenic overlooks, and stone walls. The trail also connects to the blue-blazed Saugatuck Trail offering longer-distance hiking opportunities.

Because the trail is located within watershed lands, recreational use is regulated by the Department of Public Health. Please respect and obey all signs. The Centennial Watershed State Forest is managed cooperatively by the Connecticut DEEP, Aquarion Water Company, and The Nature Conservancy.

35

▌ *Pets are not permitted on the Aspetuck Trail.*

▌ *This trail is restricted to hiking activities only. No other trail uses permitted.*

▌ *Hunting is permitted in state forests intersected by this trail. Please use caution and wear orange during hunting season.*

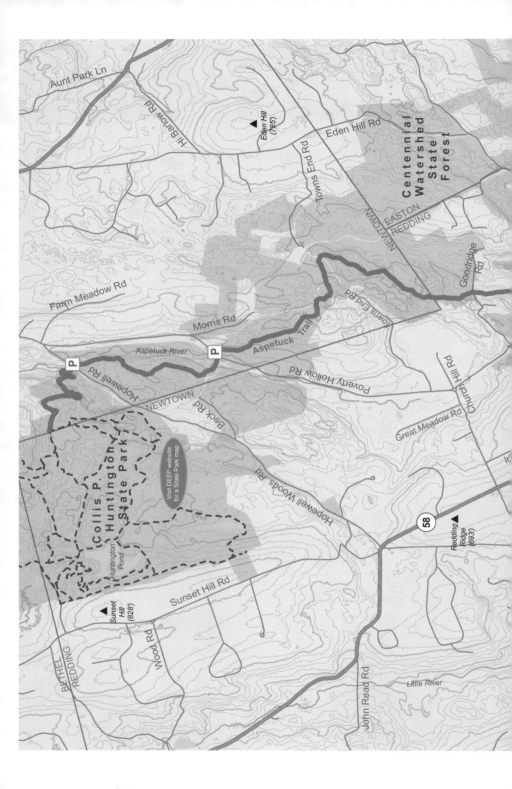

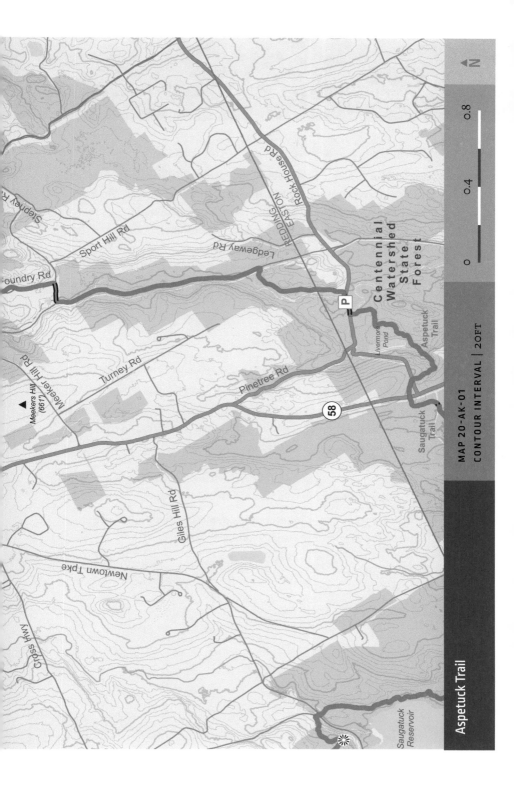

Aspetuck Trail

MAP 20-AK-01
CONTOUR INTERVAL | 20FT

0   0.4   0.8

N

Centennial Watershed State Forest

Saugatuck Reservoir

Saugatuck Trail

Aspetuck Trail

Livermore Pond

P

58

Rock House Rd

REDDING
EASTON

Ledgeway Rd

Sport Hill Rd

Foundry Rd

Stepney R

Turney Rd

Meeker Hill Rd

Meekers Hill
(661')

Pinetree Rd

Giles Hill Rd

Newtown Tpke

Cross Hwy

Chatfield Trail

LENGTH 4.3 miles   **BLAZE COLOR** Blue

Located south of Chatfield Hollow State Park in Killingworth, the Chatfield Trail travels through portions of the Cockaponset State Forest and Forster Pond State Park as well as private lands. The trail winds its way through a mixed forest and features large boulders, rocky ledges, babbling brooks, and passes the Fat Man Squeeze (a narrow vertical crack in a cliff). Cliffs and rocky, uneven terrain make this trail a fun challenge.

SIDE TRAILS

Chatfield Alternate Trail

LENGTH 0.7 miles   **BLAZE COLOR** Blue/Orange

This alternate trail, near the north end of the Chatfield Trail, offers a shorter loop option over interesting terrain. The hiker will pass around a freshwater wetland, cross a brook, pass a small waterfall, and come close to a huge vertical rock slab.

▌ *Do not disturb nearby youth group recreational activities at Deer Lake Camp on southern section of trail.*

▌ *Hunting is permitted in state forests intersected by this trail. Please use caution and wear orange during hunting season.*

Hikers should remember to wear orange during the fall hiking season.
Photo courtesy Liane Stevens.

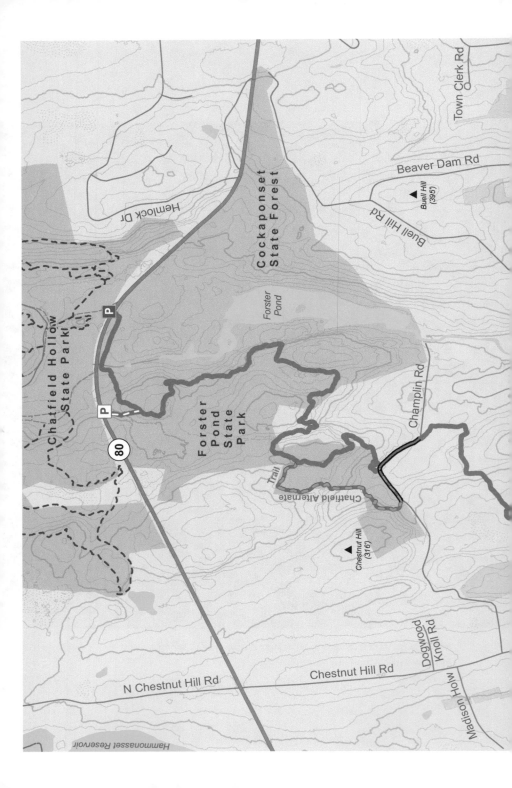

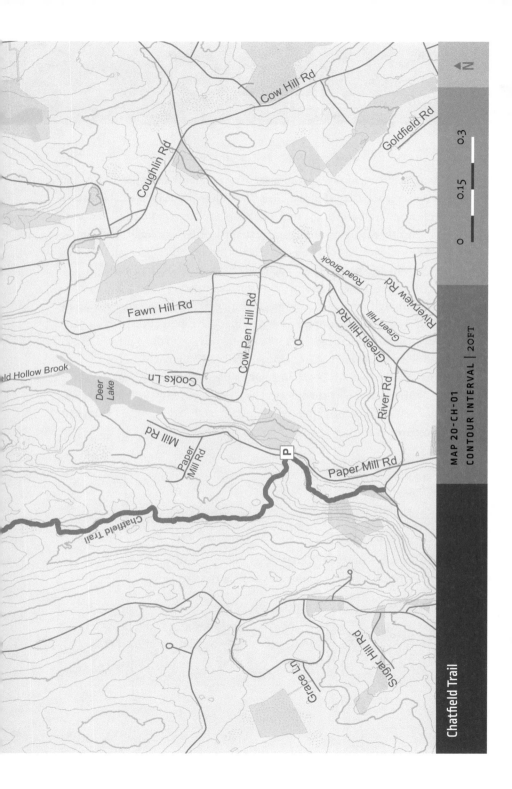

Chatfield Trail

MAP 20-CH-01
CONTOUR INTERVAL | 20FT

0   0.15   0.3

N

Cow Hill Rd

Coughlin Rd

Goldfield Rd

Road Brook

Riverview Rd

Fawn Hill Rd

Cow Pen Hill Rd

Green Hill Rd

Green Hill

River Rd

eld Hollow Brook

Deer
Lake

Cooks Ln

Mill Rd

Paper
Mill Rd

Chatfield Trail

P

Paper Mill Rd

Grace Ln

Sugar Hill Rd

Cockaponset Trail

LENGTH 7.6 miles   **BLAZE COLOR** Blue

The first parts of the Cockaponset Trail were built in 1934 as a Civilian Conservation Corps (CCC) project. The fruits of CCC labors can be seen on the northern parts of the trail. Look for excellent grading and enduring rockwork. Also, east of the trail just north of Jericho Road, you can see the footings of the old CCC-constructed Turkey Hill Observation Tower. The trail also passes several defunct charcoal-production sites.

Traveling along beautiful rolling terrain, crossing brooks, and wandering through mature forest, the Cockaponset Trail is a true gem. Many multi-use trails, both marked and unmarked, intersect and occasionally overlap the Cockaponset Trail. To ensure you are on the right trail, follow the blue blazes on the Cockaponset Trail and blue/red blazes on the loop trails. All loop trails begin and end on the Cockaponset Trail.

Visit the Connecticut DEEP website for Cockaponset State Forest maps as well as for information on swimming and parking at the Pattaconk Recreation Area.

SIDE TRAILS

South Pattaconk Trail (see Map 20-CK-01)

LENGTH 1.5 miles   **BLAZE COLOR** Blue/Red

The South Pattaconk Trail is generally easy walking. There is a stream crossing on stepping stones and one short, steep ledge.

 Things change, trails move, closures happen.
For the most up-to-date trail information, parking, and trail notices, visit our interactive trail map.

North Pattaconk Trail (see Map 20-CK-01)

LENGTH 1.2 miles   **BLAZE COLOR** Blue/Red

The North Pattaconk Trail can be picked up just west of the Pattaconk Reservoir parking lots. The trail follows the western shore of the reservoir and also crosses Pattaconk Brook.

Old Forest Trail (see Map 20-CK-02)

LENGTH 0.5 miles   **BLAZE COLOR** Blue/Red

The Old Forest Trail utilizes an old woods road for most of its length.

Wildwood Trail (see Map 20-CK-02)

LENGTH 1.4 miles   **BLAZE COLOR** Blue/Red

The Wildwood Trail commences at Wildwood Junction on the Cockaponset Trail and follows along the base of ledges. It is a series of moderate ascents and descents.

43

❚ *Hunting is permitted in state forests intersected by this trail. Please use caution and wear orange during hunting season.*

Mileage Table

COCKAPONSET TRAIL

0.0	Ct Rte 148 (P)
0.1	South jct South Pattaconk Trail (blue/red)
1.7	State Forest Rd (P)
1.8	North jct South Pattaconk Trail (blue/red) / South jct North Pattaconk Trail (blue/red)
2.9	Join North Pattaconk Trail (blue/red)
2.9	Leave North Pattaconk Trail (blue/red)
3.3	North jct North Pattaconk Trail (blue/red)
3.5	Spur to Collier hut site (300 ft)
3.9	Charcoal hearth
4.1	Begin roadwalk—Old County E Rd
4.2	End roadwalk—Old County E Rd (P)
4.2	South jct Old Forest Trail (blue/red)
4.9	Jct local trail (purple)
4.9	North jct Old Forest Trail (blue/red)
5.0	Charcoal hearth
5.1	Jericho Rd (P)
5.2	South jct Wildwood Trail (blue/red)
6.0	Jericho Rd
6.6	Charcoal hearth
6.8	Jericho Road (P)
7.3	North jct Wildwood Trail (blue/red)
7.6	Beaver Meadow Rd (P)

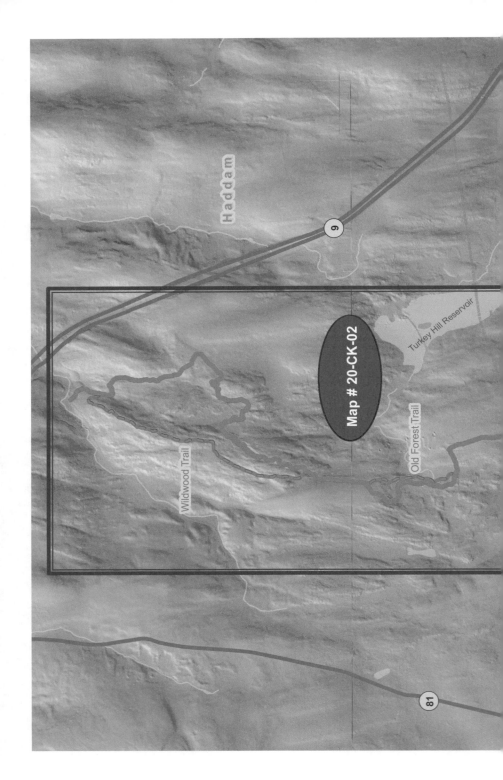

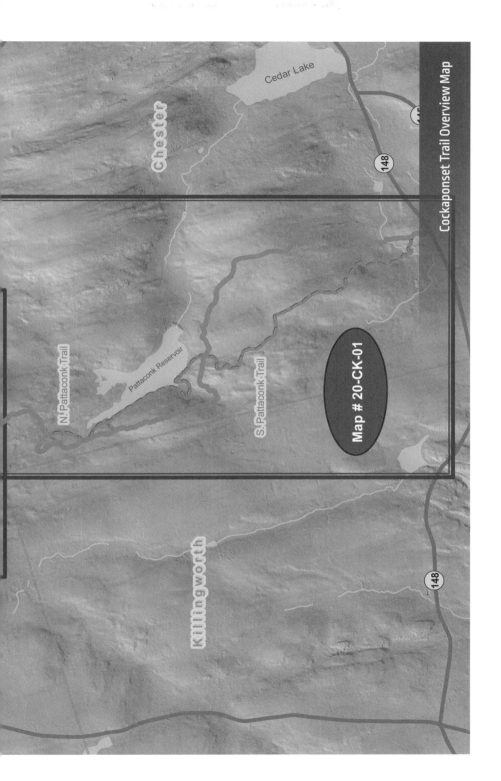

Cedar Lake

Chester

148

N.Pattaconk Trail

Pattaconk Reservoir

S.Pattaconk Trail

Map # 20-CK-01

Killingworth

148

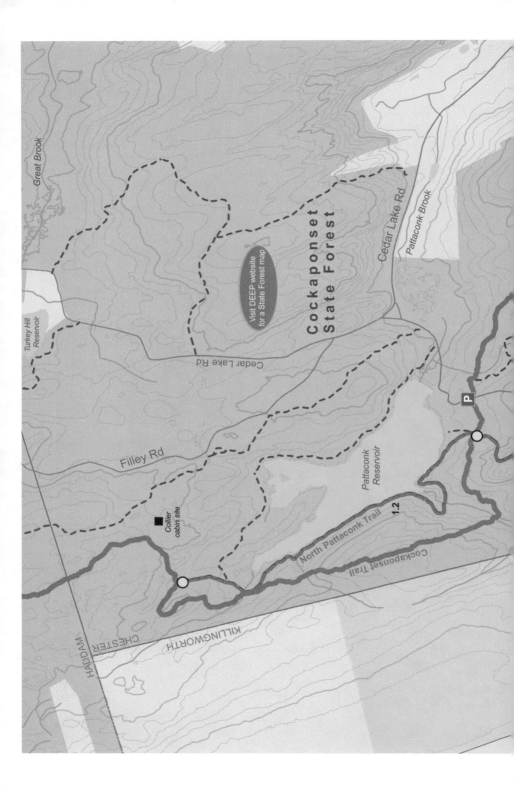

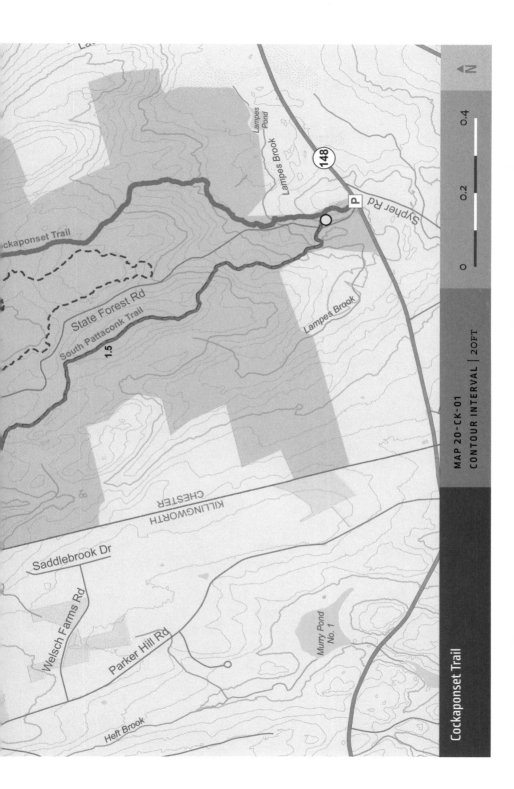

Cockaponset Trail

MAP 20-CK-01
CONTOUR INTERVAL | 20FT

N

0   0.2   0.4

ckaponset Trail

State Forest Rd

South Pattaconk Trail

1.5

8

Lampes Brook

Lampes Brook

Lampes Pond

148

Sypher Rd

P

KILLINGWORTH
CHESTER

Saddlebrook Dr

Welsch Farms Rd

Parker Hill Rd

Murry Pond No. 1

Heft Brook

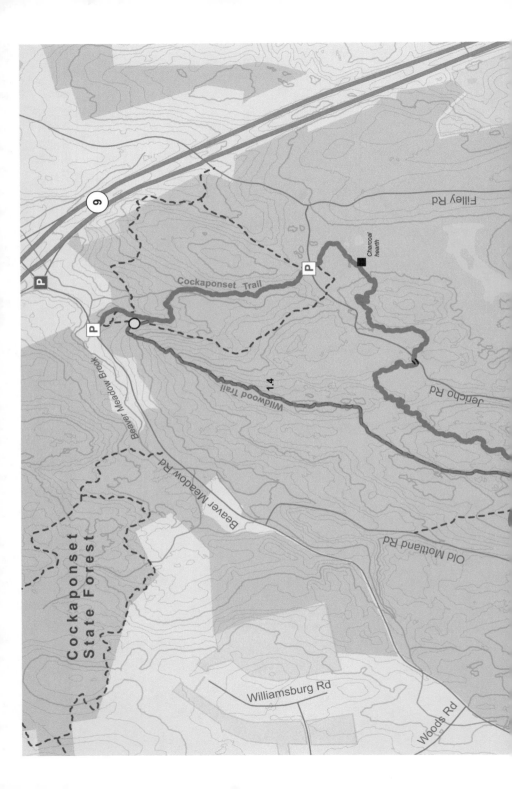

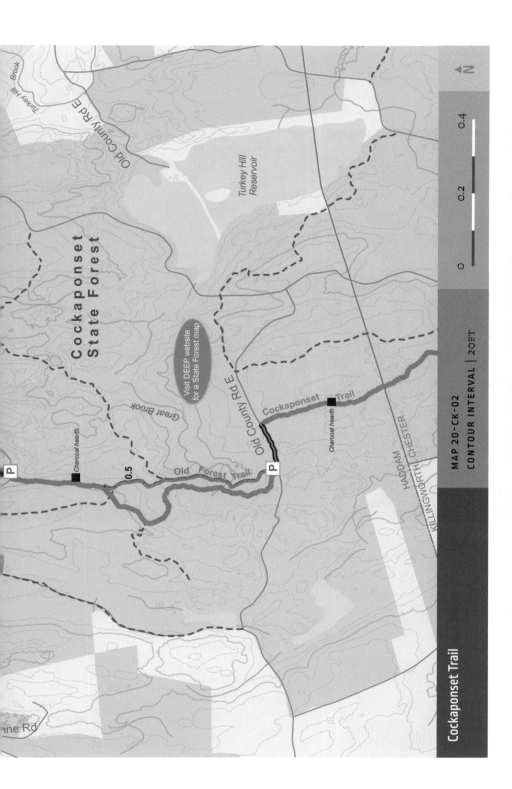

Turkey Hill Brook

Old County Rd E

Cockaponset
State Forest

Turkey Hill
Reservoir

Visit DEEP website
for a State Forest map

Great Brook

Old County Rd E

Charcoal hearth

Cockaponset   Trail

Charcoal hearth

Old   Forest   Trail

0.5

P

P

HADDAM   CHESTER

KILLINGWORTH

ne Rd

N

0   0.2   0.4

Cockaponset Trail

MAP 20-CK-02
CONTOUR INTERVAL | 20FT

There are a handful of overnight options for hikers looking
for a longer adventure. Photo courtesy CFPA.

Falls Brook Trail

LENGTH 1.4 miles   **BLAZE COLOR** Blue

The Falls Brook Trail is a short trail that winds through a mature forest located in the northern Tunxis State Forest. Falls Brook features numerous waterfalls, cascades, and pools that reward hikers with a cool and shady walk on warm summer days. After the first quarter-mile, the trail splits to form a 1.1 mile lollipop loop and meanders along both sides of the brook, which flows southeasterly to the Barkhamsted Reservoir. In the spring, hikers will be treated to pockets of wildflowers along the brook. Because of its short length, the trail is a good hike for families, although the water crossings and rocky areas can be tricky for the youngest of hikers. In the winter, the frozen waterfalls are especially beautiful and a wonderful reward for a cold-weather outing.

▮ *Spring thaws and/or heavy rains have been known to make the brook crossing impassable.*

▮ *Hunting is permitted in state forests intersected by this trail. Please use caution and wear orange during hunting season.*

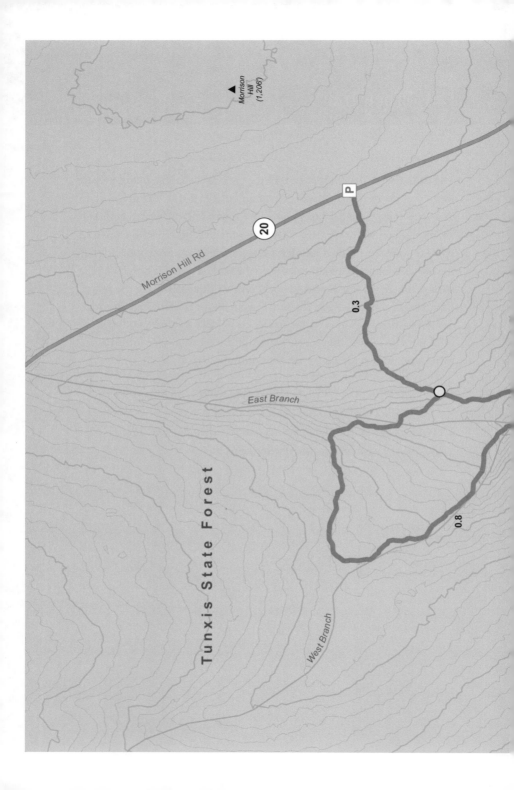

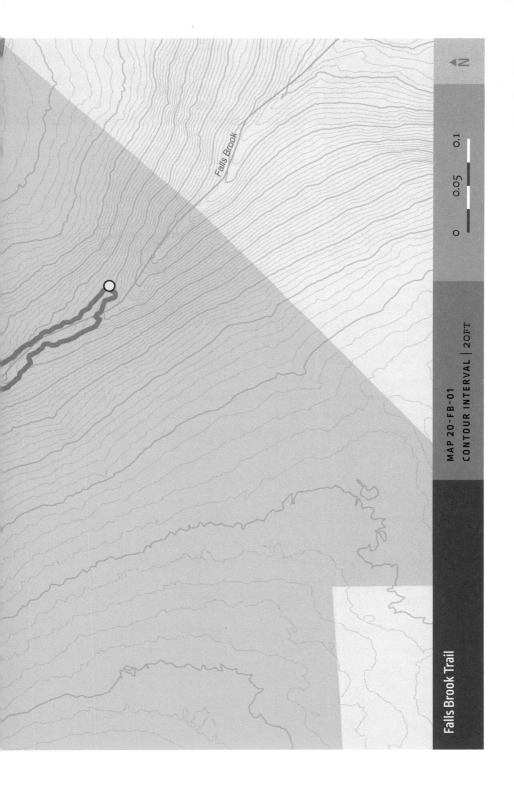

Falls Brook

Falls Brook Trail

MAP 20-FB-01
CONTOUR INTERVAL | 20FT

0   0.05   0.1

N

Field Forest Trails

LENGTH 2.2 miles   **BLAZE COLOR** Varied

Towering tulip poplars, shaded woodland trails, a vernal pool brimming with aquatic and amphibian life, streams harboring fish, a range of bird species including wild turkeys, red-eyed vireos, and pileated woodpeckers, views of the traprock ridge, and magnificent trees—you may be lucky enough to encounter all of these on your visit to the 152-acre Field Forest.

This property was given to CFPA by Howard Brigham Field, Jr. after his death in 1999. Field was a conservationist and longtime resident of Durham who loved the property and wanted it to be protected for the community. Members of the Field family still maintain an important connection to the property today.

Stone walls, cedar posts, and remnants of wire fencing indicate that the property was once agricultural land. Abandoned at the end of the nineteenth century, the farm fields subsequently grew into forest. Today, the dominant ecological process is forest succession. The wooded property consists of a variety of mixed hardwood trees which provide important wildlife habitat.

Field Forest Trail

LENGTH 1.6 miles   **BLAZE COLOR** Blue

The main trail at this site, the Field Forest Trail sweeps around the property and offers a nice ramble through beautiful woodland terrain.

Valley View Trail

LENGTH 0.3 miles   **BLAZE COLOR** Blue/Yellow

This short trail leads into a meadow and offers views of the adjoining valley.

Blue/Red Trail

LENGTH 0.3 miles   **BLAZE COLOR** Blue/Red

Connecting from the parking area on Bear Rock Road to the blue-blazed Field Forest Trail, the Blue/Red Trail features the property's unique vernal pool.

Beech Grove Trail

LENGTH 0.1 miles   **BLAZE COLOR** Blue/Orange

This is a short connector on the Field Forest Trail.

▮ *Trails are open to hiking activities only.*

▮ *Private horse use is allowed on a single trail through an agreement with a neighbor. No other uses are allowed.*

▮ *Hunting occurs on this property by permit only. Please use caution and wear orange during hunting season.*

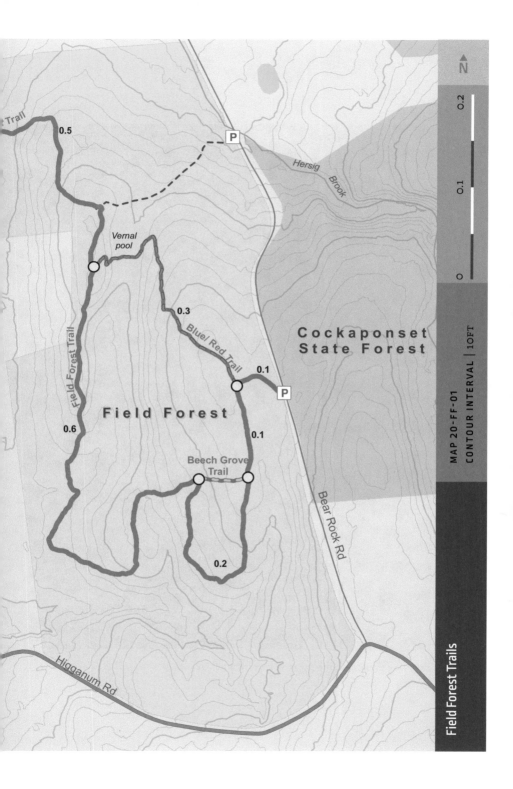

Trail

0.5

P

Hersig Brook

Vernal pool

0.3

Blue/ Red Trail

0.1

Cockaponset State Forest

P

Field Forest Trail

Field Forest

0.6

0.1

Beech Grove Trail

Bear Rock Rd

0.2

Higganum Rd

N

0   0.1   0.2

MAP 20-FF-01
CONTOUR INTERVAL | 10FT

Field Forest Trails

Enjoying the trail in the summer is fun for all ages.
Photo courtesy Jeb Stevens.

Finch Brook Trail

LENGTH 2.6 miles   **BLAZE COLOR** Blue

The Finch Brook Trail is an easy loop trail. The sole access point is the trailhead at the end of Barbara Drive in Wolcott. The trail meanders through a combination of wetlands and gently rolling hills, almost completely under a forest canopy dominated by oak species and interspersed with hickory, maple, and birch. A stretch of the central wetlands of this preserve is crossed by a lovely 125-foot-long bog bridge, affording the hiker an intimate wetlands experience. Further to the north, the trail follows a section of the Old Finch Road, a very old woods road said to have been once walked by Abraham Lincoln.

The Finch Brook Preserve, totaling just over 64 acres, has been permanently protected by the Wolcott Land Conservation Trust. Visit wolcottlandct.org for more information on trust properties.

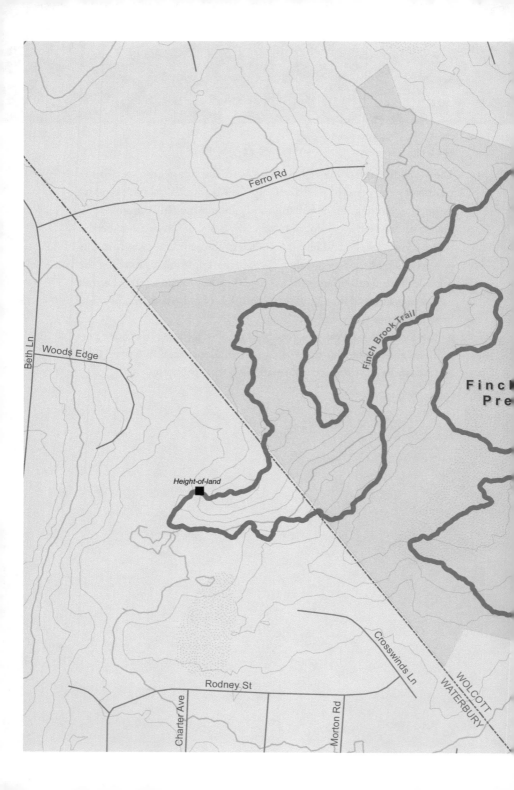

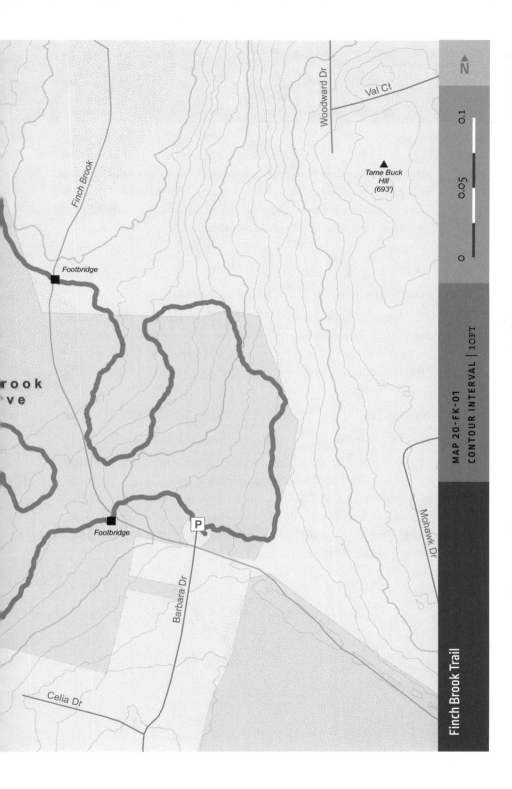

Hancock Brook, Jericho, and Whitestone Cliffs Trails

These Waterbury-area trails are located in the watershed of the Naugatuck River north of Waterbury and traverse the wooded hills east and west of Route 8. Lying primarily in Mattatuck State Forest, these footpaths follow diverse terrain over rocky ridges and through deep hemlock ravines, a refreshing respite from the urban landscape below.

Hancock Brook Trail

LENGTH 2.6 miles   **BLAZE COLOR** Blue

The Hancock Brook Trail parallels Hancock Brook as it cuts through a deep hemlock ravine, rises sharply to traverse rugged ledges, and meanders beneath high cliffs. When you reach Lion Head summit (660 feet), hikers will be rewarded with fine westerly views of the Naugatuck Valley.

Jericho Trail

LENGTH 3.1 miles   **BLAZE COLOR** Blue

The Jericho Trail traverses a section of the Mattatuck State Forest known as the Cave Block because of its numerous ledge overhangs, interesting rock formations, and intricate caves and passageways. The trail crosses Jericho Brook and winds through the site of a 1986 forest fire. The trail links to the Mattatuck Trail near one of the Leatherman's caves and features a handful of seasonal vistas.

Jericho-Whitestone Connector

LENGTH 1.5 miles   **BLAZE COLOR** Blue/Yellow

The Jericho-Whitestone Connector crosses the Naugatuck River to provide a link between the Whitestone Cliffs Trail on the east and the Jericho Trail on the west. The trail ascends a steep ridge and follows portions of an old trolley bed.

Whitestone Cliffs Trail

LENGTH 1.3 miles   **BLAZE COLOR** Blue

The Whitestone Cliffs Trail forms a short loop in Mattatuck State Forest. This short trail is incredibly diverse. Explore streams, wetlands, and rocky knolls and be rewarded with outstanding views of the Naugatuck Valley. Whitestone Cliffs Trail gets its name from the brilliant white rocky outcrop visible from Route 8.

63

▮ *Hunting is permitted in state forests intersected by these trails. Please use caution and wear orange during hunting season.*

Help us out! Report all illegal motorized vehicle use on the trails *immediately when you see it* by contacting the local police or, if on state land, the State Environmental Conservation Police, at 860-424-3333.

›

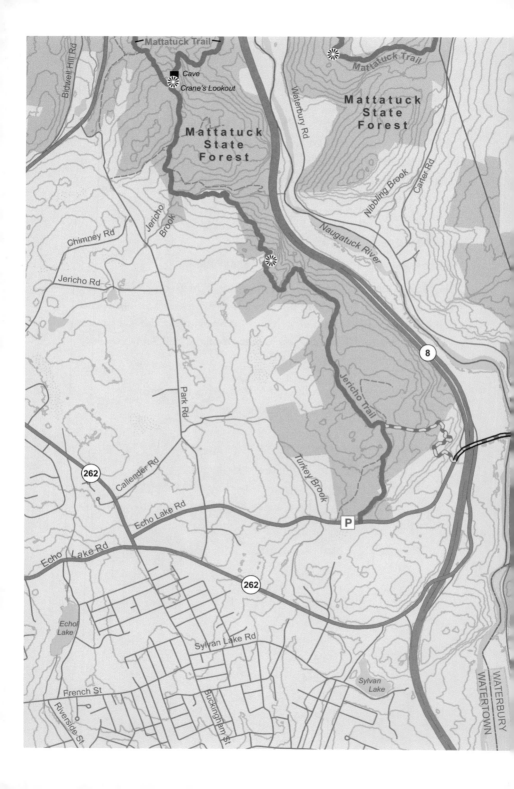

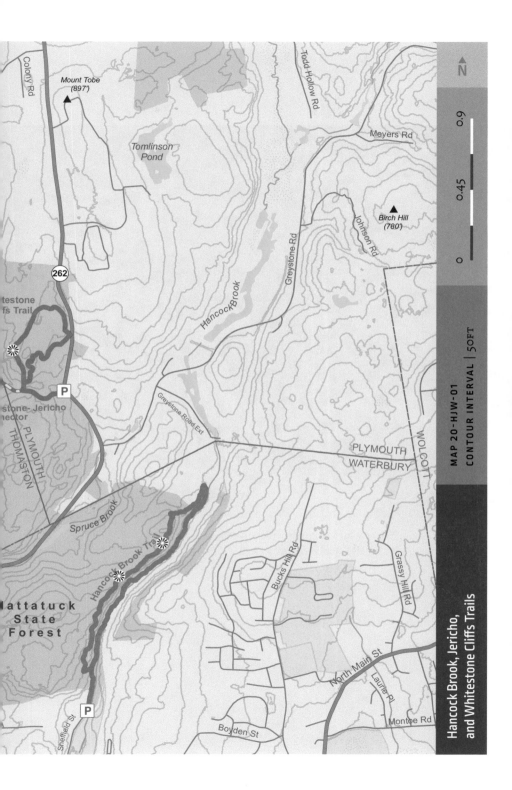

Mount Tobe
(897')

Colony Rd

Todd Hollow Rd

Tomlinson
Pond

Meyers Rd

Birch Hill
(780')

Greystone Rd

Johnson Rd

Hancock Brook

262

testone
fs Trail

Greystone Road Ext

stone- Jericho
nector

P

PLYMOUTH
THOMASTON

PLYMOUTH
WATERBURY

WOLCOTT

Spruce Brook

Hancock Brook Tra

Bucks Hill Rd

Grassy Hill Rd

Mattatuck
State
Forest

North Main St

Laurel Pl

Sheffield St

P

Boyden St

Montoe Rd

Hancock Brook, Jericho,
and Whitestone Cliffs Trails

Hiking is fun in all seasons, whether on your own or
with a hiking club. Photo courtesy CFPA.

Hibbard Trail

LENGTH 1.5 miles **BLAZE COLOR** Blue

The Whitney Forest is an 84-acre gem of protected woodland, nestled in the heart of Lebanon. It was donated to CFPA in 1998 by Dorothy D. Whitney of Avon, Connecticut. It was the desire of the Whitney family that the property be managed as a working forest in perpetuity. The forest will now serve as an educational site for sustainable forestry practices. CFPA undertook a timber harvest on the property in 2015 to improve the forest for oak and pitch-pine regeneration. The same year, CFPA's trails program built the loop trail to better showcase the property to the public. The trail features red maple swamps, fieldstone corrals, a tumbling stream, and views over a neighboring marsh.

The loop trail is named for John Hibbard, one of Connecticut's premier conservation heroes. Hibbard served as CFPA's executive director and secretary/forester from 1963 to 2000. Trained as a forester at the University of Connecticut, Hibbard was a visionary who worked on big legislative issues that have had long-lasting impacts on conservation and recreation across the state. His forceful advocacy was integral to providing tax relief for farm, forest, and open-space lands (PA 490), which currently total 484,000 acres statewide. He worked on legislation that established town conservation commissions to protect our local air, water, and open-space resources. It is our hope that, as you walk this trail, you will be both aware of the path that John Hibbard blazed and inspired to make a difference yourself.

▐ *Trails are open to foot travel only.*

▐ *Hunting occurs on the property. Please take necessary precautions during hunting season.*

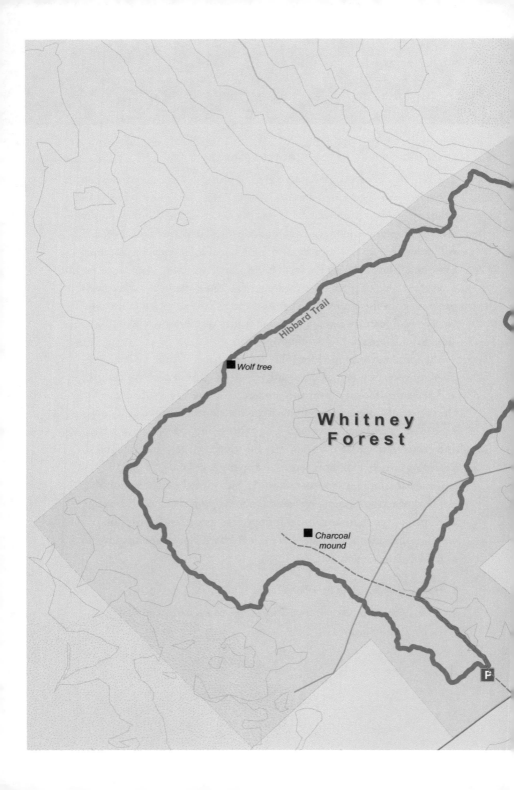

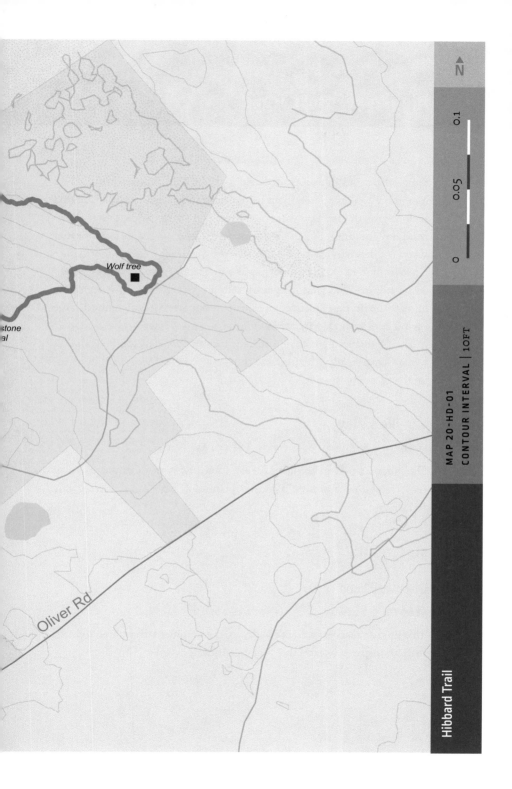

Wolf tree

stone
al

Oliver Rd

Hibbard Trail

MAP 20-HD-01
CONTOUR INTERVAL | 10FT

0   0.05   0.1

N

LENGTH 3.5 miles   **BLAZE COLOR** Varied

Situated behind CFPA's headquarters on the Middletown/Middlefield line, the Highlawn Forest is a gem. The trail system winds through a second-growth forest on what once were open farm fields, and features conifer plantations, mixed hardwood forest, and red maple swamps that support a diverse array of wildlife species. The trails follow many old fire lanes from the time the property was a tree farm and offer multiple loop opportunities. These flat and gentle trails are great for young or beginning hikers. The property also features an outdoor amphitheater, pond, large vernal pool with an observation platform, and a universal access trail.

70

The Highlawn Forest is protected from further development thanks to the Camp family, who placed a conservation easement (held by CFPA) on the property in 1987.

Camille's Way

LENGTH 2.2 miles   **BLAZE COLOR** Blue

The longest trail in Highlawn Forest, Camille's Way loops the property, features evidence of an old conifer plantation, and links to other side trails.

SIDE TRAILS

Discovery Loop

LENGTH 0.2 miles   **BLAZE COLOR** Blue/Red

This universal access trail is a wide, crushed-stone path situated right off the parking area behind the CFPA headquarters.

Camelia's Trail

LENGTH 0.7 miles   **BLAZE COLOR** Blue/Orange

Utilizing an old cart path on the property, Camelia's Trail is wide and relatively flat.

Sarah's Path

LENGTH 0.3 miles   **BLAZE COLOR** Blue/Violet

This connector trail links to the pond on the property and bisects other longer trails.

Ruth's Crossover

LENGTH 0.1 miles   **BLAZE COLOR** Blue/Green

This link trail offers a short loop opportunity between Camille's Way and Camelia's Trail.

▎ *Hunting is permitted on this property. Please use caution and wear orange during hunting season.*

▎ *Trails are open to hiking activities only.*

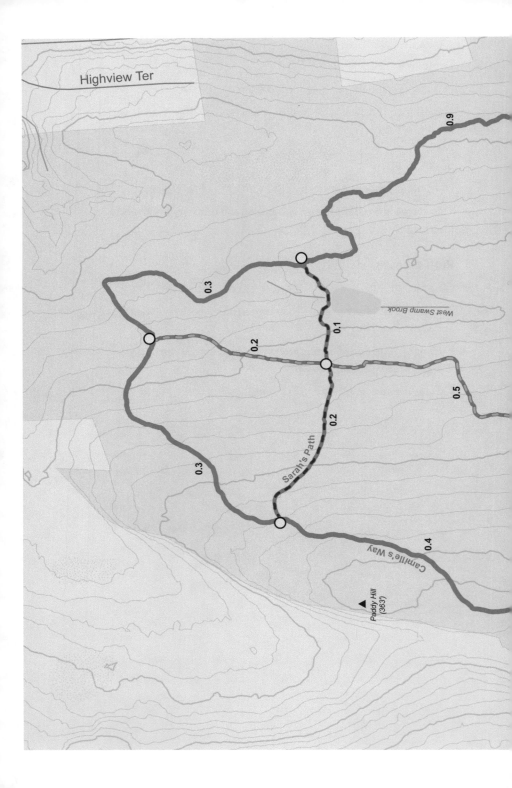

Highview Ter

0.9

0.3

West Swamp Brook

0.1

0.2

0.5

0.2

Sarah's Path

0.3

Camille's Way

0.4

Paddy Hill
(363)

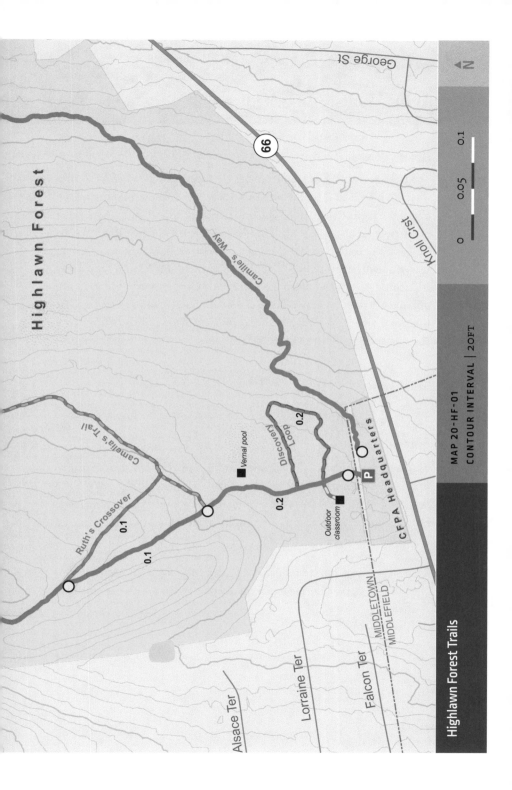

Highlawn Forest

Camille's Way

Camille's Trail

Ruth's Crossover

0.1

0.1

Vernal pool

Discovery Loop

0.2

0.2

Outdoor classroom

CFPA Headquarters

P

66

George St

Knoll Crst

Alsace Ter

Lorraine Ter

Falcon Ter

MIDDLETOWN
MIDDLEFIELD

N

0   0.05   0.1

0.1

MAP 20-HF-01
CONTOUR INTERVAL | 20FT

Highlawn Forest Trails

Housatonic Range Trail

LENGTH 6.2 miles **BLAZE COLOR** Blue

The Housatonic Range Trail traverses the forested plateau of the North-west Highlands and follows the route of a former Indian footpath high above the Housatonic River. The trail parallels Route 7 and offers views of the river as it flows through Marble Valley. From Gaylord Road in New Milford, the trail extends south across Boardman Mountain and over Pine Knob to its terminus at Candlewood Mountain. A 1.4-mile one-way trip from Route 37 south to the summit of Candlewood Mountain is a popular and challenging hike. A short side trail (blue/red blazed) near the Candlewood Mountain summit leads to Kelly's Slide, a huge rock slide on the east side of the mountain.

SIDE TRAIL

Tory's Cave Trail

LENGTH 0.3 miles **BLAZE COLOR** Blue/Yellow

This trail descends south to Route 7 and passes Tory's Cave, a natural, tunnel-like opening in the limestone that leads beneath the surface to a large cavern. Tory's Cave is the only marble solution cave in Connecticut but it is currently closed to the public for safety and habitat reasons. Please admire from a distance.

■ *There are numerous steep climbs and sharp ledge scrambles that become extremely slippery during inclement weather. Please use caution and plan accordingly.*

There are all kinds of things to discover flying around in the woods. Photo courtesy Brian Stewart.

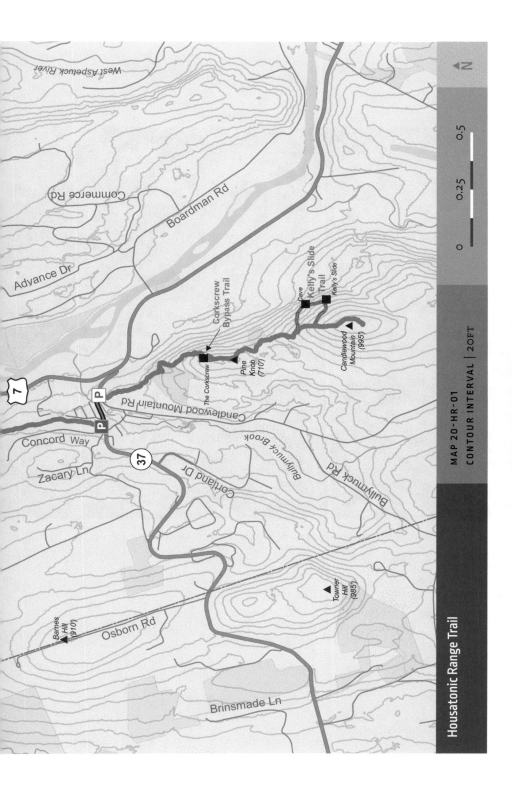

West Aspetuck River

Commerce Rd

Boardman Rd

Advance Dr

Corkscrew Bypass Trail

Cave

Kelly's Slide Trail

Kelly's Slide

The Corkscrew

Pine Knob (710)

Candlewood Mountain (995)

7

P P

Candlewood Mountain Rd

Concord Way

Zacary Ln

37

Cortland Dr

Bullymuck Brook

Bullymuck Rd

Towner Hill (985)

Barnes Hill (910)

Osborn Rd

Brinsmade Ln

N

0   0.25   0.5

MAP 20-HR-01
CONTOUR INTERVAL | 20FT

Housatonic Range Trail

See a register box on the trail, sign in and let us know you passed through. Photo courtesy CFPA.

Iron Trail

LENGTH 4.0 miles   **BLAZE COLOR** Blue

The Iron Trail runs through Housatonic State Forest and the Canaan Mountain Natural Area Preserve. From the southern terminus at a metal gate on Canaan Mountain Road in Canaan, the trail heads north and west to the Beckley Furnace Industrial Monument on the banks of the Blackberry River in North Canaan. The trail crosses mostly through mixed hardwoods—including white oak, black cherry, and beech—punctuated by islands of pine and hemlock. In the nineteenth and early twentieth centuries, the area was regularly cut to produce charcoal to feed nearby iron furnaces, including Beckley, which produced iron between 1847 and 1919. Repeated coppice cutting has resulted in many multiple-trunked trees. Visible in a couple of places are flattened areas where mounds of wood were stacked and "cooked" with slow, smoky fires to produce charcoal. About halfway along the trail is a pile of stones that was probably once the fireplace of a collier's hut. From Wangum Road the trail follows a broad woods road bounded in places by stone walls. Upstream of a narrow brook crossing there is a beaver flowage. Upon veering west, the trail narrows and winds through thick woods while skirting the edge of Canaan Mountain. The last three-quarters of a mile descend to Beckley Furnace along a narrow charcoal road. The upper part features beautiful rock outcroppings. Pieces of slag from the furnace can be found on the lower part of the trail, which passes slag piles overgrown with vegetation just before crossing the Blackberry River and arriving at the stone furnace stack. Picnic tables and interpretive signs make this a nice spot to spend some time learning about a part of Connecticut's industrial history.

▌ *There is a neighboring but different "Iron Trail" in Great Mountain Forest.*

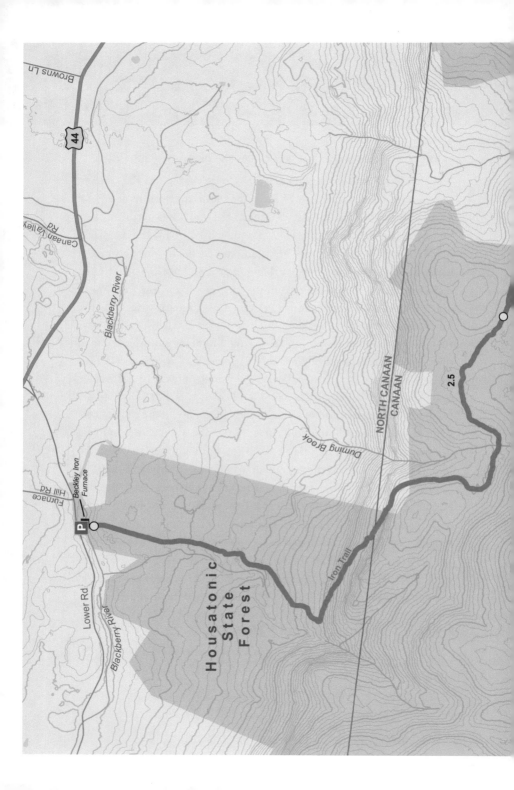

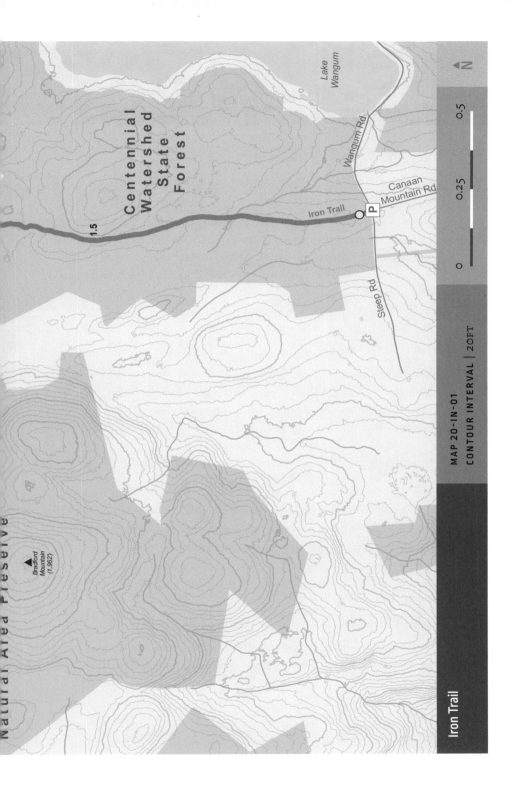

Natural Area Preserve

▲ Bradford Mountain (1,962')

Centennial Watershed State Forest

1.5

Iron Trail

Lake Wangum

Wangum Rd

Canaan Mountain Rd

Steep Rd

P

N

0   0.25   0.5

MAP 20-IN-01
CONTOUR INTERVAL | 20 FT

Iron Trail

Kettletown State Park Trails

LENGTH 6+ miles   BLAZE COLOR Varied

The hiking trails in the 600-acre Kettletown State Park offer breathtaking views of Lake Zoar and the surrounding countryside. The varied trail system has some rocky and steep climbs but also meanders along streams and ridges. The park offers multiple activities including swimming, fishing, picnicking, and camping. Visit the Connecticut DEEP website for park hours and additional information.

Miller Trail

LENGTH 1.8 miles   BLAZE COLOR Blue

The Miller Trail generally follows old woods roads and offers a nice loop hiking opportunity. A short bypass trail (blue/red) offers the opportunity to shorten the hike by about 0.5 miles. Seasonal views of Lake Zoar are possible from the blue/orange spur trail.

Brook Trail

LENGTH 0.4 miles   BLAZE COLOR Blue/Yellow

The Brook Trail begins opposite the Pomperaug Trail on the campground road, follows Kettletown Brook, and joins the park's nature trail for a short distance, passing several large glacial boulders on the way. The trail ends on the park road opposite the trailhead for the Miller Trail.

Crest Trail

LENGTH 1.7 miles   BLAZE COLOR Blue/White

The Crest Trail was built in 1980 by the Youth Conservation Corps. It runs parallel to the Pomperaug Trail, while traversing the crest of the ridge overlooking Lake Zoar. Two viewpoints offer seasonal views of Lake Zoar. The trail passes a charcoal hearth site and, north of the Campground Trail, a large glacial erratic boulder.

Campground Trail

LENGTH 0.25 miles   BLAZE COLOR Blue/Orange

The Campground Trail connects the park's campground loop with the Crest Trail.

Pomperaug Trail

LENGTH 4.6 miles   BLAZE COLOR Blue

The Pomperaug Trail connects Kettletown State Park in Southbury with the Jackson Cove Recreation Area in Oxford. The Oxford Land Trust also hosts a section of the trail. Meandering through wetlands and woods and passing several charcoal hearth sites, the Pomperaug Trail ascends high, rocky ridges over Lake Zoar providing wonderful views. Rocks in some spots are studded with industrial-grade garnets, which were harvested in the former garnet mine below the trail.

An unblazed roadwalk of approximately 1.5 miles south on Fiddlehead Road can be used to connect over the Stevenson Dam to the blue-blazed Paugussett Trail in Monroe.

Visit the Connecticut DEEP website for additional information on visiting Kettletown State Park.

SIDE TRAIL

Oxford Loop Trail

LENGTH 0.6 miles   BLAZE COLOR Blue/White

The Oxford Loop Trail follows the shore of Lake Zoar to form a picturesque hiking loop when combined with the Pomperaug Trail.

Zoar Trail

BLAZE COLOR Blue

The Zoar Trail is entirely within the 1,200-acre lower block of Paugussett State Forest in Newtown. The trail passes through a mixture of hardwood trees and shady hemlock groves and offers a diverse 6.5-mile loop hike with small beaches. Water views are a dominant feature of the trail, which is named for the lake that it parallels. Lake Zoar is a 975-acre reservoir created in 1919 by the construction of the Stevenson Dam on the Housatonic River. The Zoar Trail follows the shore for 2.4 miles north of the Great Quarter Road trailhead, rewarding hikers with frequent views of the lake, along with the forested slopes of Kettletown State Park across the water. By following the trail loop clockwise, most of the climbing is concentrated in the first two-thirds of the hike, leaving the last 2.4 miles as a series of rolling changes in terrain.

South of the junction of the Zoar Trail and the blue/white-blazed Alternate Trail is Prydden Brook Falls, which tumbles down to Lake Zoar in a series of dramatic cascades. One can view the entire falls from an unmarked trail that parallels the cascades down to Lake Zoar. On the inland side of the forest, the Zoar Trail crosses Prydden Brook, which can be difficult to navigate at times of high water. South of Prydden Brook are a few overlooks with views south across the lake.

SIDE TRAILS

Leopard Road Connector

LENGTH 0.8 miles   **BLAZE COLOR** Blue/Red

This side trail connects to Leopard Road.

Great Quarter Road Connector

LENGTH 0.1 miles   **BLAZE COLOR** Blue/Yellow

This short connector trail links to Great Quarter Road.

84

Hunting is common in many state forests, wildlife management areas, and on private conservation lands. Make sure to wear bright orange during hunting season and follow all posted signage.

Paugussett Road Connector

LENGTH 0.5 miles   **BLAZE COLOR** Blue/Yellow

This side trail connects to Paugussett Road.

Alternate Trail

LENGTH 0.3 miles   **BLAZE COLOR** Blue/White

The Alternate Trail can be used to bypass the steep and rugged inland section of the Zoar Trail.

▮ *Hunting is permitted in the state forest intersected by these trails. Please use caution and wear orange during hunting season.*

▮ *Footing can be icy and uncertain along the lake, even well into spring, so plan accordingly.*

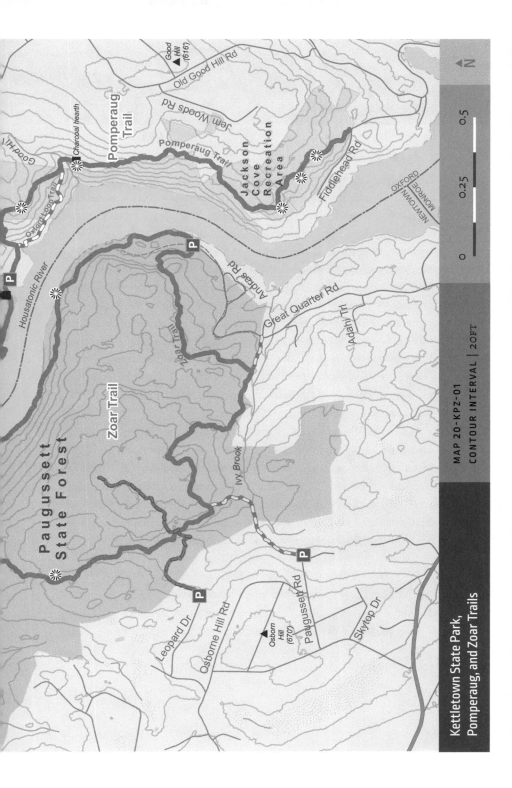

Kettletown State Park,
Pomperaug, and Zoar Trails

MAP 20-KPZ-01
CONTOUR INTERVAL | 20FT

N

0   0.25   0.5

Good
Hill
(616')

Old Good Hill Rd

Jem Woods Rd

Charcoal hearth

Pomperaug
Trail

Pomperaug Trail

Good Hill

Oxford Loop Trail

Housatonic River

Jackson
Cove
Recreation
Area

Fiddlehead Rd

OXFORD

NEWTOWN
MONROE

P

Andkas Rd

Great Quarter Rd

Adahi Trl

Zoar Trail

Zoar Trail

Paugussett
State Forest

Ivy Brook

Leopard Dr

Osborne Hill Rd

Osborn
Hill
(670')

Paugussett Rd

Skytop Dr

P

P

P

Lillinonah Trail

LENGTH 6.2 miles   **BLAZE COLOR** Blue

Located entirely within the 800-acre upper block of the Paugussett State Forest in Newtown, the Lillinonah Trail is surrounded on three sides by water. The trail parallels Lake Lillinonah, a 1,547-acre lake created in 1955 by the construction of the Shepaug Dam, which can be seen regularly from the trail. Another water feature is the Pond Brook inlet, a narrow waterway that stretches back to the trailhead at Hanover Road. The Lillinonah Trail is a rugged trail with frequent changes in elevation as it mostly follows the edge of the state forest property. The Connecticut DEEP has designated a 3.1-mile section near the lakeshore as a scenic trail because of the excellent views of Lake Lillinonah, the Shepaug River inlet, the Shepaug Dam, and the three towns bordering the lake (Newtown, Bridgewater, and Southbury). The trail also passes through an extensive maple sugaring operation in the vicinity of the Echo Valley Road parking area.

Within the forest are other multi-use trails. The Upper Gussy Trail, a 1.8-mile trail created for mountain bikers and equestrians, and Brody Road, named for conservationist Polly Brody (who convinced the state to purchase the land), both offer hikers numerous loop opportunities. Al's Trail, marked with dark blue arrows, coincides with the Lillinonah Trail from the Pond Brook inlet to the trailhead near Echo Valley Road. Visit the Al's Trail website (www.alstrail.org) for more details.

▌ *Hunting is permitted in the state forest intersected by this trail. Please use caution and wear orange during hunting season.*

▌ *The "scenic trail" section is a nesting habitat for bald eagles and the lakeshore portion is closed from December 15 to March 15. Use Brody Road as an alternative to complete the loop.*

Trailhead kiosk at Chittenden Park on the Menunkatuck Trail.
Check the map before you start your hike. Photo courtesy CFPA.

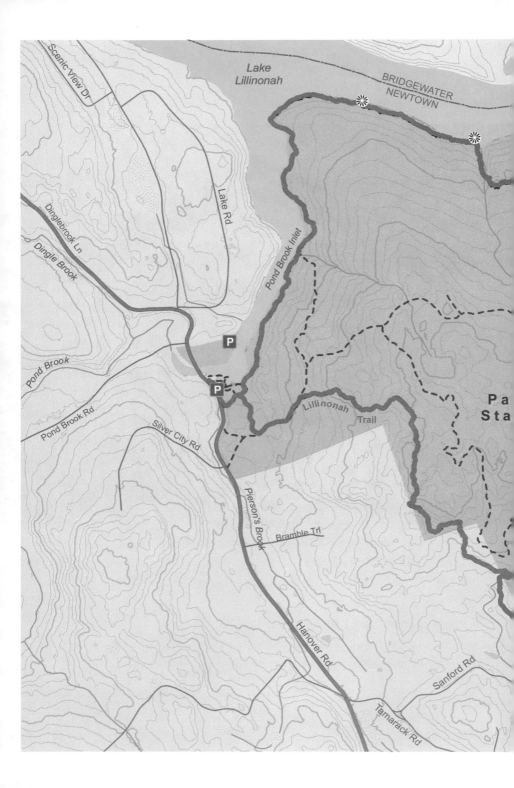

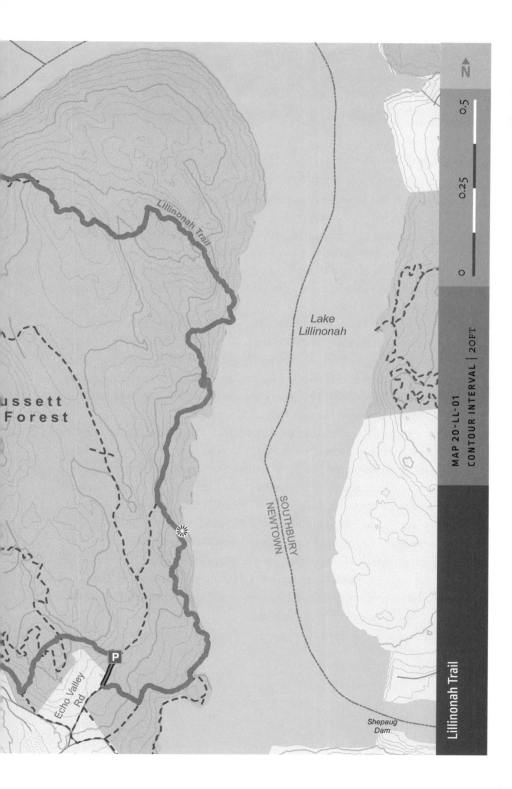

Lillinonah Trail

ussett
Forest

Lillinonah Trail

Lake
Lillinonah

SOUTHBURY
NEWTOWN

Echo Valley
Rd

P

Shepaug
Dam

N

0   0.25   0.5

MAP 20-LL-01
CONTOUR INTERVAL | 20FT

Macedonia Brook State Park Trails

LENGTH 12.8 miles **BLAZE COLOR** Varied

Macedonia Brook State Park is situated on 2,300 acres of rugged terrain in Kent, less than a mile east of the New York border. The bulk of the property was originally gifted to the state from the White Memorial Foundation of Litchfield in 1918. The land was once the domain of the Scatacook Indians. After Kent was settled in 1738, the native inhabitants and settlers shared the area harmoniously. During the Revolutionary War, Scatacook volunteers operated a signal system along the summits of the river valley.

During the state's iron boom, the Kent Iron Company operated both in Kent and the village of Macedonia. Remains of a forge and a stamping works are still visible at the southern end of the park. In 1865, competition from larger mines forced the Macedonia furnace to close. Many years later, the National Park Service established a Civilian Conservation Corps camp at the park to undertake park improvements.

The park has over 12 miles of foot trails, all originating at the graveled park road (Macedonia Brook Road). Several side trails cross or connect with the blue-blazed Macedonia Ridge Trail, an oval loop encompassing much of the park. In general, trails east of the park road are not as steep as those to the west. The Macedonia Ridge Trail offers outstanding views of the Taconic Range and Catskill Mountains from Cobble Mountain (elevation 1,380 feet), located on the west side of the park. In the valley below, numerous streams tumble into Macedonia Brook, which winds its way south through the park and is flanked on both sides by peaks and ridges over 1,000 feet high. Numerous springs and streams in the park add to the great hiking experience.

Macedonia Ridge Trail

LENGTH 6.6 miles   BLAZE COLOR Blue

The Macedonia Ridge Trail includes former sections of the Appalachian Trail, which once passed through the northern end of Macedonia Brook State Park. The sections east and west of Macedonia Brook Road are about the same length, with the finest views from the western side. The steep ascent and descent of the north slope of Cobble Mountain should be approached with caution. This section is not easily negotiated in wet or icy conditions and is not recommended for children.

Orange Trail

LENGTH 3.3 miles   BLAZE COLOR Orange

This side trail can be combined with other park trails for moderate to challenging loop hikes over varied terrain.

93

Cobble Mountain Trail

LENGTH 0.8 miles   BLAZE COLOR White

The Cobble Mountain Trail briefly parallels the park road, crosses a stream, then ascends the steep east face of Cobble Mountain. This trail is steep, can be treacherous when wet, and is difficult to negotiate when ice and snow are present. Due to the relatively steep terrain, it is not recommended for young children.

Yellow Trail

LENGTH 0.5 miles   BLAZE COLOR Yellow

This side trail features a rugged 450-foot climb from the main park road to the blue-blazed Macedonia Ridge Trail on the east side of the park. The trail offers an east-side access to the Macedonia Ridge Trail for a loop around the park, or a connection with the Green Trail for a shorter loop back to the parking lot.

Trail relocations and building new trail connections take an amazing amount of volunteer power. Photo courtesy CFPA.

Who builds these trails? Who maintains them? Volunteers do! In 2016, volunteers contributed over 20,000 hours to maintenance and upkeep of the Blue-Blazed Hiking Trails—what an amazing effort! Want to dig in and help out? Visit our website for current volunteer opportunities.

Green Trail

LENGTH 1.6 miles   **BLAZE COLOR** Green

The Green Trail connects across the center of the park, linking the east and west sides of the Macedonia Ridge Trail. The trail also overlaps with the Orange Trail. The 0.2-mile climb from the park road to the Macedonia Ridge Trail on the western side of the park is incredibly steep.

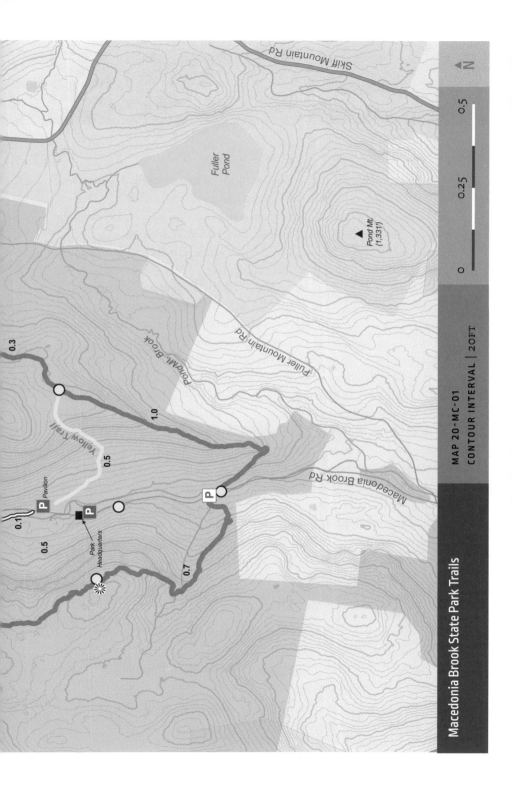

Macedonia Brook State Park Trails

MAP 20-MC-01
CONTOUR INTERVAL | 20 FT

0   0.25   0.5

N

Skiff Mountain Rd

Fuller Pond

Pond Mt. (1,331')

Pond Mt. Brook

Fuller Mountain Rd

Macedonia Brook Rd

Yellow Trail

Pavilion

Park Headquarters

0.3

1.0

0.5

0.1

0.5

0.7

LENGTH 60.8 miles   **BLAZE COLOR** Blue

The Mattabesett Trail (Mattabesett is the Indian name for Middletown) roughly forms a large horseshoe beginning at River Road in Middletown and extending to the Berlin Turnpike in Berlin. The trail begins traveling in a southerly direction, gradually becomes more westerly, then finally assumes a northerly direction. The trail was one of the first conceived by early Connecticut trail builders and remains popular today.

The eastern sections of the Mattabesett Trail contain high ledges and bald knobs with vistas of the Connecticut River. A picturesque terrain of tumbled ledges, frequent brooks, shallow bogs, vernal pools, mountain laurel, and hardwood forest adds to the trail's beauty. The western sections offer some of the finest ridge walking and cliff views in the state as the trail traverses the southern end of the traprock ridges that extend north into Massachusetts. Some of the notable features hikers will encounter include the Chinese Wall in Middletown, Pisgah Mountain in Durham, Bluff Head in Guilford, Beseck Mountain in Middlefield, Mount Higby in Middletown, and Chauncey Peak and Lamentation Mountain in Meriden.

Across its length, the trail connects some incredible open spaces. State forests and parks, land trust preserves, municipal parks, and conserved land are all linked by the trail. The Reservoir, Bear Hill, and Seven Falls sections at the eastern end include 5 miles of loop trails. The trail intersects other major trail systems and offers additional loop opportunities in Millers Pond State Park and Mica Ledges in Durham, the Rockland Preserve in Madison, Braemore Preserve in Guilford, and Giuffrida Park in Meriden.

The Mattabesett Trail is part of the 215-mile New England National Scenic Trail (NET). The NET was designated as a national scenic trail in 2009 and connects Long Island Sound to the Massachusetts/New Hampshire border. The NET is comprised of the Menunkatuck, Mattabesett,

Metacomet, and Metacomet-Monadnock Trails. The *New England Trail Map and Guide*, published by the Appalachian Mountain Club, provides a detailed resource for hikers. For more information about the NET, visit newenglandtrail.org.

❚ *Hunting is permitted in state forests and other properties intersected by this trail. Please use caution and wear orange during hunting season.*

SIDE TRAILS

Reservoir Loop (see Map 20-MB-01)

LENGTH 1.4 miles   **BLAZE COLOR** Blue/Yellow

The Reservoir Loop Trail begins on Brooks Road in Middletown, approximately 100 yards east of the Mattabesett Trail crossing. This trail crosses moderate terrain surrounding the eastern and southern shoreline of the reservoir. Great views abound along the reservoirs.

Bear Hill Loop (see Map 20-MB-01)

LENGTH 2.2 miles   **BLAZE COLOR** Blue/Yellow

This loop trail features a pond, mountain laurel, and rocky outcroppings. It has a few steep climbs and crosses several streams.

Seven Falls Loop (see Map 20-MB-01)

LENGTH 1.1 miles   **BLAZE COLOR** Blue/Yellow

Beginning at the Seven Falls Roadside Park, the Seven Falls Loop offers a short loop with the Mattabesett Trail that features ledges and two short rock scrambles. It passes a talus cave and offers some nice views.

Bear Rock Bypass (see Map 20-MB-02)

LENGTH 0.1 miles   **BLAZE COLOR** Blue/Red

The bypass begins 40 yards east of Bear Rock and rejoins the main Mattabesett Trail in 0.1 miles. It should be used when trail conditions are wet or icy, as the descent from Bear Rock to the south and west is particularly difficult under these conditions. Bear Rock, with its expansive view, can still be enjoyed by following the main trail 40 yards to the summit and then retracing your steps to the bypass trail.

Cream Pot Road Access Trail (see Map 20-MB-03)

LENGTH 0.1 miles   BLAZE COLOR Blue/Red

This short trail uses an unimproved section of Cream Pot Road in Durham to provide access to the Mattabesett Trail. It continues for another 0.9 miles as a blue/red-blazed trail called the Selectmen's Path. This trail provides additional access to the Mica Ledges Preserve, managed by the Madison Land Conservation Trust and the Middlesex Land Trust. Selectmen's Path crosses the Mattabesett Trail and uses unimproved roads to access Whitney Pond and the Selectmen's Stones, which mark the point where the town boundaries of Durham, Madison, and Guilford meet.

Lone Pine Trail (see Map 20-MB-03)

LENGTH 4.4 miles   BLAZE COLOR Blue/Red

The Lone Pine Trail passes through Guilford's Braemore, Myerhuber, and James Valley Preserves, and the Guilford Land Conservation Trust's Bluff Head Preserve. This large area, called the Northwoods, is a gem of protected lands in north Guilford. This trail can be combined with the Mattabesett Trail for a longer hike and reaches the high summit plateau of Totoket Mountain (elevation 720 feet).

George Etzel–Meyerhuber Trail (see Map 20-MB-03)

LENGTH 1.0 mile   BLAZE COLOR Blue/ Yellow

This trail offers a link between the Mattabesett Trail at Bluffhead and the Lone Pine Trail. The trail, which parallels Route 77, has a short roadwalk and wanders through some beautiful woodlands.

Bluff Head Alternate Route (see Map 20-MB-03)

LENGTH 1.0 miles   BLAZE COLOR Blue/Orange

The alternate trail to Bluff Head begins at the Route 77 parking area. It provides a more moderate, yet still challenging, climb to Bluff Head ridge.

North Slope Trail (see Map 20-MB-03)

LENGTH 0.5 miles   BLAZE COLOR Blue/White

This trail links the Lone Pine Trail at Hemlock Brook to the Mattabesett Trail by following a woods road with a moderate slope. Historically this was an old wagon road that climbed from the valley up to the plateau. It, along with the George Etzel–Meyerhuber Trail, provides some loop-hike opportunities of varying length around Bluff Head.

Route 66 Connector (see Map 20-MB-05)

LENGTH 0.1 miles   BLAZE COLOR Blue/Red

This short trail connects the Mattabesett Trail to a major parking area on Route 66, the main trailhead for Mount Higby.

Tynan Park Connector (see Map 20-MB-05)

LENGTH 0.9 miles   BLAZE COLOR Blue/Red

This trail travels through Middletown's Tynan Park and offers access to the Mattabesett Trail.

Footit Drive Connector (see Map 20-MB-05)

LENGTH 0.1 miles   BLAZE COLOR Blue/Red

This connector links a parking area in Middletown's Wilcox Park to the Mattabesett Trail.

Chauncey Peak Bypass (see Map 20-MB-05)

LENGTH 0.1 miles   BLAZE COLOR Blue/Red

This short trail provides access to an interesting mountain-top ravine and "slot" while bypassing the main view on Chauncey Peak.

Mileage Table

MATTABESETT TRAIL

0.0	River Rd (P)
2.7	Reservoir Rd
3.4	Rock Pile Cave
3.6	Reservoir overlook
3.9	Reservoir Rd / Jct Reservoir Loop (blue/yellow)
4.2	Jct Reservoir Loop (blue/yellow)
4.8	Brooks Rd / Jct Reservoir Loop (blue/yellow, 300 ft, P)
5.0	Bear Hill Rd (P)
5.2	Jct Bear Hill Loop (blue/yellow)
6.4	Jct Bear Hill Loop (blue/yellow)
7.2	Join Bear Hill Loop (blue/yellow)
7.2	Leave Bear Hill Loop (blue/yellow)
7.6	Jct Bear Hill Loop (blue/yellow)
8.9	Jct Bear Hill Loop (blue/yellow)
9.0	Aircraft Rd (P)
9.1	Freeman Rd
9.3	East jct Seven Falls Loop (blue/yellow)
10.1	Cave
10.5	West jct Seven Falls Loop (blue/yellow)
10.5	Begin roadwalk
10.5	Join Thayer Rd / Ct Rte 154 (P)
10.6	Join Nedobity Rd
11.5	Join Brainard Hill Rd
12.4	Leave Brainard Hill Rd (P)
12.4	End roadwalk
13.5	View
14.9	Begin roadwalk
14.9	Join Foot Hills Rd (P)
15.6	Join Wiese Albert Rd
15.6	Leave Wiese Albert Rd
15.6	End roadwalk
15.8	Join local trail (white, 0.3 mi, P)
16.4	Leave local trail (white)
17.7	North jct Bear Rock Bypass (blue/red, 200 ft)
17.7	Summit, Bear Rock (652 ft)
17.8	South jct Bear Rock Bypass Trail (blue/red, 200 ft)
18.4	Harvey Rd (P)
18.7	Higganum Rd (P)
20.3	Coginchaug Cave
20.8	Begin roadwalk
20.8	Join Old Blue Hills Rd (P)
21.6	Ct Rte 79 / Join Sand Hill Rd
21.6	Join Pisgah Rd
22.1	Leave Pisgah Rd (P)
22.1	End roadwalk
22.7	Summit, Mount Pisgah (641 ft)
22.9	Spur to Lookout (200 ft)
23.6	Cream Pot Rd Access Trail (blue/red, 0.1 mi, P)
23.8	The Pyramid / Jct local trail (orange)
24.1	View at Mica Ledges
24.2	Jct local trail (orange)
24.6	Jct local trail (orange)
24.6	Selectmen's Stones
25.8	Jct local trail (red)
25.9	East jct Lone Pine Trail (blue/red)
26.0	Godman Group Campsite
27.4	Jct Menunkatuck Trail (blue)
27.6	Vernal pool
28.6	Jct George Etzel–Meyerhuber Trail (blue/yellow)
28.8	Ct Rte 77 (P)
28.9	South jct Bluff Head Alternate Trail (blue/orange)
29.2	View / North jct Bluff Head Alternate Trail (blue/orange)
29.5	View
29.7	Spur to View (250 ft)
30.4	Jct North Slope Trail (blue/white)
31.9	West jct Lone Pine Trail (blue/red)
32.7	Begin roadwalk
32.7	Join Stagecoach Rd (P)
32.9	Join Ct Rte 17
33.2	Leave Ct Rte 17 (P)
33.2	End roadwalk
34.4	View
35.1	Howd Rd (P)
39.0	Cattails Shelter
39.1	Begin roadwalk—Ct Rte 68
39.3	End roadwalk—Ct Rte 68 (P)
40.4	View
41.1	Powerline
41.6	Jct local trail (orange)
42.2	Powder Ridge Ski Area
45.4	Ct Rte 147 / Ct Rte 66 (P)
46.1	Jct Rte 66 Connector (blue/red, P)
47.0	Ridgeline views

LONE PINE TRAIL

103

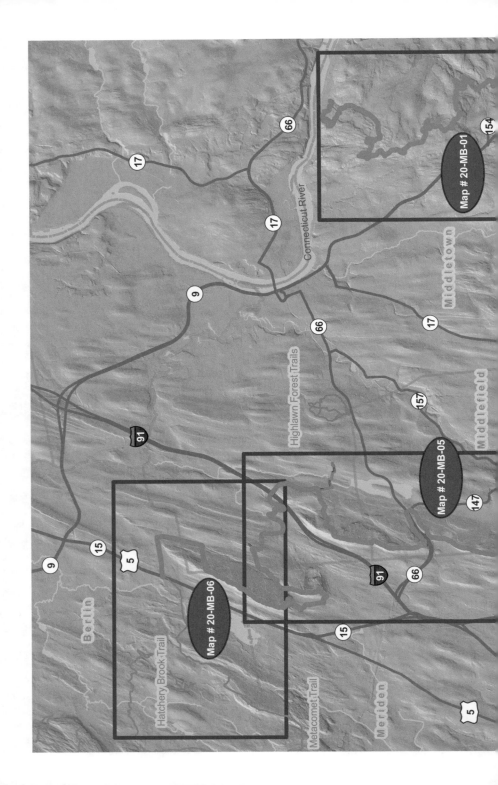

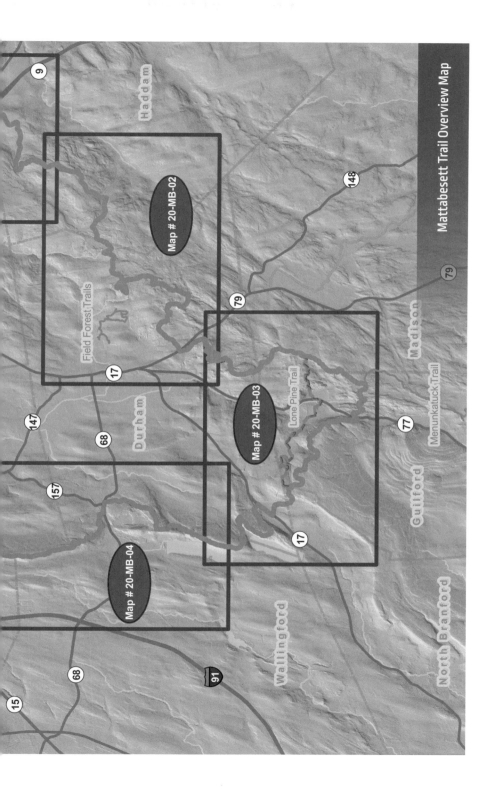

Mattabesett Trail Overview Map

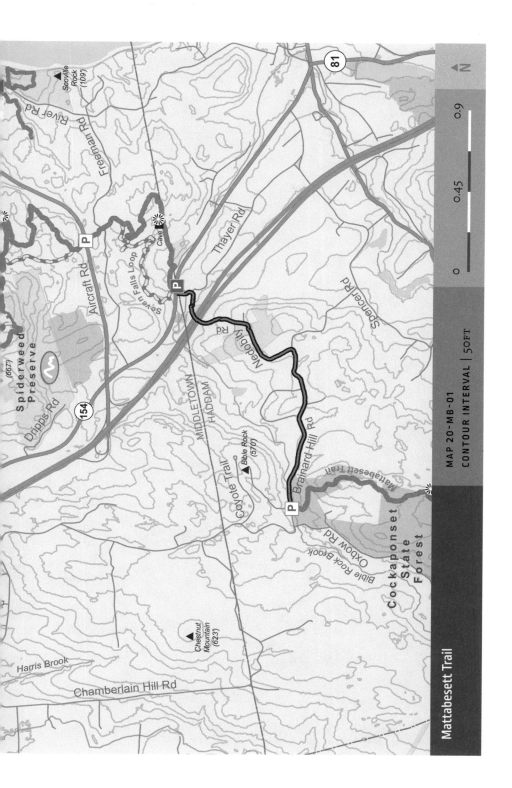

Mattabesett Trail

MAP 20-MB-01

CONTOUR INTERVAL | 50FT

N

0   0.45   0.9

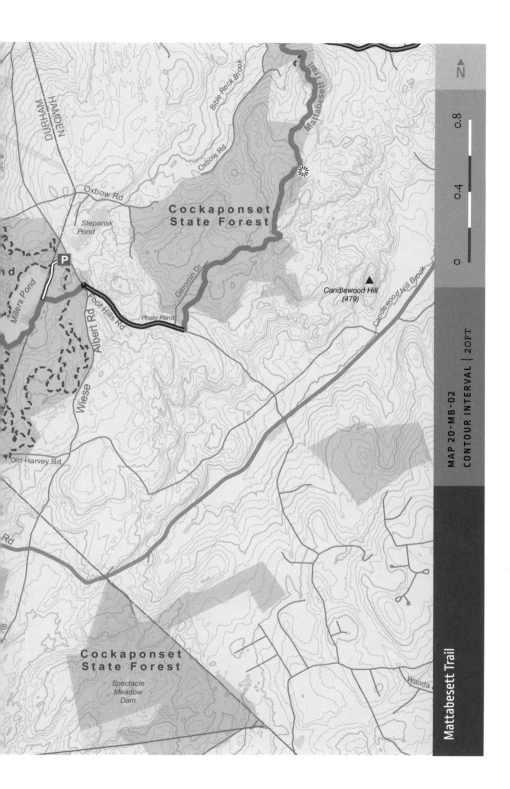

Bible Rock Brook

Mattabesett Trail

Oxbow Rd

Cockaponset
State Forest

Oxbow Rd

Stepansk
Pond

Geromin Dr

Candlewood Hill
(479)

Candlewood Hill Brook

P

Millers Pond

Foot Hills Rd

Photo Pond

Albert Rd

Wiese

Old Harvey Rd

Rd

Cockaponset
State Forest

Spectacle
Meadow
Dam

Wanda

HAMDEN

DURHAM

nd

0   0.4   0.8

CONTOUR INTERVAL | 20FT

Mattabesett Trail

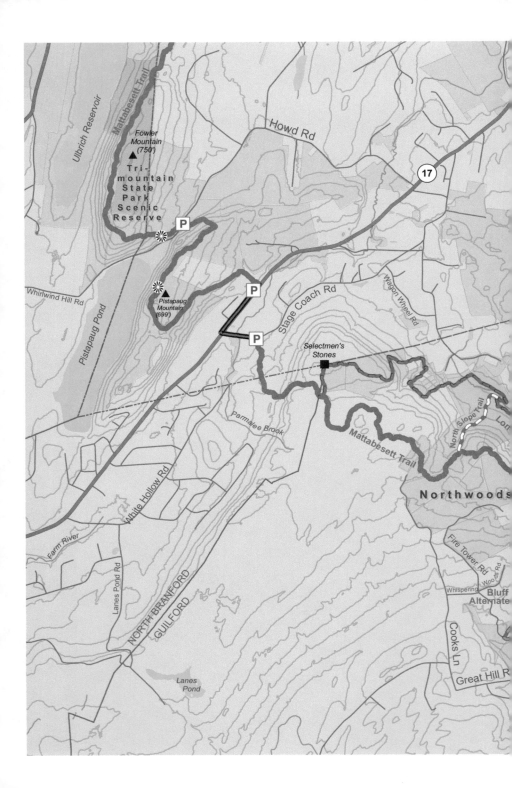

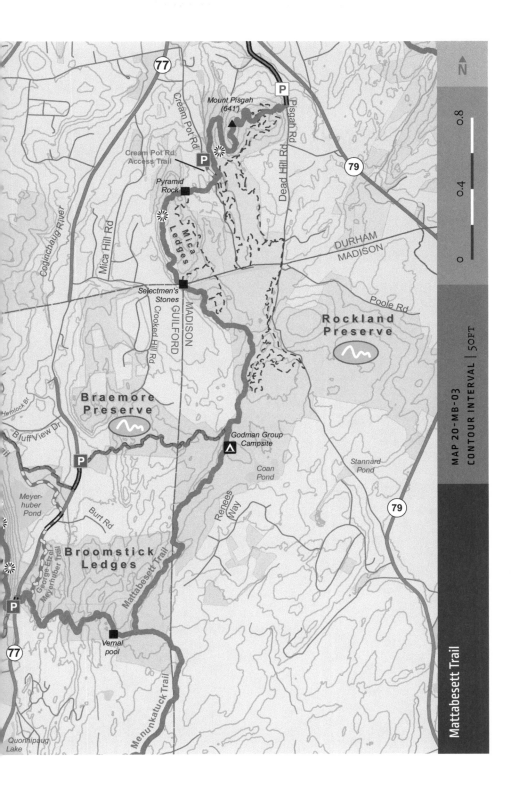

77

Mount Pisgah
(641')

P

Pisgah Rd

Cream Pot Rd

Cream Pot Rd
Access Trail

P

Dead Hill Rd

79

Pyramid
Rock

Coginchaug River

Mica Hill Rd

Mica Ledges

DURHAM
MADISON

Selectmen's
Stones

MADISON
GUILFORD

Crooked Hill Rd

Poole Rd

Rockland
Preserve

Braemore
Preserve

Hemlock Br

Bluff View Dr

P

Godman Group
Campsite

Coan
Pond

Stannard
Pond

79

Meyer-
huber
Pond

Burt Rd

Renees Way

Broomstick
Ledges

George Etzel
Meyerhuber Trail

Mattabesett Trail

P

Vernal
pool

77

Menunkatuck Trail

Quonnipaug
Lake

MAP 20-MB-03
CONTOUR INTERVAL | 50FT

0.8

0.4

0

Mattabesett Trail

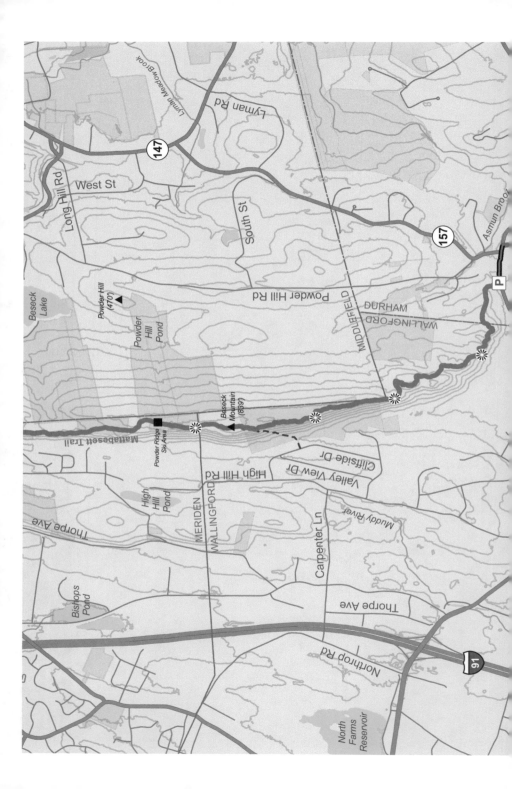

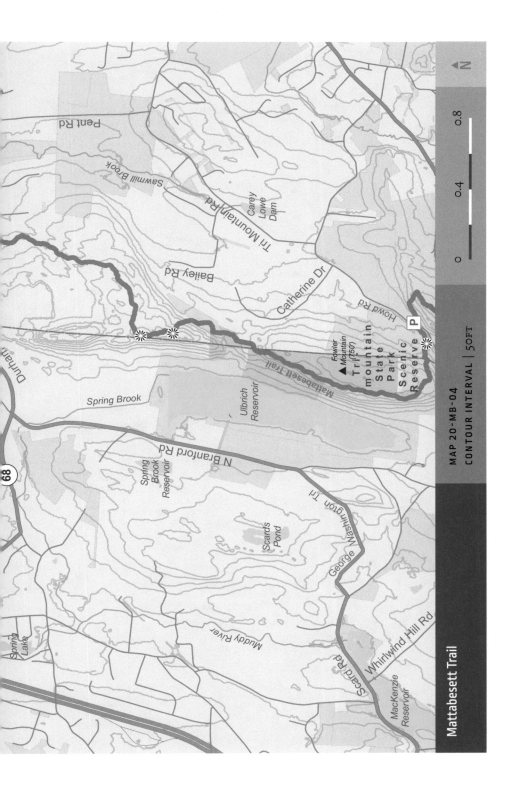

Pent Rd

Sawmill Brook

Carey
Lowe
Dam

Tri Mountain Rd

Bailey Rd

Catherine Dr

Howd Rd

Fowler
Mountain
(750')
▲ Tri-
mountain
State
Park
Scenic
Reserve

P

Mattabesett Trail

Durham

Spring Brook

Ulbrich
Reservoir

N Branford Rd

Spring
Brook
Reservoir

Scards
Pond

George Washington Trl

68

Spring
Lake

Muddy River

Whirlwind Hill Rd

Scard Rd

MacKenzie
Reservoir

N

0   0.4   0.8

MAP 20-MB-04
CONTOUR INTERVAL | 50FT

Mattabesett Trail

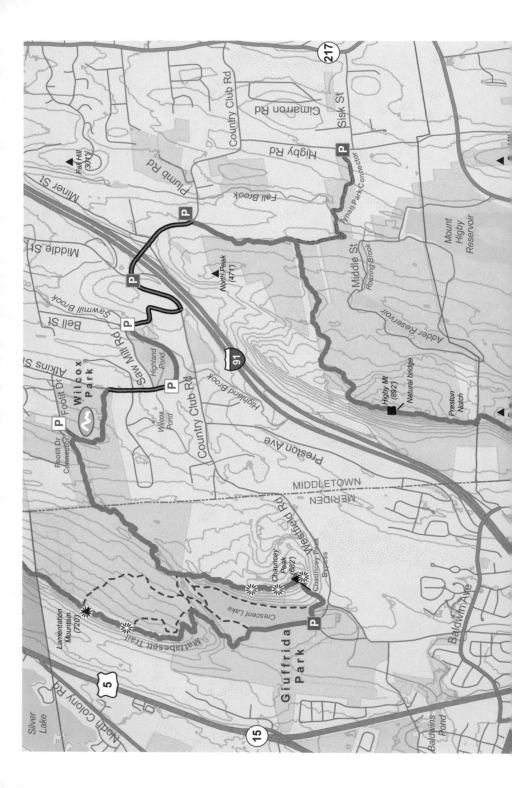

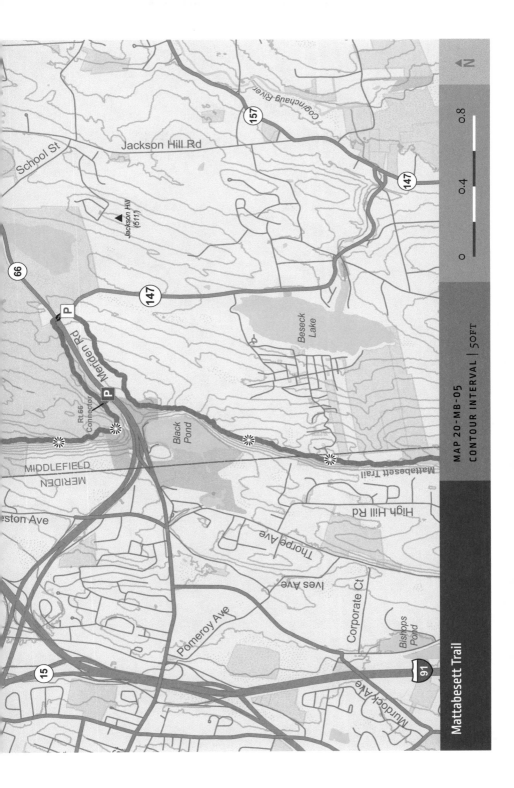

School St

Jackson Hill Rd

Coginchaug River

157

147

66

147

Meriden Rd

Rt 66
Connector

Jackson Hill
(511)

Beseck
Lake

P

P

MIDDLEFIELD
MERIDEN

ston Ave

Black
Pond

Mattabesett Trail

High Hill Rd

Thorpe Ave

Ives Ave

Corporate Ct

Bishops
Pond

Pomeroy Ave

15

91

Murdock Ave

N

0   0.4   0.8

MAP 20-MB-05
CONTOUR INTERVAL | 50FT

Mattabesett Trail

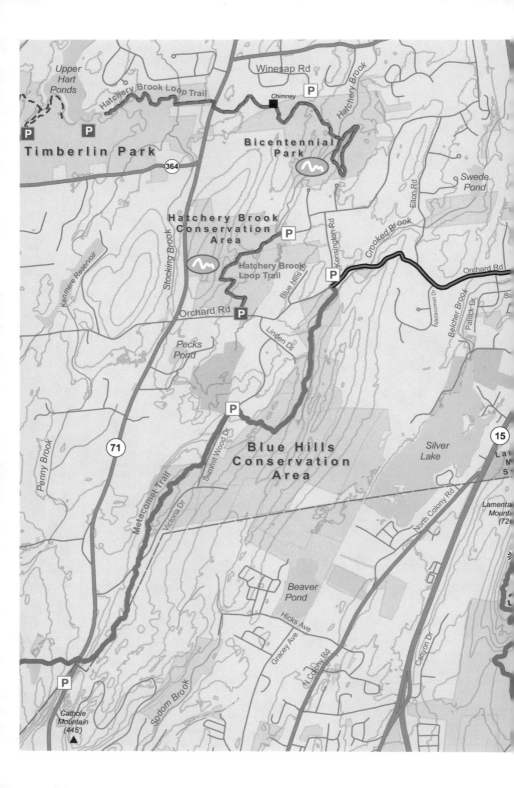

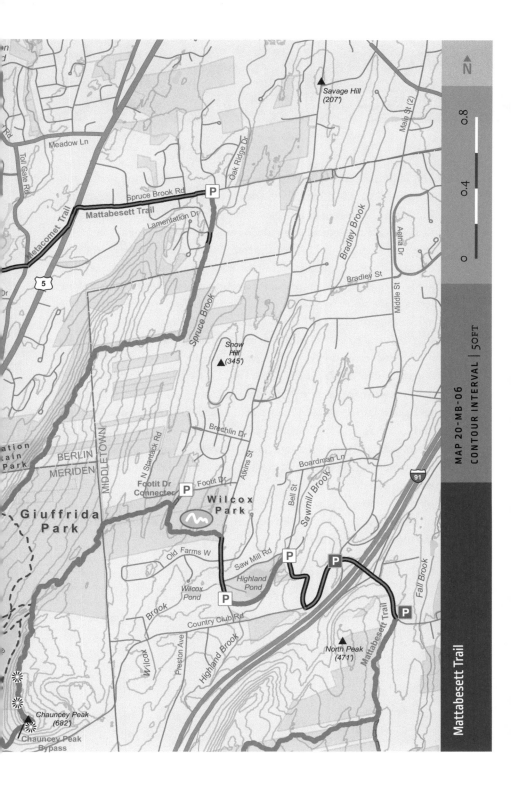

MAP 20-MB-06
CONTOUR INTERVAL | 50FT

N

0.8

0.4

0

Savage Hill
(207')

Main St (2)

Meadow Ln

Toll Gate Rd

Spruce Brook Rd

Mattabesett Trail

Metacomet Trail

Lamentation Dr

Oak Ridge Dr

Bradley Brook

Aetna Dr

Bradley St

Middle St

5

Spruce Brook

Snow
Hill
(345')

Brechlin Dr

Boardman Ln

91

BERLIN

MERIDEN

MIDDLETOWN

N Stantack Rd

Atkins St

Footit Dr
Connector

Footit Dr

Bell St

Sawmill Brook

Wilcox
Park

Giuffrida
Park

Old Farms W

Saw Mill Rd

Highland
Pond

Wilcox
Pond

Fall Brook

Brook

Country Club Rd

Preston Ave

Wilcox

Highland Brook

North Peak
(471')

Mattabesett Trail

Chauncey Peak
(682')

Chauncey Peak
Bypass

Mattabesett Trail

Mattatuck Trail

LENGTH 42.2 miles   **BLAZE COLOR** Blue

The Mattatuck Trail features a woodland footpath beside ponds and streams, descends through a ravine framing the spectacularly terraced Buttermilk Falls, meanders past a cave frequented by the legendary Leatherman, and crosses one of Connecticut's highest peaks. From its southern terminus in Wolcott, the trail follows a northwesterly route to the Mattatuck State Forest and Black Rock State Park. The trail ascends along the western ridges of the Waterbury reservoirs with breathtaking views to the north. In Litchfield the Mattatuck Trail passes through the White Memorial Conservation Center, a 4,000-acre wildlife sanctuary that includes a network of supplementary side trails.

The trail resumes in Warren in the Wyantenock State Forest. It quickly enters the City of Waterbury's Shepaug Reservoir land and Warren Land Trust open-space property. The trail traverses rugged terrain featuring mountain laurel, seasonal views of the reservoirs to the east, streams and marshes, and thick woodlands. The northernmost section of the Mattatuck Trail travels through the Mohawk State Forest in Cornwall, one of the most scenic woodland areas in Connecticut. Meandering beside streams and through rock walls, the trail climbs Mohawk Mountain and offers outstanding panoramic views of western Connecticut and the hills of New York. The Mattatuck's northern terminus is at its junction with the blue-blazed Mohawk Trail.

∎ *The Waterbury reservoir lands are open to foot travel only.*

∎ *Pets must be leashed on the Waterbury reservoir lands at all times.*

∎ *Hunting is permitted in state forests and conservation lands intersected by this trail. Please use caution and wear orange during hunting season.*

Prospect Mountain Trails (see Map 20-MT-04)

LENGTH 4.75 miles   BLAZE COLOR Varied

The Prospect Mountain Preserve includes 340 acres located west of the Borough of Litchfield. The preserve features most of a locally prominent hill with a spectacular viewpoint near its 1,350-foot summit, as well as a large pond to the west. The property is mostly forested, with several meadows indicating past agricultural uses. The area was subject to significant nickel-mining explorations in the nineteenth century. A number of mine shafts still exist on the property. Many are filled with water and visitors are cautioned to approach them with care. The preserve is managed by the Litchfield Land Trust; learn more at www.litchfieldlandtrust.org.

Prospect Mountain Trail

LENGTH 1.9 miles   BLAZE COLOR Blue

The Prospect Mountain Trail transects the preserve. This trail was once a portion of the blue-blazed Mattatuck Trail. Highlights include rocky terrain, mountain laurel, a stand of young black birch (regeneration from tornado destruction in 1989), a steep ravine, and Prospect Mountain's south and north summits, each with long views.

Graham Thompson Trail

LENGTH 1.3 miles   BLAZE COLOR White

This trail begins moderately, passing wetlands, an old pine plantation, then open forest. It crosses several stone-wall barways before gradually

 Did you know that every year during the first weekend in June CFPA hosts Connecticut Trails Day, the largest trails celebration in the nation? Visit our website for more details and join us for this special weekend of trail events.

becoming steeper and more irregular. It eventually intersects the blue-blazed trail near the south summit.

Yellow Trail

LENGTH 0.7 miles   **BLAZE COLOR** Yellow

This trail forms a loop with the blue-blazed trail, traveling through a predominantly birch forest. It crosses seasonal wetlands and ascends steeply to meet the Prospect Mountain Trail near the mountain's 1,350-foot summit.

Mileage Table

MATTATUCK TRAIL

0.0	Mad River Rd / Peterson Park (P)
1.3	Bound Line Rd
1.8	Spindle Hill Rd (P)
2.7	Charlie Krug Cave
2.9	Indian Jack Cave
2.9	Spur to lookout (blue/yellow)
3.5	Begin roadwalk
3.5	Join Wolcott Rd (P)
3.6	Join Allentown Rd
4.1	Leave Allentown Rd
4.1	End roadwalk
4.5	Dam
4.6	Buttermilk Falls
4.7	Begin roadwalk
4.7	Join Lane Hill Rd (P)
4.9	Join S Main St
4.9	Join S Eagle St
5.2	Leave S Eagle St (P)
5.2	End roadwalk
6.1	Jct Town Hill Rd Connector (blue/white, 0.5 mi, P)
6.9	Begin roadwalk
6.9	Join Todd Hollow Rd / Ed's Big Pebble
7.4	Join Keegan Rd (P)
7.5	Leave Keegan Rd
7.5	End roadwalk
7.8	Spur to beaver pond (blue/yellow)
9.1	Begin roadwalk
9.1	Join Ct Rte 262 (P)
9.3	Join Wilton Rd (P)
9.8	Join Carter Rd (P)
9.9	Leave Carter Rd
9.9	End roadwalk
11.1	Begin roadwalk
11.1	Join Waterbury Rd
11.4	Join W Hill Rd
11.5	Leave W Hill Rd
11.5	End roadwalk
11.8	Begin roadwalk
11.8	Join Waterbury Rd
12.0	Join Old Waterbury Rd
12.4	Leave Old Waterbury Rd / Reynolds Bridge Rd (P)
12.4	End roadwalk
12.6	Jct Branch Brook Trail (blue/yellow)
12.7	Spur to quarry (150 ft)
13.6	Cave
13.7	Jct Jericho Trail (blue)
13.7	Crane's Lookout / View

Red Trail

LENGTH 0.7 miles   **BLAZE COLOR** Red

This moderately easy trail passes along the southern and western shores of Granniss Pond, then through a pine plantation, up an old farm road, and through an abandoned meadow. Hikers will pass through several stone-wall barways along the way. The trail finally descends across a wooded slope back to the pond's eastern side before returning back to the trailhead.

14.5	US Rte 6 (P)	27.7	Valley Rd
14.8	Bidwell Hill Rd (P)	31.7	Hardscrabble Rd (P)
15.6	Spur to Black Rock (180 ft, view)	34.9	Jct Blue/White Trail (0.2 mi, P)
16.3	Northfield Rd (0.1 mi, P)	35.2	Shepaug River
18.5	Gilbert Rd	35.4	Flat Rocks Rd / Great Hollow Rd (P)
18.9	Waterfall	36.6	Begin roadwalk—College St
19.2	View	36.8	End roadwalk—College St
19.6	Begin roadwalk	38.3	Begin roadwalk
	19.6 Join Ct Rte 109		38.3 Join Great Hill Rd (P)
	19.6 Join Pitch Rd (P)		38.4 Join Camp Rd
	19.9 Leave Pitch Rd		38.8 Leave Camp Rd
19.9	End roadwalk	38.8	End roadwalk
20.0	Waterfall	39.5	Begin roadwalk—Wadhams Rd
20.6	Farnham Rd	39.6	End roadwalk—Wadhams Rd
21.6	Slab Meadow Rd (P)	40.4	Wadhams Rd
24.6	Ct Rte 63 (P)	40.8	Summit, Mohawk Mtn (1,684 ft) /
25.8	Webster Rd		Mohawk Tower (P)
26.5	Whites Wood Rd (P)	42.0	Begin roadwalk—Toumey Rd
26.7	Begin roadwalk—Whitehall Rd	42.1	End roadwalk—Toumey Rd (P)
27.0	End roadwalk—Whitehall Rd / Bissell Rd	42.2	Jct Mohawk Trail (blue)
27.7	Bissell Rd (P)		

BREAK IN TRAIL Trail mileage continues on Map 20-MT-06 in Warren.

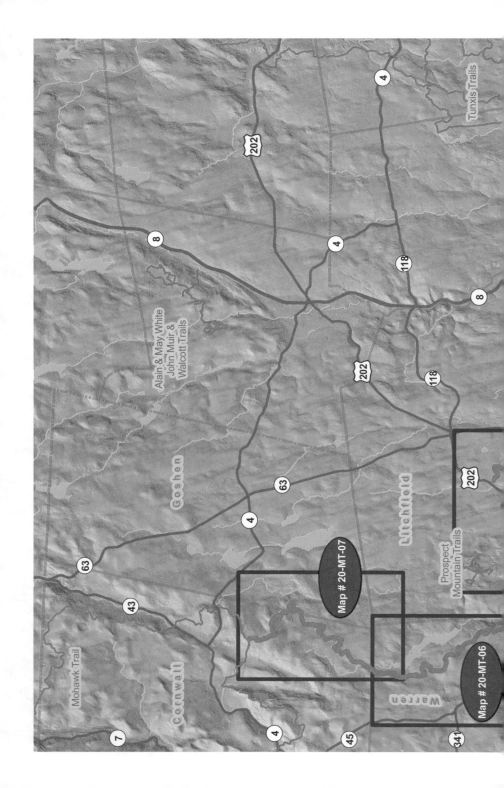

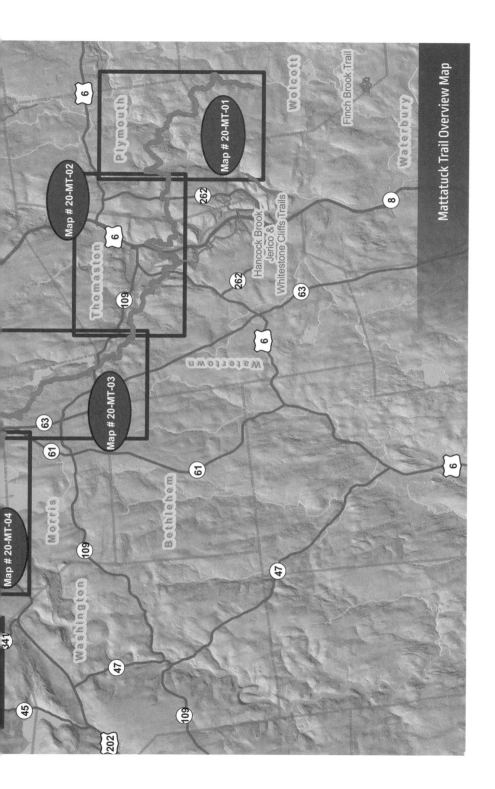

Mattatuck Trail Overview Map

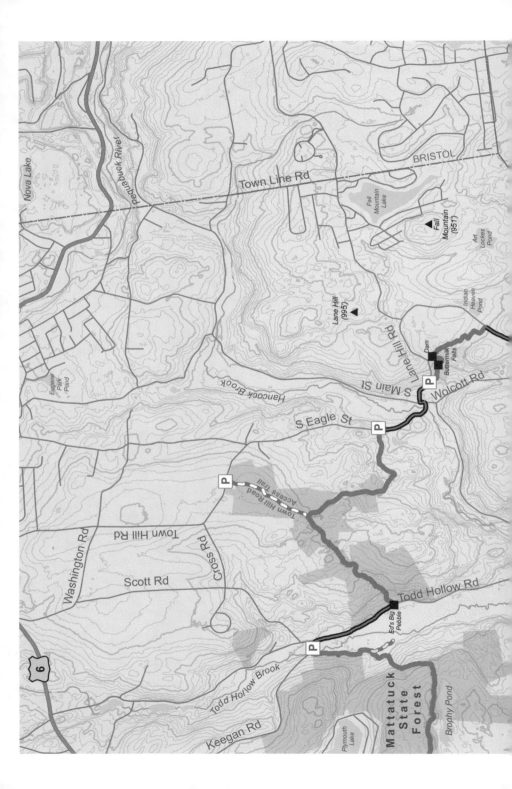

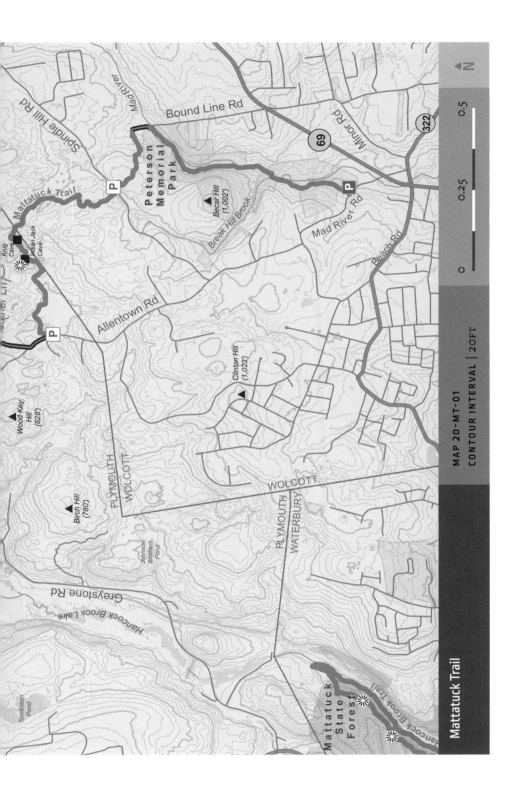

Mattatuck Trail

MAP 20-MT-01
CONTOUR INTERVAL | 20FT

N

0   0.25   0.5

Bound Line Rd

Spindle Hill Rd

Mad River

Mattatuck Trail

Peterson Memorial Park

Becar Hill
(1,002)

Break Hill Brook

69

Minor Rd

Mad River Rd

Beach Rd

322

Knig Cave

Indian Jack Cave

Allentown Rd

Clinton Hill
(1,023)

P

Wood Key Hill
(828)

PLYMOUTH
WOLCOTT

WOLCOTT

PLYMOUTH
WATERBURY

Birch Hill
(780)

Johnson Brothers Pond

Greystone Rd

Hancock Brook Lake

Tomlinson Pond

Mattatuck State Forest

Hancock Brook Trail

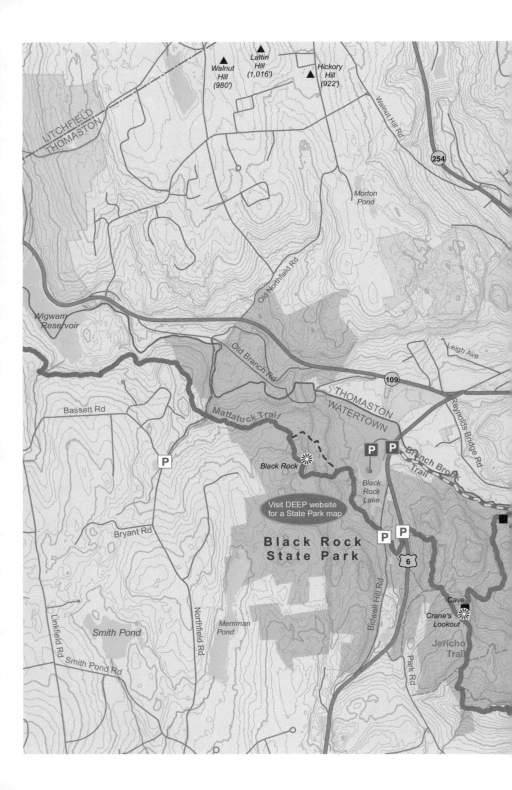

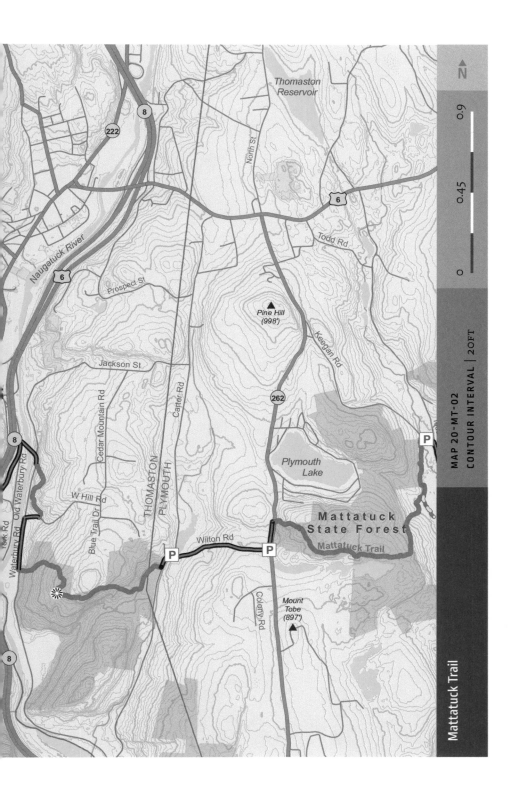

Thomaston
Reservoir

8

222

North St

6

Todd Rd

Naugatuck River

6

Prospect St

Pine Hill
(998')

Keegan Rd

Jackson St

Cedar Mountain Rd

Carter Rd

262

THOMASTON
PLYMOUTH

Plymouth
Lake

8

York Rd

Old Waterbury Rd

Waterbury Rd

W Hill Rd

Blue Trail Dr

P

Wilton Rd

P

Mattatuck
State Forest

Mattatuck Trail

P

8

Colony Rd

Mount
Tobe
(897')

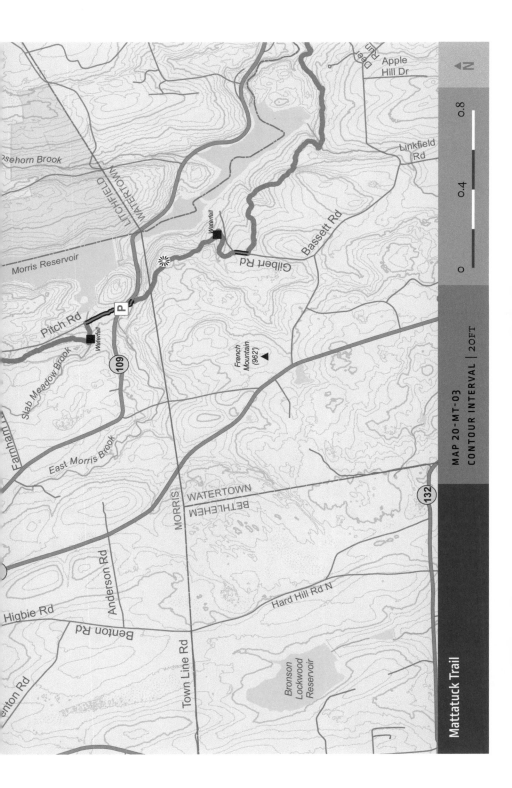

MAP 20-MT-03
CONTOUR INTERVAL | 20 FT

Mattatuck Trail

N

0   0.4   0.8

Apple
Hill Dr

Linkfield
Rd

Bassett Rd

Gilbert Rd

Waterfall

French
Mountain
(962')

Morris Reservoir

sehorn Brook

LITCHFIELD
WATERTOWN

Pitch Rd

P

Waterfall

109

Slab Meadow Brook

Farnham L

East Morris Brook

MORRIS
WATERTOWN
BETHLEHEM

Anderson Rd

Benton Rd

Higbie Rd

enton Rd

Town Line Rd

Hard Hill Rd N

Bronson
Lockwood
Reservoir

132

Deer
Run

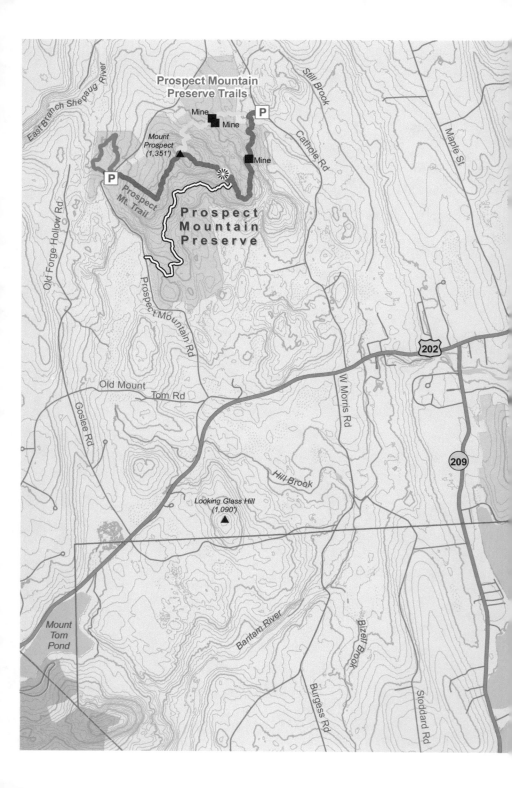

Prospect Mountain
Preserve Trails

Mine
Mine

P

Mount
Prospect
(1,351')

Mine

East Branch Shepaug River

Still Brook

Cathole Rd

Maple St

P

Prospect
Mt. Trail

Prospect
Mountain
Preserve

Old Forge Hollow Rd

Prospect Mountain Rd

Old Mount Tom Rd

Goslee Rd

W Morris Rd

202

209

Hill Brook

Looking Glass Hill
(1,090')

Mount
Tom
Pond

Bantam River

Bizell Brook

Burgess Rd

Stoddard Rd

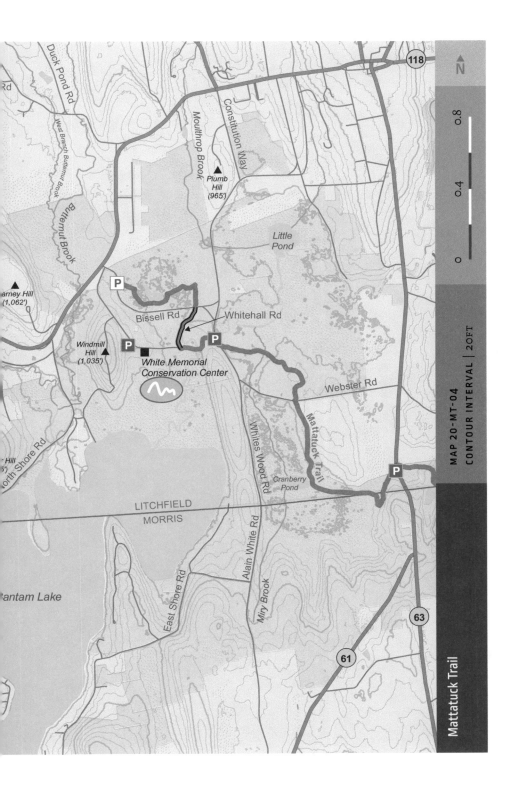

118

N

0.8

0.4

0

MAP 20-MT-04
CONTOUR INTERVAL | 20 FT

Mattatuck Trail

Duck Pond Rd

Rd

West Branch Butternut Brook

Butternut Brook

arney Hill
(1,062')

Bull

Moulthrop Brook

Constitution Way

Plumb
Hill
(965')

Little
Pond

P

Bissell Rd

Whitehall Rd

P

Windmill
Hill
(1,035')

P

White Memorial
Conservation Center

Webster Rd

r Hill
')
orth Shore Rd

Mattatuck Trail

Whites Wood Rd

Cranberry
Pond

P

LITCHFIELD
MORRIS

antam Lake

East Shore Rd

Alain White Rd

Miry Brook

63

61

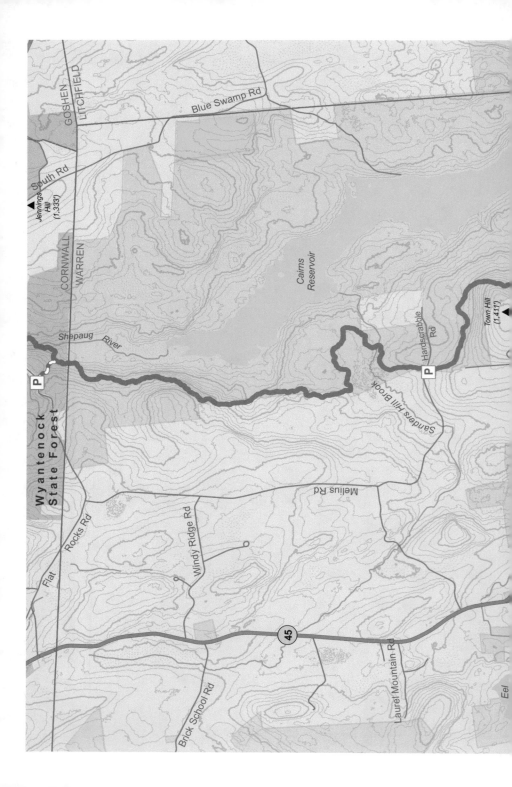

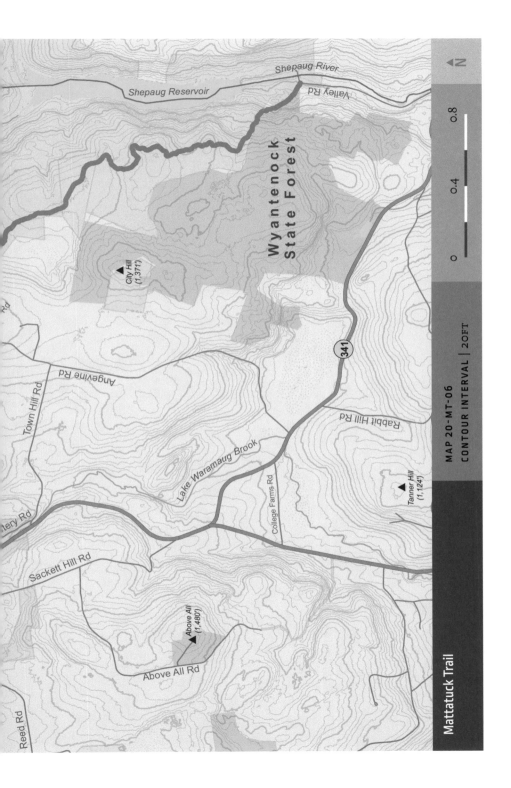

Shepaug River

Shepaug Reservoir

Valley Rd

Wyantenock
State Forest

City Hill
(1,371')

341

Angevine Rd

Town Hill Rd

Rabbit Hill Rd

Lake Waramaug Brook

College Farms Rd

Tanner Hill
(1,124')

...tery Rd

Sackett Hill Rd

Above All
(1,480')

Above All Rd

Reed Rd

...Rd

N

0   0.4   0.8

MAP 20-MT-06
CONTOUR INTERVAL | 20FT

Mattatuck Trail

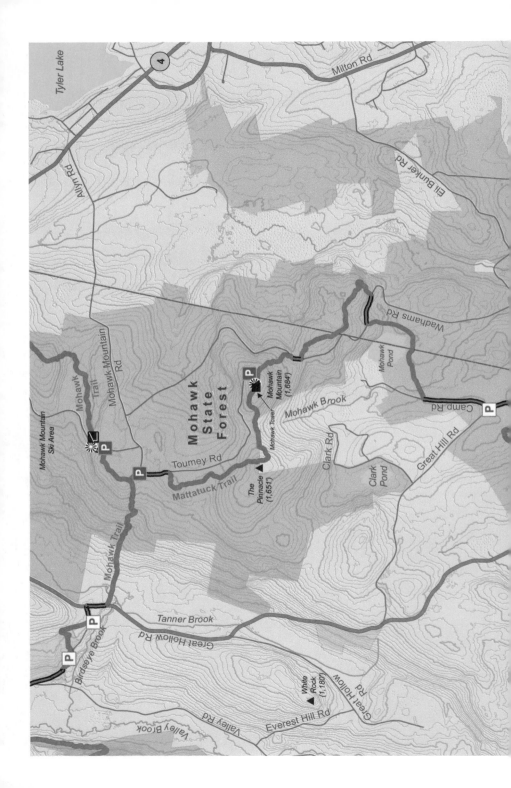

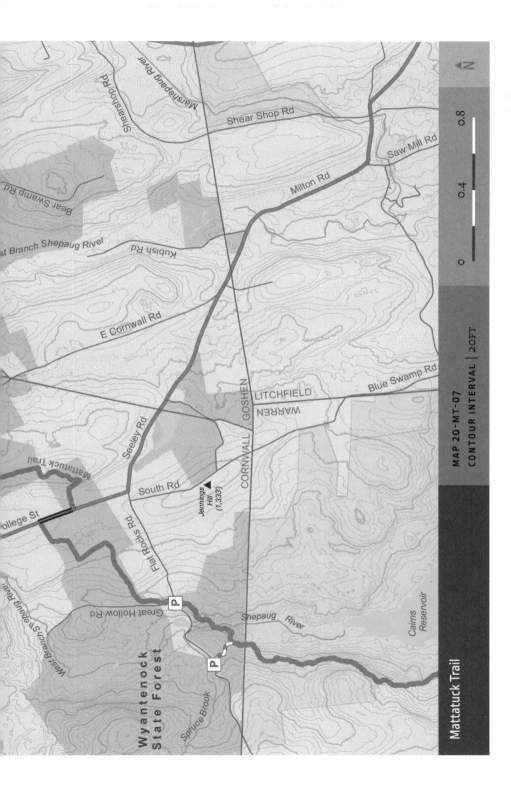

Mattatuck Trail

MAP 20-MT-07
CONTOUR INTERVAL | 20FT

0   0.4   0.8

N

Marshepaug River
Shearshop Rd
Shear Shop Rd
Saw Mill Rd
Milton Rd
Bear Swamp Rd
st Branch Shepaug River
Kubish Rd
E Cornwall Rd
Blue Swamp Rd
GOSHEN
LITCHFIELD
WARREN
CORNWALL
Seeley Rd
Mattatuck Trail
South Rd
Jennings Hill (1,333')
ollege St
Flat Rocks Rd
Great Hollow Rd
Shepaug River
Cairns Reservoir
Wyantenock State Forest
West Branch Shepaug River
Spruce Brook

LENGTH 17.5 miles   **BLAZE COLOR** Varied

The McLean Game Refuge is a privately owned and operated wildlife sanctuary, established in 1932 by the will of Senator George P. McLean. Senator McLean wished his refuge to be "a place where some of the things God made may be seen by those who love them as I have loved them and who may find in them the peace of mind and body that I have found." The refuge consists of more than 4,400 acres of forests, fields, and streams. It is open from 8:00 a.m. to 8:00 p.m. in summer and 8:00 a.m. until sunset during the spring, fall, and winter. There is no charge for admission.

The land of the McLean Game Refuge was shaped by the glaciers of the ice ages. Rounded highlands of ancient crystalline rock, jutting traprock ridges, sandy flats, and kettle ponds where mountains of ice melted, characterize its geological footprint. Two tributaries of the Farmington River, Bissell Brook and Salmon Brook, help define this unique landscape and offer the visitor a variety of terrains to enjoy.

Permitted activities include hiking, jogging, nature study, and photography. Visit the refuge website for more details, mcleangamerefuge.org.

- *Hunting, fishing, trapping, and camping are not allowed.*
- *No motorized vehicles of any description are permitted.*
- *Flowers, shrubs, and trees should not be picked or disturbed.*
- *Smoking and the building of fires are allowed in the picnic grove only.*
- *Dogs must be leashed at all times.*
- *To ensure safety on the trails, bicycles are prohibited.*
- *Horseback riding is allowed only on yellow-blazed trails; the riding season begins April 15 and ends November 30.*

Eastern Division Trails

North Trail

LENGTH 2.8 miles   BLAZE COLOR Purple

This trail links the Blue Loop to the Creek Trail and the Lower Trail. Hikers can extend their trip by continuing from the southern end of the North Trail onto the gray-blazed Firetown Trail.

Creek Trail

LENGTH 0.3 miles   BLAZE COLOR Blue

This short trail connects the yellow-blazed Horse Trail with the purple-blazed North Trail.

Lower Trail

LENGTH 0.4 miles   BLAZE COLOR Blue   137

This short connector trail links the Lower Trail via an unmarked trail to the blue-blazed Spring Pond Trail.

Werbitzkas Loop Trail

LENGTH 1.2 miles   BLAZE COLOR Green

This self-contained loop in the northeastern portion of the refuge offers a nice ramble.

Spring Pond Trail

LENGTH 0.3 miles   BLAZE COLOR Blue

Following the western shoreline of Spring Pond, this trail connects hikers to the Spring Pond Cabin and via unmarked paths to the North Trail, the Horse Trail, and the Lower Trail.

Summit Trail

LENGTH 0.7 miles   BLAZE COLOR Blue

Leaving the North Trail, this trail ascends to a nice summit and views to the west.

Eastern Division Loop Trails

The Blue, Orange, and Red Loop Trails begin as one trail, diverge at different points to form three counterclockwise loops, then converge onto a woods road and return to the trailhead, ending as one trail. All three loop trails pass the Senator McLean cabin (no public access), parallel Salmon Brook, cover rolling terrain with seasonal views, and travel along the shore of Trout Pond. Mix and match portions of these loops to create a short or longer hike.

138 ### Blue Loop Trail

LENGTH 2.1 miles   BLAZE COLOR Blue

Orange Loop Trail

LENGTH 1.9 miles   BLAZE COLOR Orange

Red Loop Trail

LENGTH 1.3 miles   BLAZE COLOR Red

Eastern Division Bridle Trails

Horseback riding is permitted on two yellow-blazed trails in the refuge, the Horse Trail and the Horse Loop Trail, from April 15 to November 30.

Horse Trail

LENGTH 3.4 miles   BLAZE COLOR Yellow

This trail travels along the southeastern boundary of the refuge.

Stop in and visit us at our office in Middlefield. Photo courtesy CFPA.

Whose land am I on? The Blue-Blazed Hiking Trails have special landowner hosts who graciously allow the trails to cross their property. Private, municipal, corporate, land-trust, and state landowners all host sections of our trail system. Please be respectful and thank any landowners you encounter. Without them, these long trails would not be connected.

Horse Loop Trail

LENGTH 1.0 mile   BLAZE COLOR Yellow

This short loop follows a stream and offers relatively flat terrain.

Western Division Trails

East Loop Trail

LENGTH 1.2 miles   BLAZE COLOR Blue

The East Loop begins and ends on Firetown Road in the western region of the refuge. It links to the Firetown Trail and the West Ledge Trail.

Eddy Loop Trail

LENGTH 2.3 miles   BLAZE COLOR White

This loop trail begins on Firetown Road and coincides with the Weed Hill Trail for a distance before breaking off to the west and looping over beautiful terrain to join the West Ledge Trail, which heads west to return to Firetown Road.

Firetown Trail

LENGTH 1.5 miles   BLAZE COLOR Gray

This trail connects the refuge's Lower Trail and East Loop Trail.

Pine Cone Trail

LENGTH 1.3 miles   **BLAZE COLOR** Black

Beginning on Weed Hill Road, this trail climbs to Pine Cone summit and has an unblazed connector to Beach Brook.

South Trail

LENGTH 0.7 miles   **BLAZE COLOR** Blue

The South Trail connects the western end of the Horse Trail at Barndoor Hills Road to the gray-blazed Firetown Trail. The trail also crosses beautiful Bissell Brook.

Weed Hill Trail

LENGTH 1.3 miles   **BLAZE COLOR** Blue

This trail, which shares footage briefly with the white-blazed Eddy Loop Trail, ascends to the summit of Weed Hill.

West Ledge Trail

LENGTH 1.6 miles   **BLAZE COLOR** Pink

This trail connects Firetown Road and Highridge Road. Sharing footage with the white-blazed Eddy Loop Trail, the West Ledge Trail travels through beautiful wooded terrain.

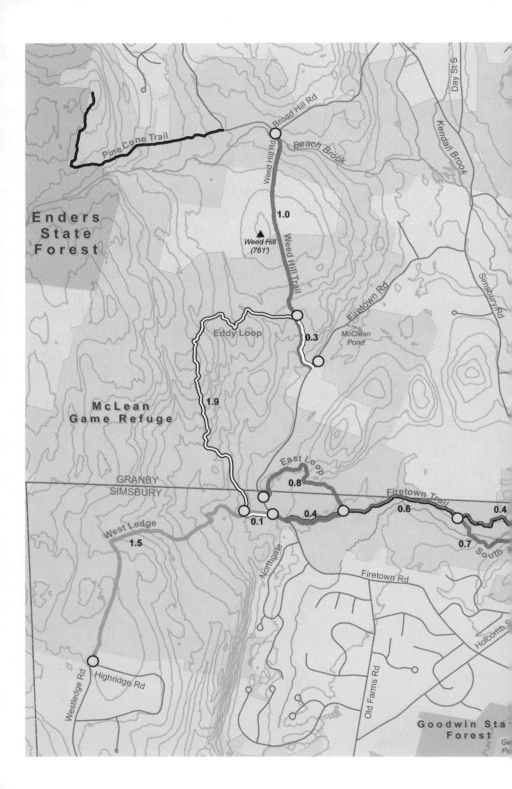

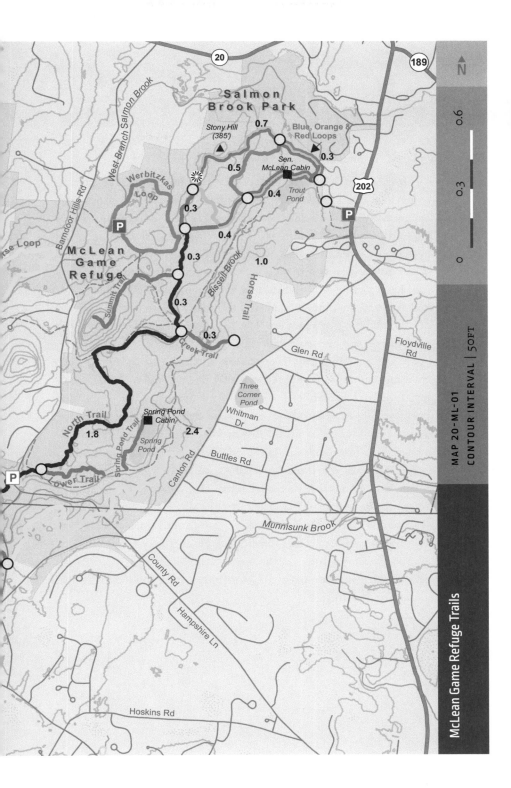

MAP 20-ML-01
CONTOUR INTERVAL | 50FT

McLean Game Refuge Trails

20
189

N

0.6

0.3

0

Salmon
Brook Park

Stony Hill
(385')

0.7

Blue, Orange &
Red Loops

Werbitzkas
Loop

0.5

Sen.
McLean Cabin

0.3

202

Barndoor Hills Rd

West Branch Salmon Brook

0.3

0.4

Trout
Pond

P

se Loop

P

McLean
Game
Refuge

0.4

0.3

Bissell Brook

1.0

Horse Trail

Summit Trail

0.3

0.3

0.3

Creek Trail

Glen Rd

Floydville
Rd

Three
Corner
Pond

North Trail

Spring Pond
Cabin

Whitman
Dr

1.8

2.4

Spring
Pond

Spring Pond Trail

Canton Rd

Buttles Rd

P

Lower Trail

Munnisunk Brook

County Rd

Hampshire Ln

Hoskins Rd

Menunkatuck Trail

LENGTH 16.7 miles   BLAZE COLOR Blue

The Menunkatuck Trail, named for the first human inhabitants of this region, represents the southernmost segment of the New England Trail, connecting the Mattabesett Trail with Long Island Sound in the town of Guilford. The trail leaves the Mattabesett 1.3 miles east of Route 77 and heads south over land owned by the South Central Connecticut Regional Water Authority, two town preserves, and various properties of the Guilford Land Conservation Trust, before emerging onto secondary roads and reaching the shoreline at Chittenden Park. Chittenden Park is the official southern gateway of the New England Trail and the park features a boardwalk and overlook platform on Long Island Sound.

The terrain of the Menunkatuck Trail is rolling, with little or no steep climbing, and consists of rocky wooded ridges, inland wetlands, scenic meadows, and residential areas. Notable features include Timberland Preserve's Upper Lake and the beautiful hayfields of East River Preserve. The Menunkatuck also has the distinction of being the only CFPA trail to pass directly through a train station (Shore Line East in Guilford)!

The Menunkatuck Trail is part of the 215-mile New England National Scenic Trail (NET). The NET was designated as a national scenic trail in 2009 and connects Long Island Sound to the Massachusetts/New Hampshire border. The NET is comprised of the Menunkatuck, Mattabesett, Metacomet, and Metacomet-Monadnock Trails. The *New England Trail Map and Guide*, published by the Appalachian Mountain Club, provides a detailed resource for hikers. For more information about the NET, visit newenglandtrail.org.

SIDE TRAILS

Guilford Historic Loop (see Map 20-MK-01)

LENGTH 0.7 miles   **BLAZE COLOR** Blue/Green

This alternate route passes through a portion of Guilford's historic district. Where the Menunkatuck Trail turns onto Lover's Lane to cross the town fairgrounds, the loop continues on Boston Street, providing access to Guilford's expansive town green, municipal offices, and nearby shops and restaurants. The loop rejoins the Menunkatuck Trail where it emerges from the Henry Whitfield State Museum.

▎ *Hunting is permitted in state forests intersected by this trail. Please use caution and wear orange during hunting season.*

Hikers on the Finch Brook Trail enjoy Trails Day together.
Photo courtesy Tom Tella.

Mileage Table

MENUNKATUCK TRAIL

0.0	Long Island Sound
0.2	Chittenden Park (P)
0.2	Join Seaside Ave
0.5	Join Whitfield St
0.5	Join Old Whitfield St
0.8	Amtrak rail station (P)
0.9	Join Old Whitfield St
1.1	Jct Historic Guilford Loop (blue/green) / Leave Old Whitfield St
1.2	Henry Whitfield State Museum (P)
1.2	Join Stone House Ln
1.4	Join Lovers Ln
1.8	Join Boston St / Ct Rte 146 / Jct Historic Guilford Loop (blue/green)
2.7	Begin roadwalk
	2.7 Join US Rte 1
	2.8 Join Tanner Marsh Rd
	3.2 Join Clapboard Hill Rd
	3.9 Leave Clapboard Hill Rd (P)
3.9	End roadwalk
4.0	View of East River
4.3	Duck Hole Rd
5.1	View of East River
5.4	Spur to Foote Bridge Rd (250 ft, P)
5.8	Spur to Sullivan Dr (500 ft, P)
6.5	Powerline
6.8	Join local trail (white dot)
6.9	Jct local trail (white Xs)
6.9	Jct local trails (blue or white Xs)
7.0	Leave local trail (white dot)
7.7	Willow Rd (P)
8.5	Begin roadwalk—North Madison Rd

8.7	End roadwalk—North Madison Rd / Timberland Preserve (P)
9.2	Join local trail (green)
9.5	Leave local trail (green) / Join local trail (white)
9.6	North jct local trail (green)
9.6	Jct local trail (white circles)
9.7	Iron Stream Bridge
9.7	Jct local trail (white Xs)
9.7	Leave local trail (white) / Join local trail (red circles)
10.0	South jct local trail (red)
10.2	Jct local trail (yellow Xs)
10.2	Leave local trail (red circles) / Join local trail (yellow)
10.5	Leave local trail (yellow) / Join local trail (red)
11.0	Jct local trail (white) / leave local trail (red) / join local trail (white)
11.2	Jct local trail (purple Xs)
11.3	Ct Rte 80 / Timberland Preserve (P)
11.8	Cave
12.6	Begin roadwalk—Hart Rd
12.7	End roadwalk—Hart Rd (P)
16.5	Jct local trail (green)
16.7	Jct Mattabesett Trail (blue)

HISTORIC GUILFORD LOOP

0.0	Jct Menunkatuck Trail (blue) / leave Old Whitfield St / join Whitfield St
0.3	Join Boston St
0.7	Jct Menunkatuck Trail (blue) / Lovers Ln

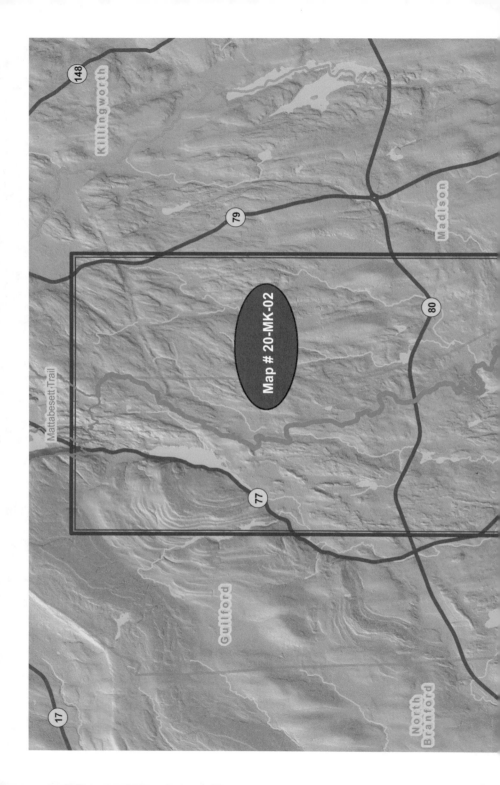

Map # 20-MK-02

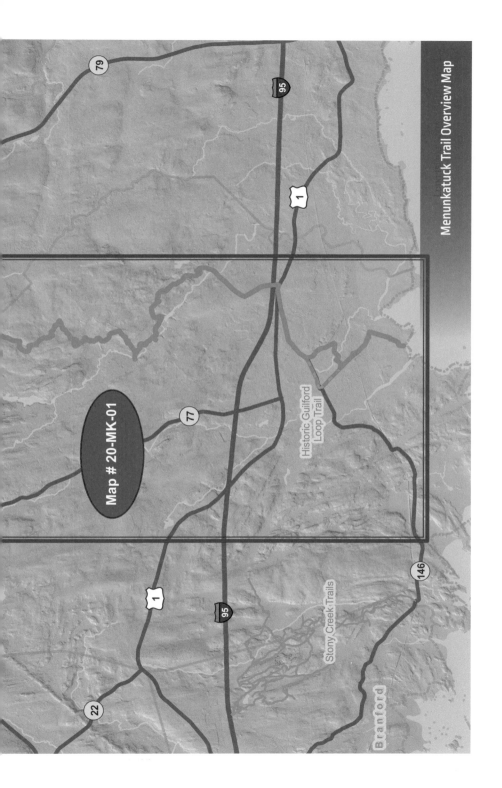

Menunkatuck Trail Overview Map

Map # 20-MK-01

Historic Guilford Loop Trail

Stony Creek Trails

Branford

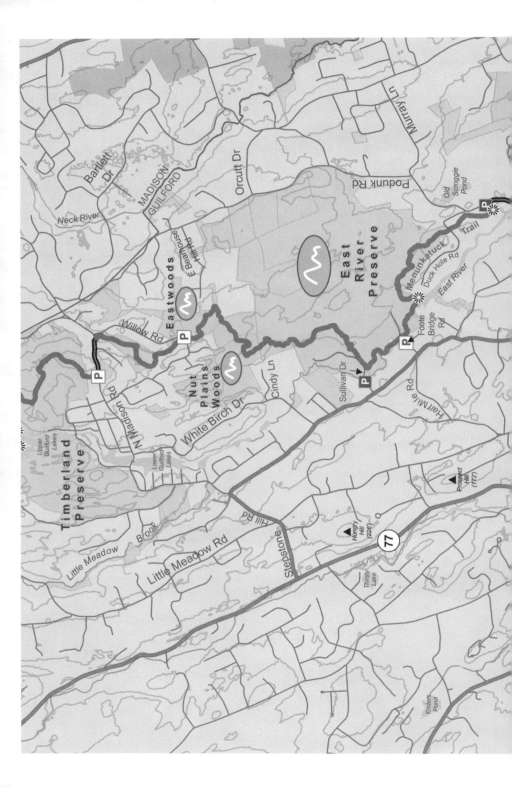

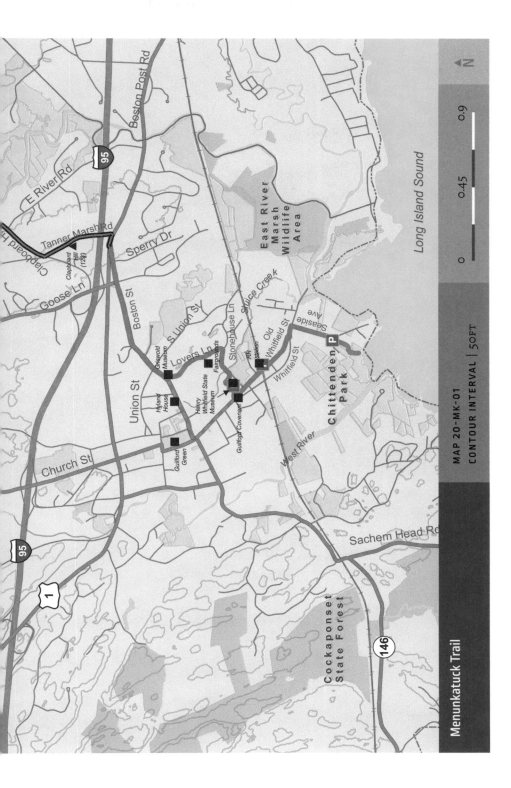

Menunkatuck Trail

MAP 20-MK-01
CONTOUR INTERVAL | 50FT

0   0.45   0.9

N

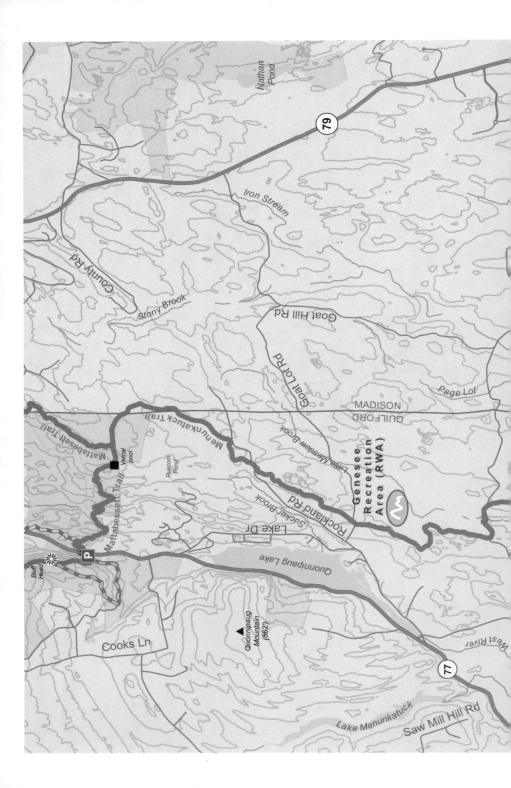

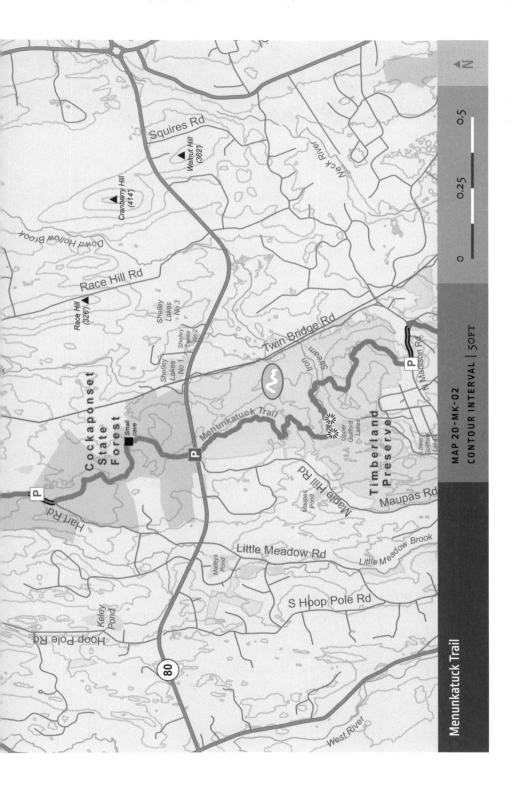

Menunkatuck Trail

MAP 20-MK-02
CONTOUR INTERVAL | 50FT

N

0   0.25   0.5

Metacomet Trail

LENGTH 62.2 miles   BLAZE COLOR Blue

The Metacomet Trail in Connecticut follows a striking traprock ridge from the Hanging Hills of Meriden to the Massachusetts border. While offering a wide variety of terrain, this trail affords incredible views, features historic landmarks, and offers the opportunity to observe a variety of wildlife. Hikers will intersect well-known and iconic landmarks on the trail, including Castle Craig in Hubbard Park, Hill-Stead Museum in Farmington, and the Heublein Tower in Simsbury's Talcott Mountain State Park. Other notable points of interest include Will Warren's Den and Pinnacle Rock in Farmington, Ragged Mountain in Berlin, the Tariffville Gorge in Tariffville, and Suffield Mountain in Suffield. Views from the northern stretch of the trail stretch west to the Barndoor Hills and north to Manituck Mountain.

A variety of loop-hike opportunities are possible where the Metacomet intersects other significant trail systems. Most notable are the adjoining trail systems in Hubbard Park in Meriden, Timberlin Park in Berlin, Crescent Lake in Southington, Ragged Mountain Preserve in Berlin, the Metropolitan District Commission (MDC) reservoirs in West Hartford, Penwood State Park on the Simsbury/Bloomfield line, and Sunrise Park in Suffield.

Along the trail, hikers will travel through beautiful forests with mature trees, encounter numerous glacial erratics, enjoy the expanded views from the traprock ridgeline, and marvel at the trailside wildflowers that abound in the spring. On the northern section of the trail, hikers will encounter unique Metacomet basalt formations, eroding into chimney-like spires along the cliff edge. In some places, the trail is distinguished by its steep and challenging nature. Other sections of the trail are more moderate, allowing for a rolling ridge walk. In West Hartford, along Reservoir 6, the trail follows a graveled path that is wide and flat for easy strolling.

The Metacomet Trail is part of the 215-mile New England National Scenic Trail (NET). The NET was designated as a national scenic trail in 2009 and connects Long Island Sound to the Massachusetts/New Hampshire border. The NET is comprised of the Menunkatuck, Mattabesett, Metacomet, and Metacomet-Monadnock Trails. The *New England Trail Map and Guide*, published by the Appalachian Mountain Club, provides a detailed resource for hikers. For more information about the NET, visit newenglandtrail.org.

SIDE TRAILS

Timberlin Connector (see Map 20-ME-01)

LENGTH 0.2 miles   **BLAZE COLOR** Blue/White

This short trail connects the Metacomet Trail on the south side of Short Mountain to the Amelia Green Trail in Timberlin Park.

Preserve Trail (see Map 20-ME-03)

LENGTH 3.2 miles   **BLAZE COLOR** Blue/Red

This trail in the Ragged Mountain Preserve can be accessed from a parking area at West Lane. It features attractive ledges and views of Hart Ponds and the Hanging Hills of Meriden, crosses streams and brooks, and overlooks some popular rock-climbing areas. To experience the full rustic beauty of Ragged Mountain Preserve, hikers can combine the Preserve Trail with the Metacomet Trail for a long and challenging 6-mile round-trip loop. The loop can be shortened by using the other blazed preserve trails described below.

Blue/Orange Trail (see Map 20-ME-03)

LENGTH 0.7 miles   **BLAZE COLOR** Blue/Orange

This trail links the Ragged Mountain Preserve Trail to the Metacomet Trail.

Blue/White Trail (see Map 20-ME-03)

LENGTH 0.5 miles   BLAZE COLOR Blue/ White

This trail links the Ragged Mountain Preserve Trail to the Metacomet Trail.

Blue/Yellow Trail (see Map 20-ME-03)

LENGTH 0.9 miles   BLAZE COLOR Blue/Yellow

This trail links the Ragged Mountain Preserve Trail to the Metacomet Trail.

Crescent Lake Connector (see Map 20-ME-03)

LENGTH 0.9 miles   BLAZE COLOR Blue/Orange

This trail descends steeply from the traprock ledge and connects to trailhead parking at Southington's Crescent Lake. Other trails off the connector can be used for further exploration.

Talcott Mountain Bypass (see Map 20-ME-06)

LENGTH 1.3 miles   BLAZE COLOR Blue/Red

This bypass trail follows flatter terrain, allowing hikers to avoid the steep ascent to Talcott Mountain. The trail leaves the Metacomet Trail at the north end of MDC's Reservoir 6 and rejoins the Metacomet Trail in Talcott Mountain State Park, creating a nice loop opportunity.

East-West Trail (see Map 20-ME-06)

LENGTH 1.3 miles   BLAZE COLOR Blue

This trail drops steeply to the west from the yellow-blazed trail on the Metacomet Ridge in Penwood State Park. The trail traverses the Tanager Hill and Owen Mortimer Preserves owned and managed by the Simsbury Land Trust. The trail currently ends at East Weatogue Street. Eventually the East-West Trail will link the Metacomet section of the New England Trail to the Appalachian Trail in Canaan.

Autumn view of Breakneck Pond from the trail in Bigelow Hollow State Park. Photo courtesy Rachael McGrath.

Hatchery Brook Loop Trail (see Map 20-ME-01)

LENGTH 3.1 miles   BLAZE COLOR Blue/Red

The nearly 150-acre Hatchery Brook Conservation Area (HBCA) lies in the heart of Berlin and is managed by the town. Featuring a winding watercourse, swamps and vernal pools, several ponds, traprock outcroppings, wildflowers, groves of stately trees, lichen-covered stone walls, historic foundations, and several pleasant viewing areas, HBCA tells a tale of Berlin once upon a time. Trails link lands that were once working farms and orchards, along with forested areas that include a 1960s-era Girl Scout camp, Merebrite. These second-growth forests were first cleared in the colonial era for heating, then were further decimated during the industrial revolution for charcoal.

Four loop trails—Red, Yellow, Blue, and Orange—wind through the HBCA. A blue/red trail is maintained as part of the Blue-Blazed Hiking Trails System. All the loops offer hikers a variety of terrain and difficulty. Plans are underway to connect the Hatchery Brook Loop Trail to the Metacomet Trail, offering more opportunities for hikers.

For more information and maps, visit Berlin's Conservation Commission website.

Mileage Table

METACOMET TRAIL

0.0	Begin roadwalk
	0.0 Ct Rte 15 / Spruce Brook Rd / Jct Mattabesett Trail (blue)
	0.1 Join Orchard Rd
	1.8 Leave Orchard Rd (P)
1.8	End roadwalk
3.2	Summit Wood Dr (P)
5.2	Ct Rte 71 (P)
5.5	Elmere Reservoir Dam
6.2	Begin roadwalk
	6.2 Join W Peak Dr / Park Dr
	6.2 Merimere Reservoir Dam
	6.3 Leave W Peak Dr
6.3	End roadwalk
7.6	Views
7.7	Castle Craig (P)
8.3	Join local trail (red)
8.3	Leave local trail (red)
8.8	Spur to lookout (450 ft)
8.8	W Peak Dr (P)
9.4	View
10.1	Pipeline
11.2	Begin roadwalk
	11.2 Join Edgewood Rd (P)
	12.7 Join Ct Rte 364
	12.7 Leave Ct Rte 364
12.7	End roadwalk
12.9	Jct Timberlin Park Connector (blue/white, P)
13.0	South jct local trail (green)
13.7	Views
14.5	North jct local trail (green)
14.6	Begin roadwalk
	14.6 Join Millbrook Ln
	14.7 Join Carey St
	14.7 Join private driveway
	14.8 Leave private driveway
14.8	End roadwalk
15.0	Base of Short Cliff
15.1	South jct Ragged Mountain Preserve Trail (blue/red)
15.5	View
16.2	Jct Blue/Yellow Trail (blue/yellow)
16.6	Jct local trail (red)

17.0	Jct Blue/Orange Trail (blue/orange)
17.7	Jct Blue/White Trail (blue/white)
17.7	North jct Ragged Mountain Preserve Trail (blue/red)
18.5	View
19.4	Spur to lookout (blue/red)
20.0	Begin roadwalk
	20.0 Andrews St / Join Long Bottom Rd
	20.8 Leave Long Bottom Rd
20.8	End roadwalk
21.8	View
21.9	Jct Crescent Lake Connector (blue/orange) / Join local trail (orange)
22.4	View
22.5	Leave local trail (orange)
22.6	Jct Ledge Road Connector (blue/red)
24.4	Begin roadwalk
	24.4 Esther St / Join Black Rock Ave
	24.5 Join Wooster St (P)
	24.7 Join Ct Rte 372
	25.6 Leave Ct Rte 372
25.6	End roadwalk
27.3	Former Nike missile base
27.4	Pinnacle Rock / View
28.5	Rattlesnake Cliffs
28.6	Will Warren's Den
28.7	TV towers
29.7	Spur to Rte 6 parking (blue/white, 0.1 mi, P)
29.7	US Rte 6
30.3	Begin roadwalk
	30.3 Join Poplar Hill Dr
	30.8 Join Mountain Rd
	30.9 Leave Mountain Rd
30.9	End roadwalk
31.5	Ct Rte 4
31.6	Prattling Pond Rd (200 ft, P)
32.0	Begin roadwalk—Prattling Pond Rd
32.3	End roadwalk—Prattling Pond Rd
32.7	Begin roadwalk—Metacomet Rd
32.9	End roadwalk—Metacomet Rd
33.0	Talcott Notch Rd
33.5	Old Mountain Rd
34.8	Kilkenny Rock
38.1	Ct Rte 44 (P)

38.3	Join MDC Reservoir 6 service road (P)
39.9	Leave MDC Reservoir 6 service road / Jct Talcott Mountain Bypass Trail (blue/red)
40.6	Powerlines
40.7	Pipeline
41.1	Paved park service road
41.5	Join local trail (red)
41.5	Heublein Tower / View
41.6	Leave local trail (red) / Join local trail (yellow)
41.7	Leave local trail (yellow)
43.2	North jct Talcott Mountain Bypass Trail (blue/red)
43.8	Ct Rte 185
43.8	Penwood State Park (P) / Begin roadwalk—park road
44.0	End roadwalk—park road
44.5	Jct local trail (red) / South jct local trail (purple)
44.8	North jct local trail (purple)
45.2	Spur to "Stone Garden" (50 ft)
45.5	Spur to stone pedestal, survey marker (75 ft)
45.7	Lake Louise
46.0	Jct local trail (white)
46.0	The Pinnacle / View / Survey marker
47.2	Wintonbury Rd (P)
49.2	Bartlett Tower (ruins)
49.5	Begin roadwalk
	49.5 Join Mountain Rd (P)
	49.8 Join Ct Rte 189
	50.1 Leave Ct Rte 189 / Old Hartford Ave (P)

50.1	End roadwalk
51.5	Chimney
52.4	Hatchett Hill Rd (P)
54.4	Begin roadwalk
	54.4 Join Holcomb St (P)
	54.5 Ct Rte 20 / Join Newgate Rd
	54.6 Leave Newgate Rd (P)
54.6	End roadwalk
56.5	Windsor Locks Scouts Primitive Tentsite
59.6	Phelps Rd (P) / Ct Rte 168
60.4	View
62.2	CT State Line / Metacomet-Monadnock Trail (white, 0.1 mi, P)

RAGGED MOUNTAIN PRESERVE TRAIL

0.0	South jct Metacomet Trail (blue) / View / Short Cliff
1.0	Jct Blue/Yellow Trail (blue/yellow) / View
1.7	Jct Blue/Orange Trail (blue/orange)
1.7	Spur to West Ln (blue/red, 250 ft, P)
2.3	Jct Blue/White Trail (blue/white)
2.4	Waterfall
3.2	North jct Metacomet Trail (blue)

TALCOTT MOUNTAIN BYPASS TRAIL

0.0	South jct Metacomet Trail (blue)
0.1	Jct service road
0.5	Pipeline
0.8	Powerline
1.0	Chimney
1.3	North jct Metacomet Trail (blue)

159

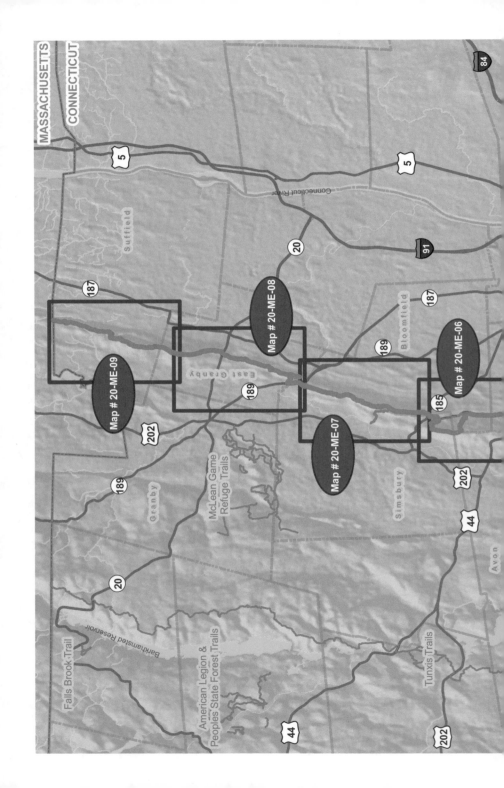

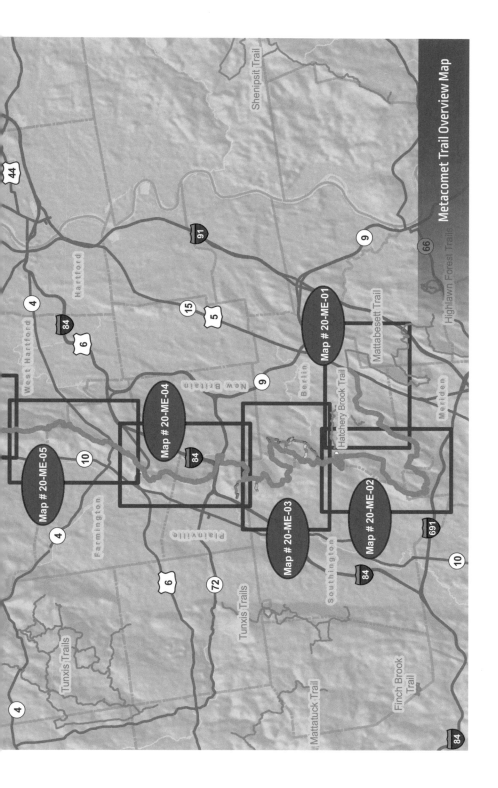

Metacomet Trail Overview Map

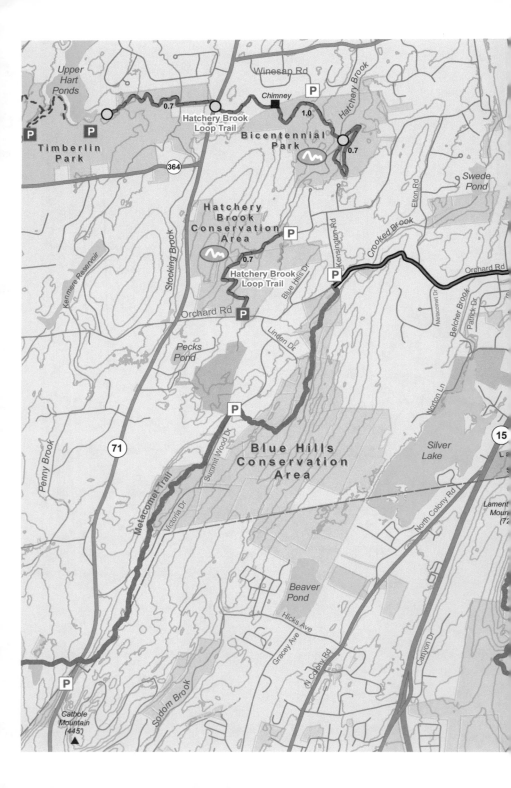

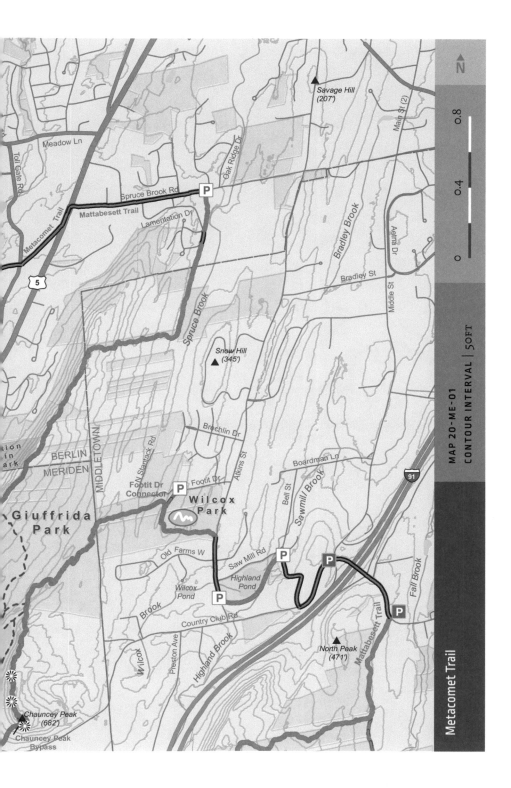

N

0   0.4   0.8

MAP 20-ME-01
CONTOUR INTERVAL | 50FT

Metacomet Trail

Meadow Ln

Toll Gate Rd

Metacomet Trail

5

Spruce Brook Rd   P

Mattabesett Trail

Lamentation Dr

Oak Ridge Dr

Savage Hill
(207')

Main St (2)

Bradley Brook

Aetna Dr

Bradley St

Middle St

Spruce Brook

Snow Hill
(345')

Brechlin Dr

BERLIN

MERIDEN

MIDDLETOWN

N Slantack Rd

Atkins St

Boardman Ln

91

ion
in
ark

Footit Dr
Connector   P   Footit Dr

Wilcox
Park

Bell St

Sawmill Brook

Giuffrida
Park

Old Farms W

Wilcox
Pond

Saw Mill Rd

Highland
Pond

P

P

Fall Brook

Brook

P

Country Club Rd

Highland Brook

Wilcox

Preston Ave

North Peak
(471')

Mattabesett Trail

Chauncey Peak
(682')

Chauncey Peak
Bypass

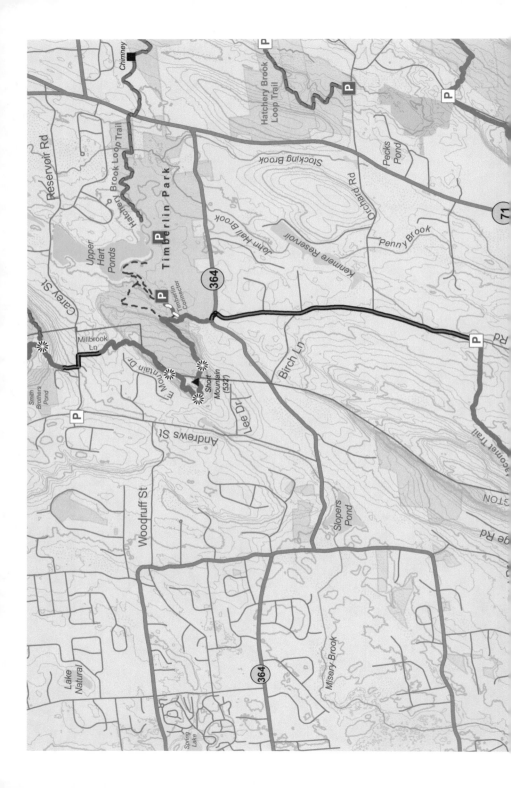

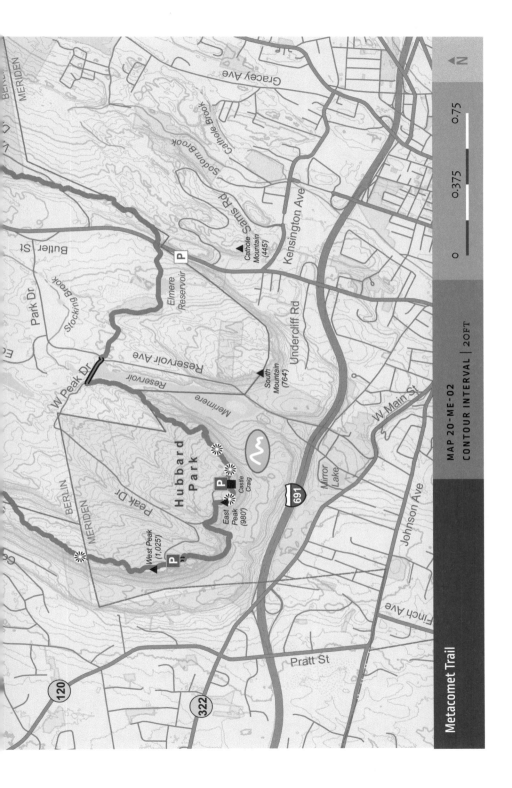

Metacomet Trail

MAP 20-ME-02
CONTOUR INTERVAL | 20FT

0   0.375   0.75

N

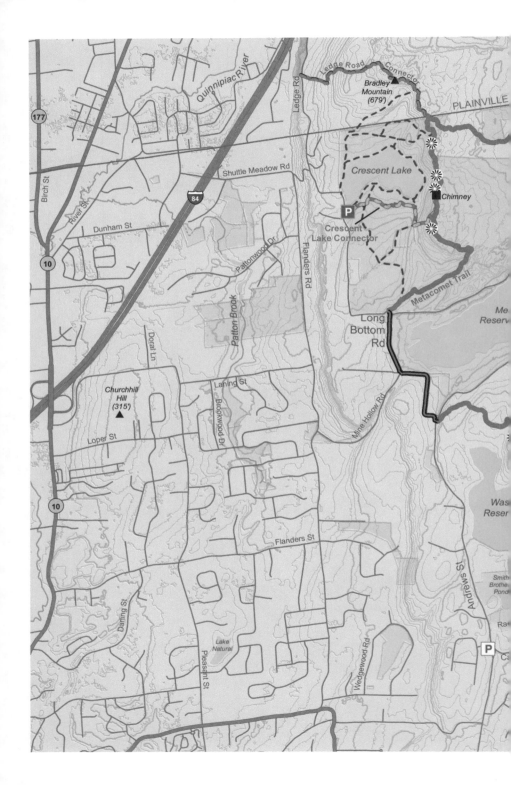

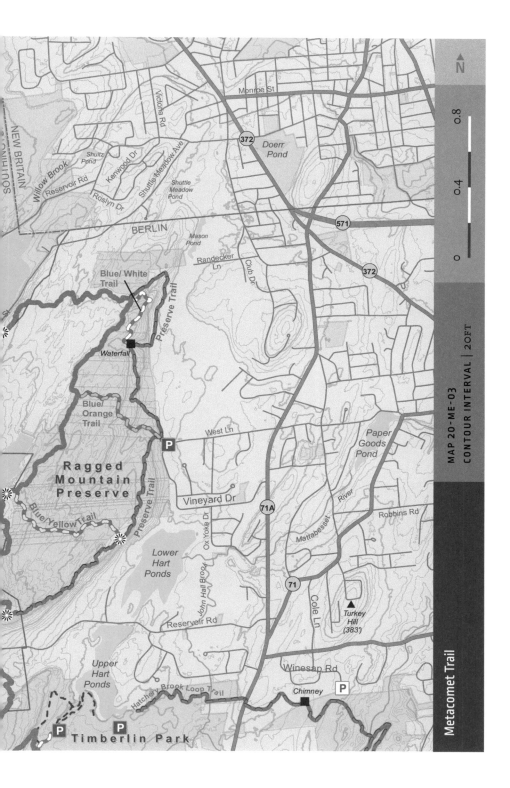

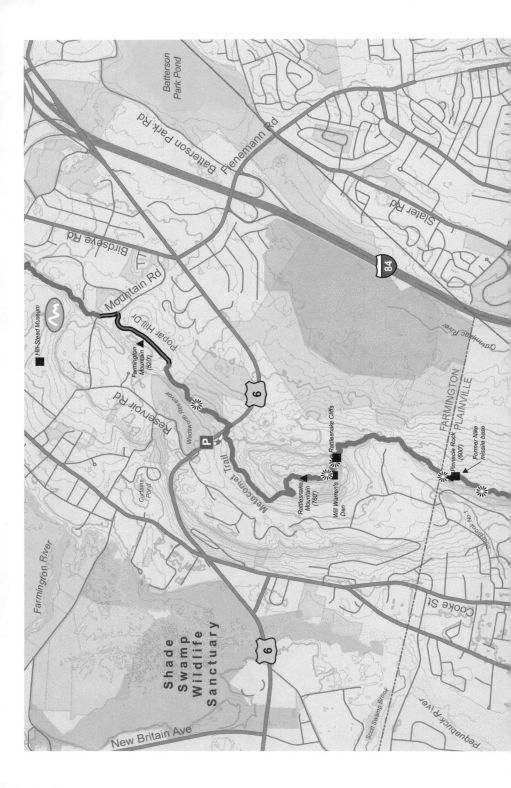

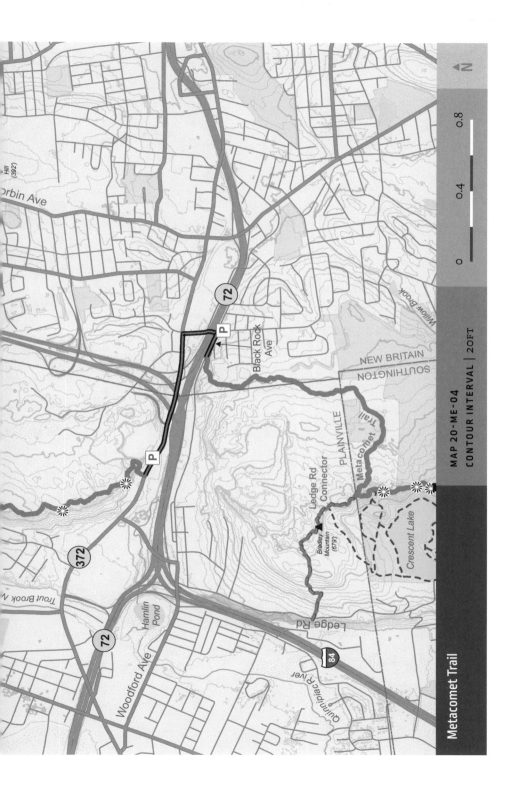

Metacomet Trail

MAP 20-ME-04
CONTOUR INTERVAL | 20FT

0   0.4   0.8

N

Hill
(392)

orbin Ave

72

Black Rock
Ave

Willow Brook

NEW BRITAIN
SOUTHINGTON

PLAINVILLE

Metacomet Trail

Ledge Rd
Connector

Bradley
Mountain
(679)

Crescent Lake

Ledge Rd

372

Trout Brook

Hamlin
Pond

72

Woodford Ave

84

Quinnipiac River

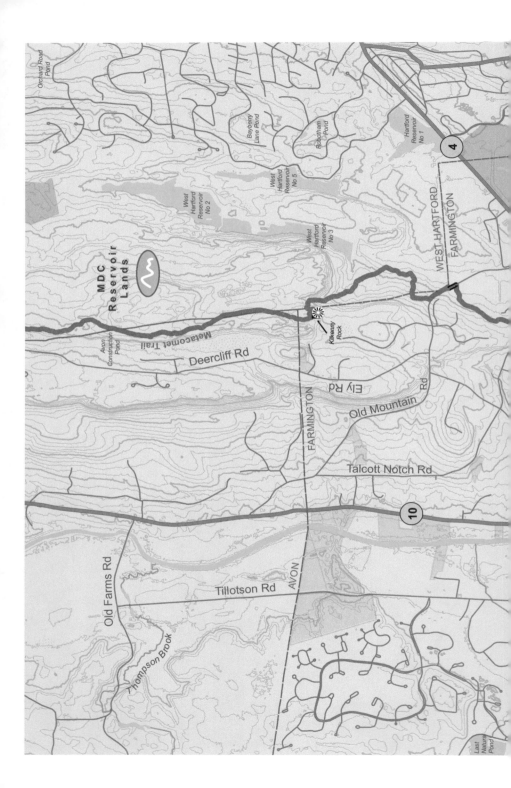

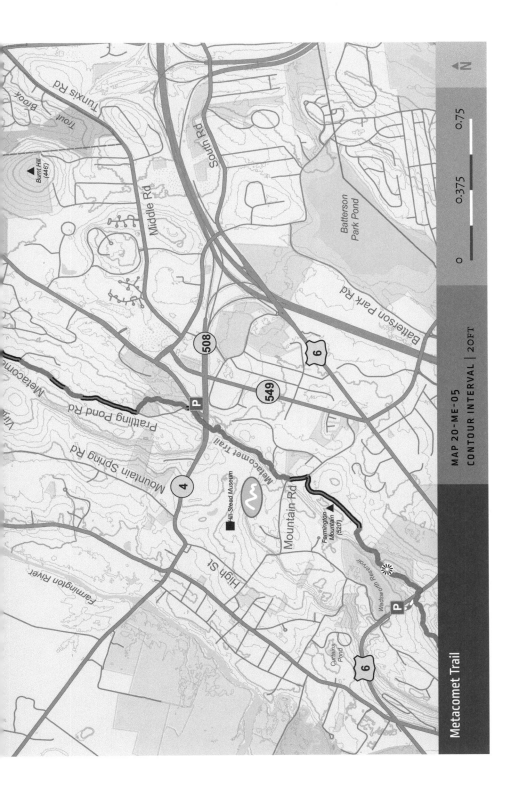

Metacomet Trail

MAP 20-ME-05
CONTOUR INTERVAL | 20FT

0   0.375   0.75

N

Burnt Hill
(446)

Trout Brook

Tunxis Rd

Middle Rd

South Rd

Batterson
Park Pond

Batterson Park Rd

508

549

6

Metacomet

Pratling Pond Rd

Mountain Spring Rd

4

Hill-Stead Museum

Metacomet Trail

Mountain Rd

Farmington
Mountain
(520)

High St

Wadsworth Reservoir

P

Farmington River

Curtains
Pond

6

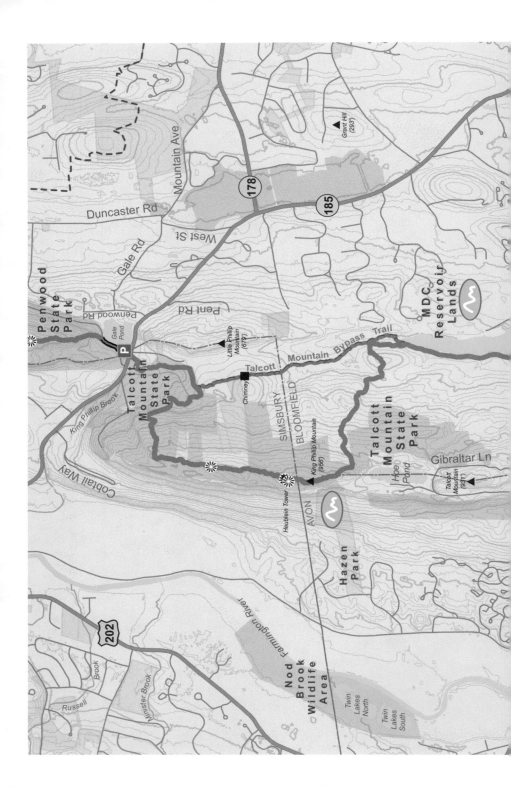

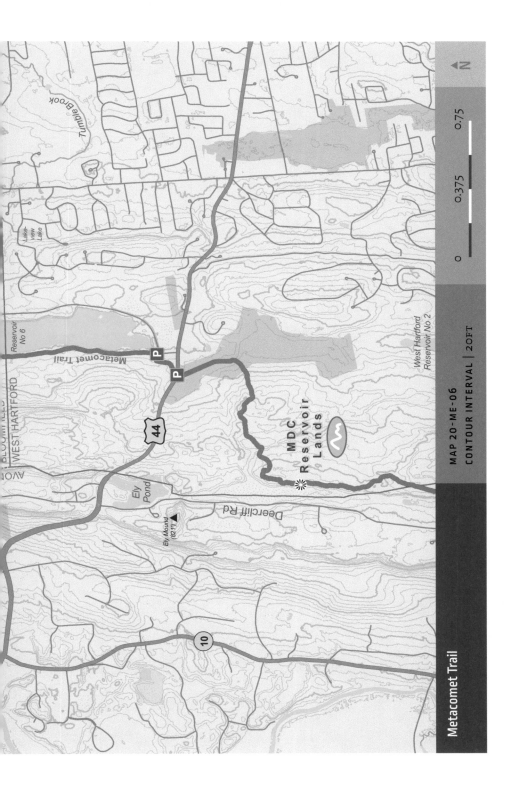

Tumblebrook Brook

Lakeview Lake

Reservoir No 6

Metacomet Trail

BLOOM...
WEST HARTFORD

AVON

44

Ely Pond

Ely Mound
(821')

Deercliff Rd

10

West Hartford
Reservoir No 2

MDC
Reservoir
Lands

MAP 20-ME-06
CONTOUR INTERVAL | 20FT

0   0.375   0.75

N

Metacomet Trail

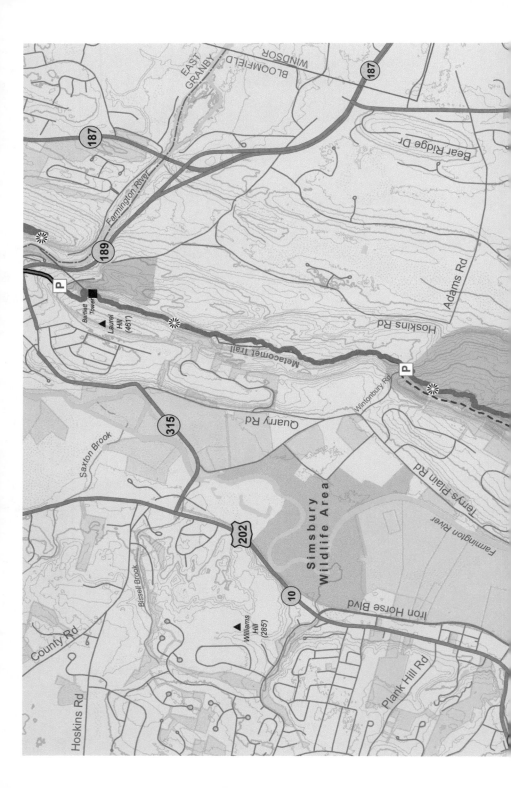

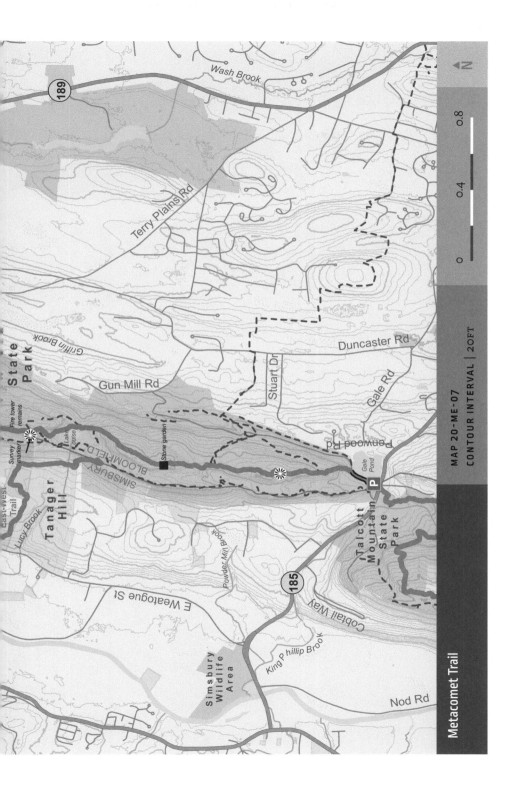

Metacomet Trail

MAP 20-ME-07
CONTOUR INTERVAL | 20FT

0   0.4   0.8

N

189

Wash Brook

Terry Plains Rd

State
Park

Griffin Brook

Gun Mill Rd

Duncaster Rd

Stuart Dr

Gale Rd

Penwood Rd

East-West
Trail

Survey
marker

Fire tower
remains

Lake
Louise

SIMSBURY
BLOOMFIELD

Stone garden

Lucy Brook

Tanager
Hill

Powder Mill Brook

Gale
Pond

P

Talcott
Mountain
State
Park

Cobtail Way

E Weatogue St

185

King Phillip Brook

Simsbury
Wildlife
Area

Nod Rd

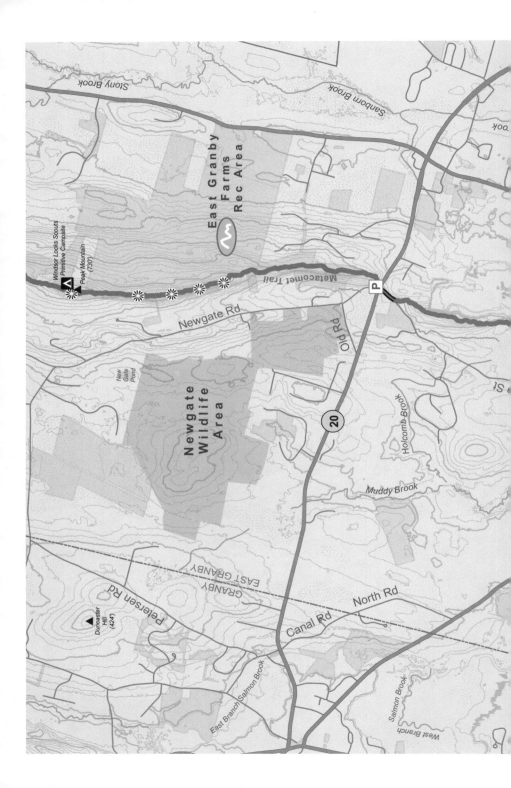

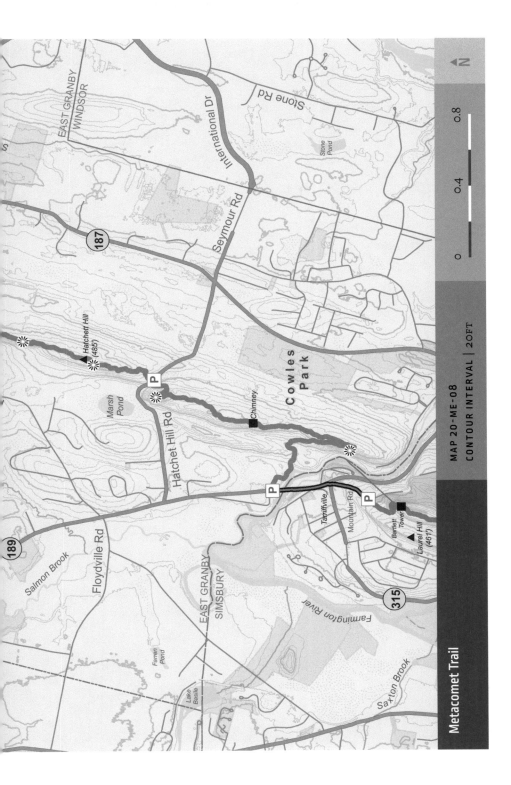

Metacomet Trail

MAP 20-ME-08
CONTOUR INTERVAL | 20FT

EAST GRANBY
WINDSOR

International Dr

Stone Rd

Seymour Rd

Stone
Pond

187

Hatchett Hill
(485')

Marsh
Pond

Hatchet Hill Rd

Chimney

C o w l e s
P a r k

P

P

P

Tariffville

Mountain Rd

Bartlett
Tower

Laurel Hill
(461')

315

189

Salmon Brook

Floydville Rd

EAST GRANBY
SIMSBURY

Farmington River

Sarton Brook

Farren
Pond

Lake
Basile

N

0   0.4   0.8

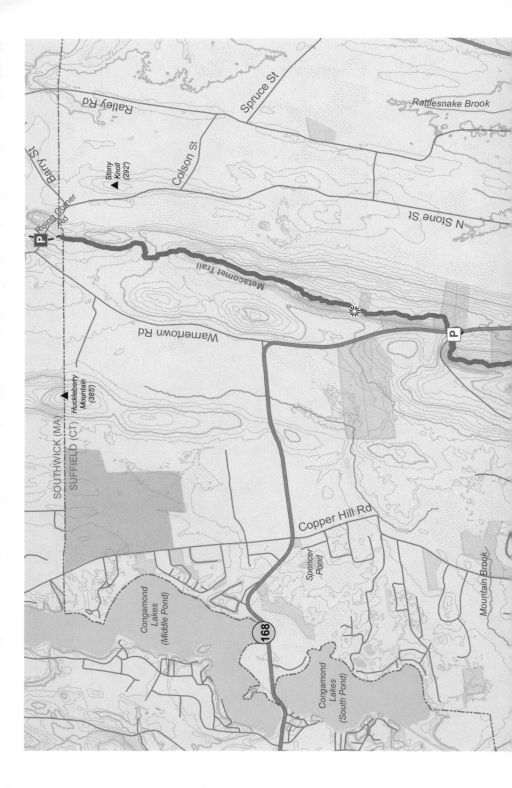

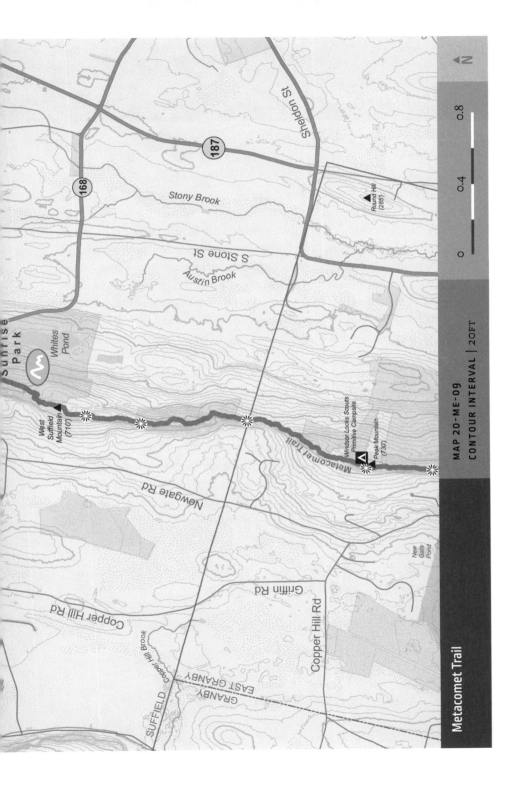

Metacomet Trail

MAP 20-ME-09
CONTOUR INTERVAL | 20 FT

0   0.4   0.8

N

Mohawk Trail

LENGTH 25.7 miles   **BLAZE COLOR** Blue

The Mohawk Trail, established as a Blue-Blazed Hiking Trail on May 8, 1988, follows the former eastern route of the Appalachian Trail. (The AT was relocated west of the Housatonic River between Route 4 and Falls Village.) The Mohawk Trail crosses Mohawk Mountain and Housatonic Meadows State Parks and the Mohawk, Wyantenock, and Housatonic State Forests. From its southern junction with the AT on Breadloaf Mountain, the trail crosses the Housatonic River and traverses multiple peaks 1,200 feet or higher in the Litchfield Hills—from Coltsfoot Mountain in Cornwall to Barrack Mountain in Canaan—then ends at the AT on the Warren Turnpike near the regional high school in Falls Village. The Mohawk Trail intersects the Mattatuck Trail on Mohawk Mountain in Cornwall. Distinctive features such as Cathedral Pines, Mohawk Mountain, Red Mountain, Dean Ravine, and Lookout Point on Barrack Mountain, as well as spectacular views from many points along the trail, make it a popular hiking destination.

Four backpacking shelters on the Mohawk Trail offer hikers the opportunity to enjoy overnight trips. These shelters are maintained by the Connecticut DEEP. Please contact the DEEP Western District office for reservations or if you have questions about shelter availability. Backpackers often enjoy connecting the Mohawk and Appalachian Trails for an extended, multiple-night loop trip.

▌ *Hunting is permitted in state forests intersected by this trail. Please use caution and wear orange during hunting season.*

Mileage Table

MOHAWK TRAIL

0.0	Jct Appalachian Trail (white)
0.1	Spur to lookout
0.8	Begin roadwalk
	0.8 Join US Rte 7 (P)
	0.9 Join Ct Rte 4 (P)
	1.2 Join Dark Entry Rd
	1.9 Leave Dark Entry Rd
1.9	End roadwalk
5.3	View
6.8	Begin roadwalk
	6.8 Join Jewell St
	7.1 Join Valley Rd
	7.3 Join Essex Hill Rd
	7.5 Leave Essex Hill Rd (P)
7.5	End roadwalk
8.0	Begin roadwalk
	8.0 Join Essex Hill Rd (P)
	8.1 Join Great Hollow Rd
	8.2 Leave Great Hollow Rd
8.2	End roadwalk
9.1	Jct Mattatuck Trail (blue)
9.5	Toumey Rd / View (P)
9.5	Shelter
10.8	Shelter
10.9	Forest road (200 ft, P)
11.0	Ct Rte 4
11.1	Spur to shelter (100 ft)
11.5	Summit, Red Mtn (1,651 ft)
11.7	View
12.7	Begin roadwalk—Johnson Rd
13.5	End roadwalk—Johnson Rd / Ct Rte 43 (P)
15.6	Lake Rd (P)
17.3	Ford Hill Rd
19.1	Mansfield Rd (P)
19.5	Yelping Hill Rd (P)
21.0	Shelter
22.5	Music Mountain Rd / Waterfall (P)
22.9	Waterfall
23.2	Begin roadwalk—Music Mountain Rd
23.4	End roadwalk—Music Mountain Rd
24.7	View
25.5	Begin roadwalk
	25.5 Join Johnson Rd
	25.5 Join Ct Rte 7
	25.5 Leave Ct Rte 7
25.5	End roadwalk
25.7	Railroad tracks
25.7	Jct Appalachian Trail (white) / Warren Tpke

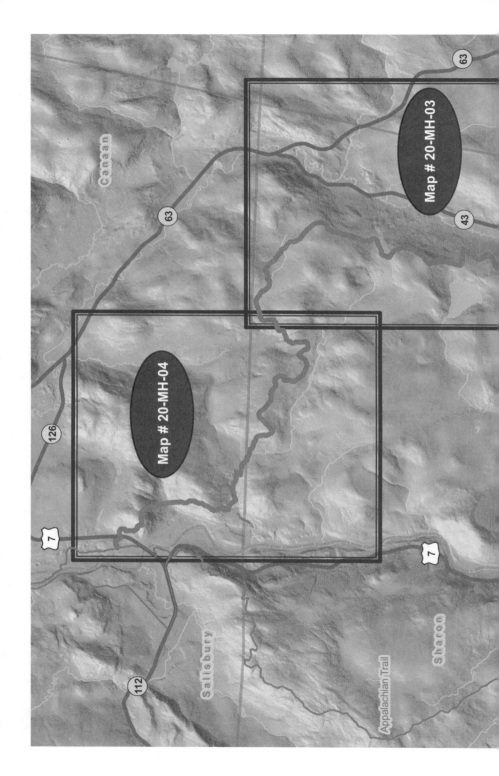

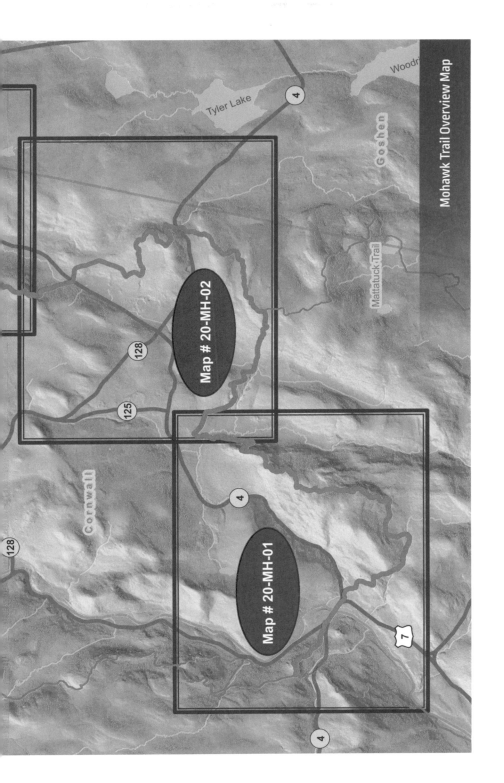

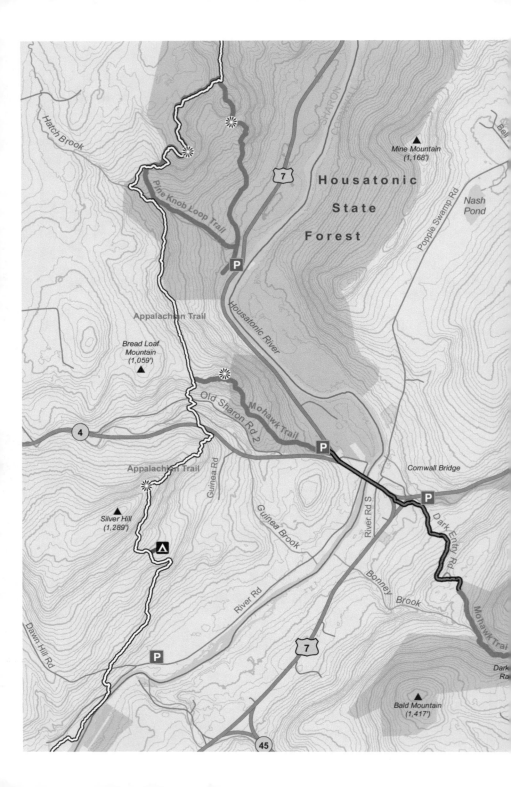

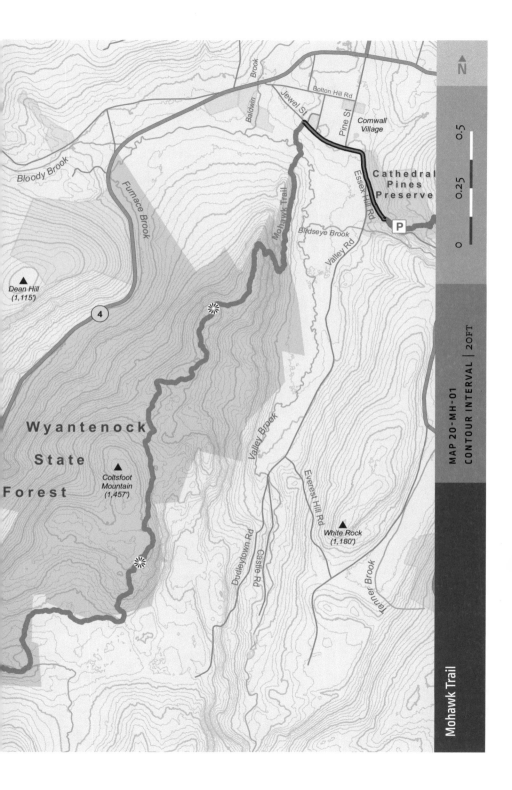

0.5

0.25

0

CONTOUR INTERVAL | 20FT

MAP 20-MH-01

Mohawk Trail

Bloody Brook

Baldwin Brook

Jewel St

Bolton Hill Rd

Pine St

Cornwall Village

Cathedral Pines Preserve

Essex Hill Rd

P

Furnace Brook

Mohawk Trail

Birdseye Brook

Valley Rd

Dean Hill (1,115')

4

Wyantenock

State

Forest

Coltsfoot Mountain (1,457')

Valley Brook

Everest Hill Rd

White Rock (1,180')

Dudleytown Rd

Castle Rd

Tanner Brook

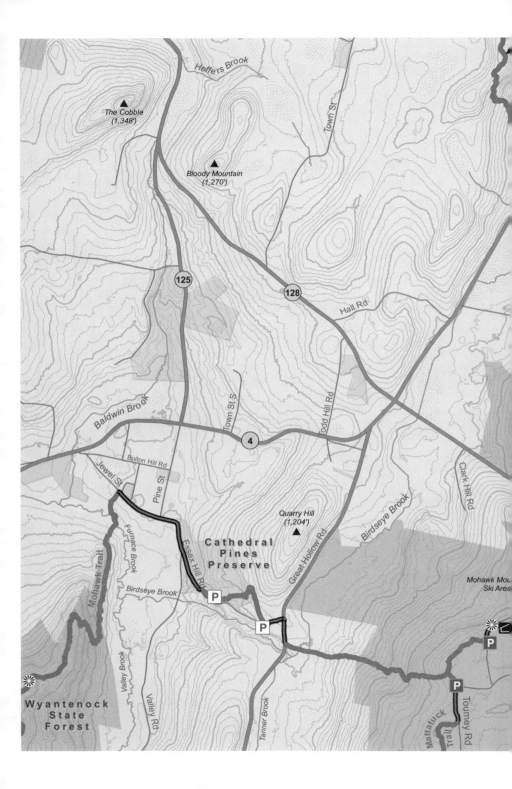

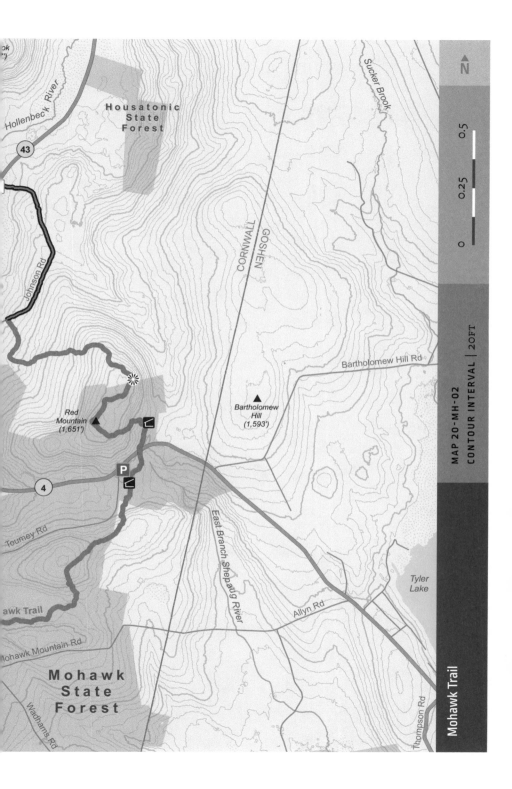

N

0   0.25   0.5

MAP 20-MH-02
CONTOUR INTERVAL | 20FT

Mohawk Trail

Hollenbeck River

Housatonic
State
Forest

43

Sucker Brook

Johnson Rd

CORNWALL

GOSHEN

Bartholomew Hill Rd

Red
Mountain
(1,651')

Bartholomew
Hill
(1,593')

P

4

Toumey Rd

East Branch Shepaug River

Tyler
Lake

awk Trail

Allyn Rd

Mohawk Mountain Rd

Mohawk
State
Forest

Wadhams Rd

Thompson Rd

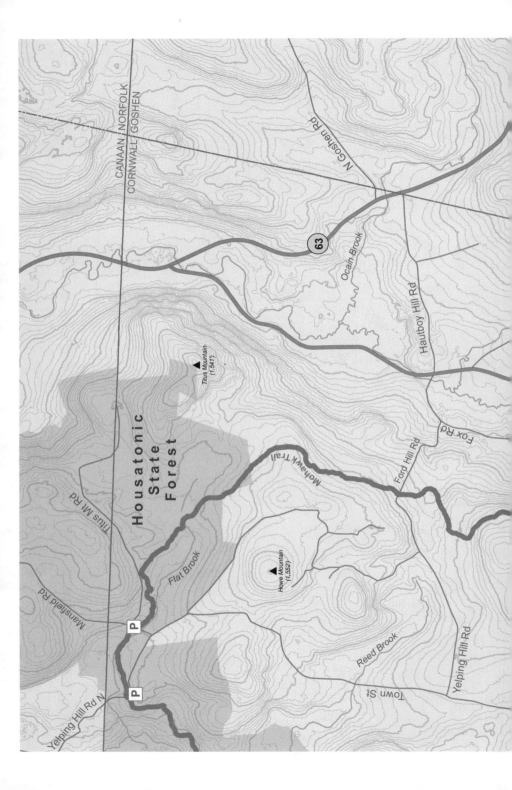

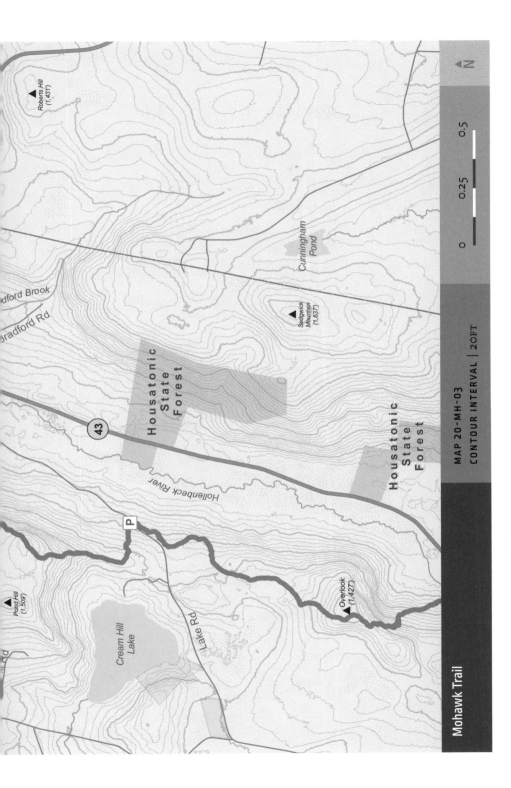

Mohawk Trail

MAP 20-MH-03
CONTOUR INTERVAL | 20FT

0   0.25   0.5

N

Roberts Hill
(1,431')

Cunningham
Pond

Sedgwick
Mountain
(1,537')

Housatonic
State
Forest

Housatonic
State
Forest

dford Brook

Bradford Rd

43

Hollenbeck River

P

Overlook
(1,427')

Pond Hill
(1,509')

Cream Hill
Lake

Lake Rd

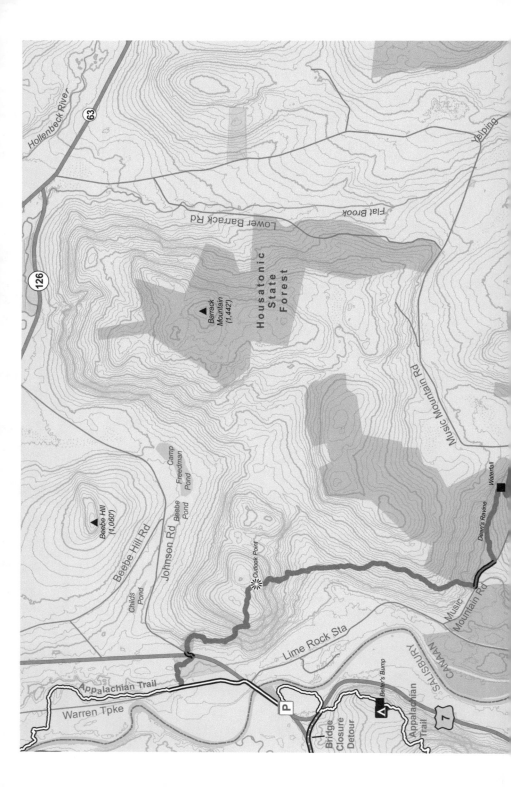

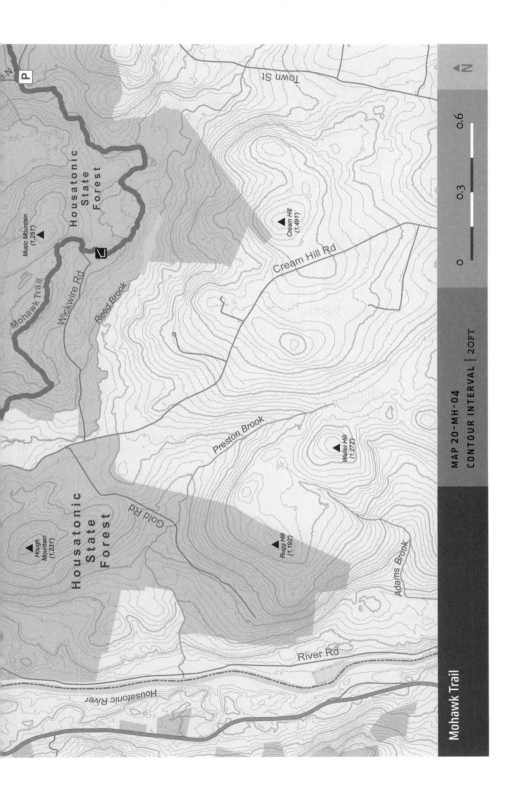

Mohawk Trail

MAP 20-MH-04
CONTOUR INTERVAL | 20FT

0   0.3   0.6

N

Music Mountain
(1,251')

Mohawk Trail

Wickwire Rd

Reed Brook

Housatonic
State
Forest

P

Cream Hill
(1,491')

Cream Hill Rd

Town St

Hough
Mountain
(1,231')

Housatonic
State
Forest

Gold Rd

Rugg Hill
(1,192')

Preston Brook

Walker Hill
(1,272')

Adams Brook

River Rd

Housatonic River

Narragansett Trail

LENGTH 15.0 miles   **BLAZE COLOR** Blue

The Narragansett Trail in Connecticut is a multifaceted trail that passes thorough rich forestland and active wildlife refuge areas. The trail follows and crosses several brooks, traverses wild ravines, and passes five ponds and lakes. The trail offers many panoramic vistas along the way, including those from the summits of Lantern Hill and High Ledge. On a clear day, hikers may be able to see all the way to Long Island Sound. The trail joins the Pachaug Trail in Pachaug State Forest; it also passes near The Nature Conservancy's Gladys Foster Preserve, and offers opportunities for loop hikes where it connects with other CFPA trails. The Narragansett Trail continues into Rhode Island at Camp Yawgoog and that section is maintained by the Appalachian Mountain Club. Along the border the trail shares footage with the Tippecansett Trail.

Longer backpacking trips can be achieved by linking the Quinebaug, Pachaug, Nehantic, and Narragansett Trails. Four overnight shelters in the state forest can be used by backpackers on a first-come, first-served basis.

 Challenge yourself to hike a little further! Join others by participating in our Blue-Blaze Hiker Challenge. You can become a 200-, 400- or 800-miler of the Blue-Blazed Hiking Trails, one step at a time.

SIDE TRAILS

Green Fall Pond Trail (see Map 20-NA-03)

LENGTH 1.6 miles   **BLAZE COLOR** Blue/Orange

Circling Green Fall Pond in the Pachaug State Forest, this loop trail connects to the blue-blazed Narragansett, Nehantic, and Pachaug Trails.

Pachaug-Narragansett Connector (see Map 20-NA-03)

LENGTH 0.3 miles   **BLAZE COLOR** Blue/Red

This short connector links the blue-blazed Pachaug and Narragansett Trails.

▌ *Hunting is permitted in state forests intersected by this trail. Please use caution and wear orange during hunting season.*

193

Mileage Table

NARRAGANSETT TRAIL

0.0	Wintechog Hill Rd (P)
0.5	Summit, Lantern Hill (493 ft) / View
1.2	Wintechog Hill Rd
3.2	Begin roadwalk
3.2	Join Ct Rte 2 (P)
3.2	Join Ryder Rd
3.3	Leave Ryder Rd (P)
3.3	End roadwalk
3.8	View
6.6	Begin roadwalk—Wyassup Lake Rd
6.7	End roadwalk—Wyassup Lake Rd (P)
10.6	Begin roadwalk
10.6	Join Legend Wood Rd (P)
11.0	Join Johnson Rd
11.1	Leave Ct Rte 49
11.1	End roadwalk

BREAK IN TRAIL. Trail mileage continues on Tom Wheeler Rd in North Stonington.

11.1	Tom Wheeler Rd (P)
12.3	Begin roadwalk—Sand Hill Rd
12.5	End roadwalk—Sand Hill Rd
12.8	Join Green Fall Pond Trail (blue/orange)
13.4	Leave Green Fall Pond Trail (blue/orange)
13.8	Spur to Peg Mill Shelter
15.0	Camp Yawgoog Rd (P)

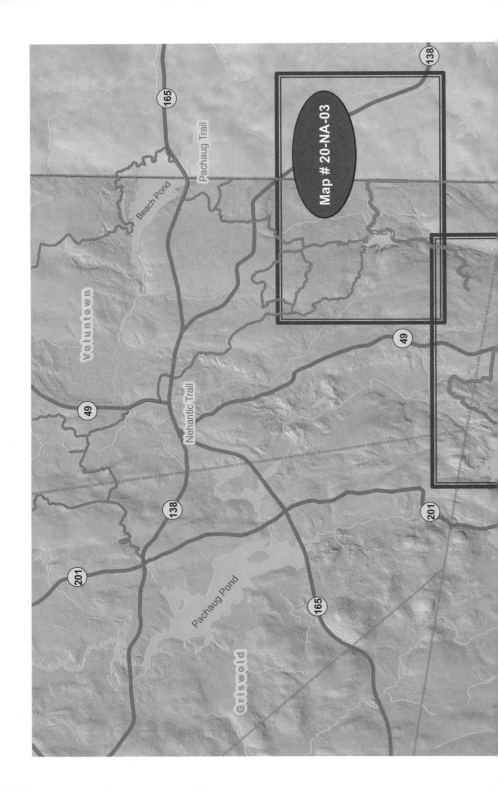

Map # 20-NA-03

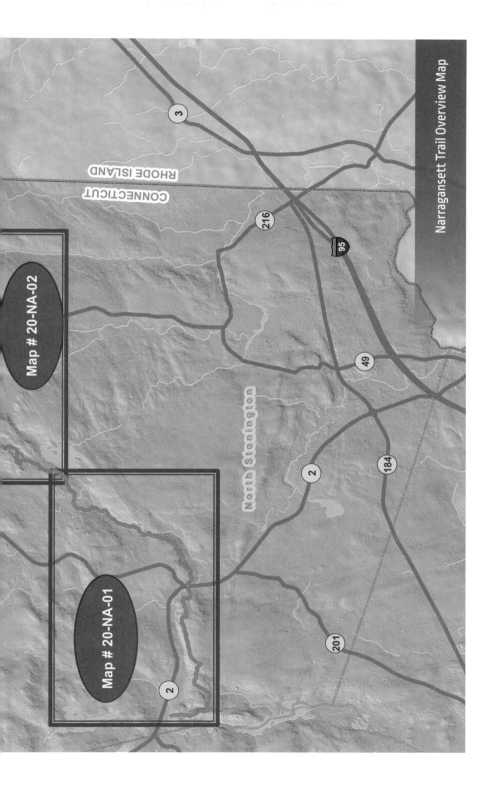

Narragansett Trail Overview Map

Map # 20-NA-02

Map # 20-NA-01

North Stonington

RHODE ISLAND
CONNECTICUT

3

216

95

49

2

184

201

2

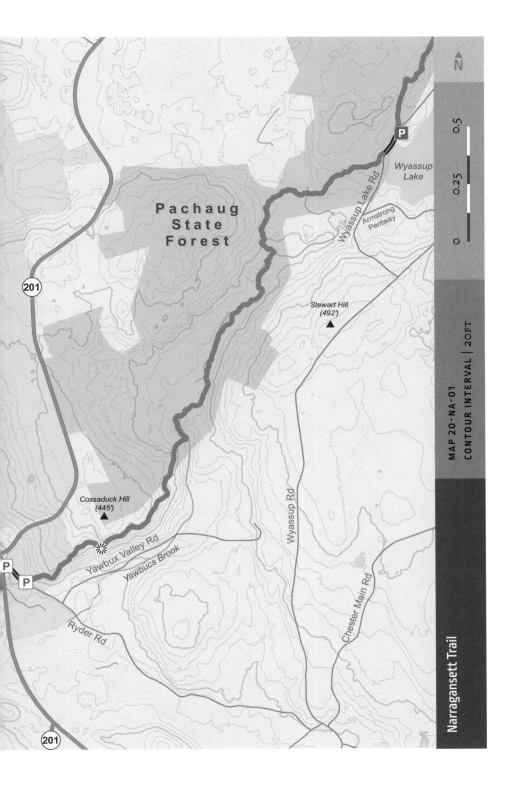

Pachaug
State
Forest

Wyassup Lake Rd

Wyassup
Lake

Armstrong
Pentway

201

Stewart Hill
(492')
▲

Cossaduck Hill
(445')
▲

Yawbux Valley Rd

Yawbucs Brook

Wyassup Rd

Chester Main Rd

Ryder Rd

201

N▲

0   0.25   0.5

MAP 20-NA-01
CONTOUR INTERVAL | 20FT

Narragansett Trail

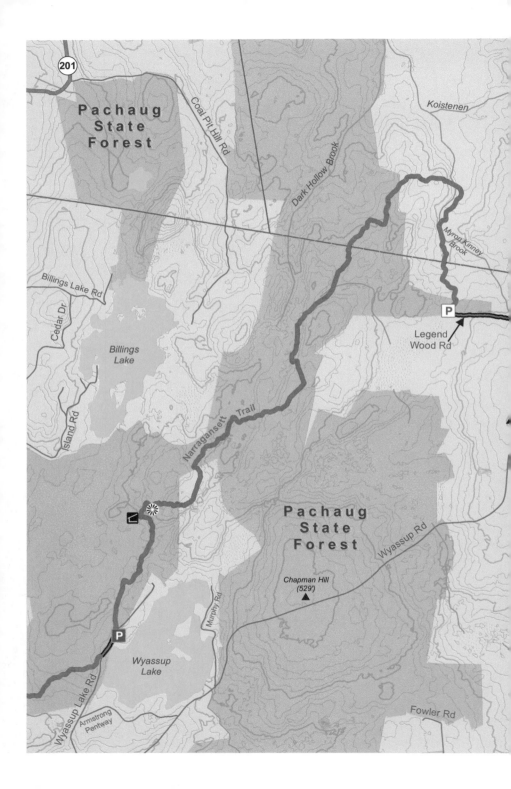

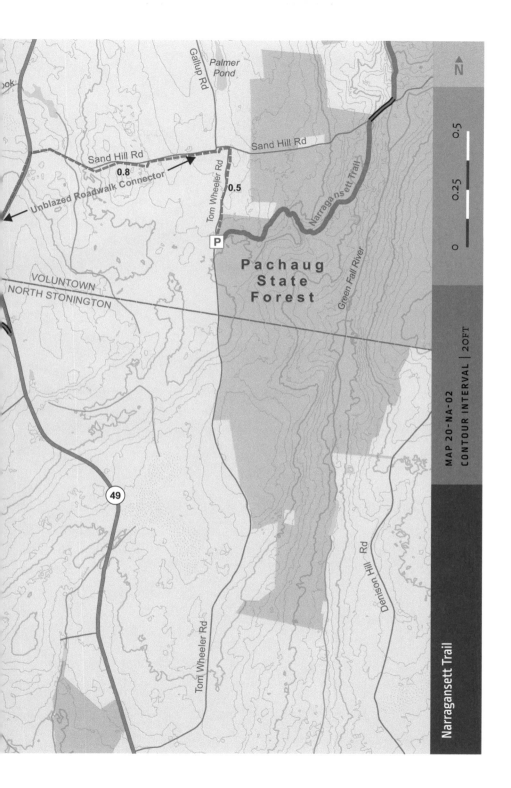

Narragansett Trail

MAP 20-NA-02
CONTOUR INTERVAL | 20FT

0   0.25   0.5

N

Gallup Rd

Palmer
Pond

Sand Hill Rd

Sand Hill Rd

0.8

Unblazed Roadwalk Connector

Tom Wheeler Rd

0.5

P

Narragansett Trail

Pachaug
State
Forest

Green Fall River

VOLUNTOWN
NORTH STONINGTON

49

Tom Wheeler Rd

Denison Hill Rd

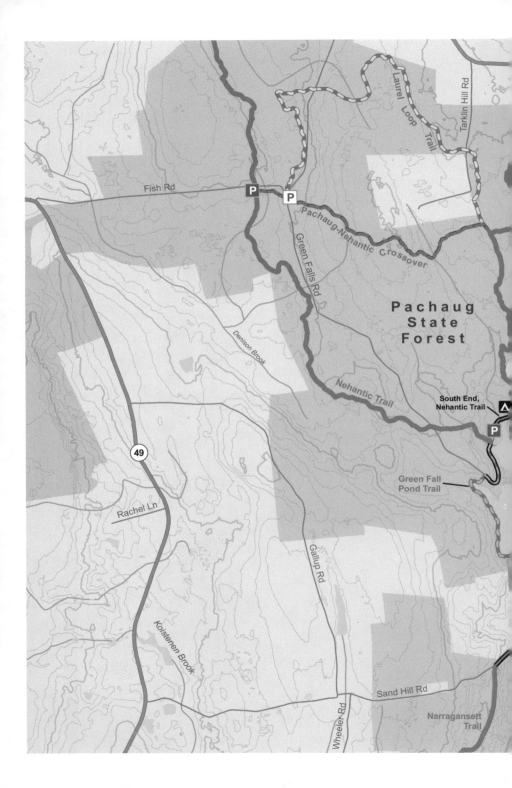

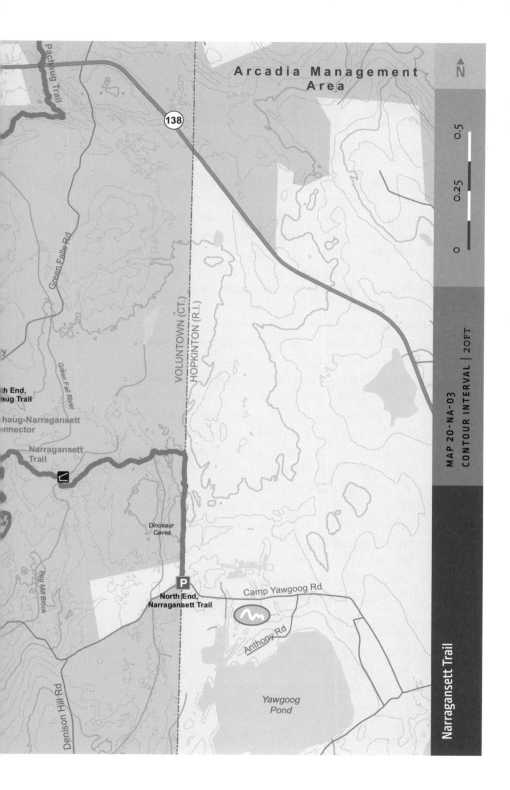

Arcadia Management Area

138

VOLUNTOWN (CT.)
HOPKINTON (R.I.)

Pachaug Trail

Green Falls Rd

Green Fall River

th End,
aug Trail

haug-Narragansett
nnector

Narragansett
Trail

Dinosaur
Caves

Reg Mill Brook

P
North End,
Narragansett Trail

Camp Yawgoog Rd

Anthony Rd

Denison Hill Rd

Yawgoog
Pond

N

0.5

0.25

0

MAP 20-NA-03
CONTOUR INTERVAL | 20FT

Narragansett Trail

Natchaug Trail

LENGTH 17.8 miles   **BLAZE COLOR** Blue

The Natchaug Trail traverses the James L. Goodwin and Natchaug State Forests. Together with the Nipmuck State Forest, Yale Forest, and several large private tracts, they combine to form one of the largest areas of contiguous forest in southern New England, supporting a large variety of wildlife.

The trail follows a short portion of the beautiful Still River and journeys along Bigelow Brook. Meandering over relatively easy terrain, it crosses several small brooks, passes stone walls, and slips through interesting stands of trees. State foresters actively manage these forests for wildlife and timber production and the trail traverses a diverse and interesting mix of trees, ranging from young seedlings to mature specimens well over 100 years old. Along streams and in the areas around Pine Acres Pond, and Black Spruce and Beaverdam Marshes, there are opportunities to catch sight of turtles, beavers, and many bird species.

The trail also passes near or through several historic sites, including old CCC Camp Fernow (1933–42) and General Nathaniel Lyon Memorial Park, which honors the first Union general to be killed in the Civil War. A short northern section coincides with the Old Connecticut Path traveled in the 1630s by settlers relocating from the Boston area to the Hartford area in one of the first major inland migrations by European settlers in America.

The Natchaug Trail joins the Nipmuck Trail in Ashford and hikers can continue exploring north to Bigelow Hollow State Park and the Connecticut/Massachusetts state line or south to Mansfield Hollow State Park.

The James L. Goodwin Conservation Education Center, on Pine Acres Pond in Hampton, offers extensive educational programming, interpretive trails, and guided walks. It maintains a native plant wildlife garden and offers both nature and history museums (www.friendsofgoodwin forest.org). This site is jointly managed by CFPA and the Connecticut DEEP.

CCC Loop Trail (see Map 20-NT-02)

LENGTH 2.8 miles **BLAZE COLOR** Blue/Yellow

This trail follows a portion of the Natchaug River, passes a large vernal pool, crosses a small underground stream, and takes hikers to the stone foundation of a former Civilian Conservation Corps (CCC) cabin. In conjunction with the Natchaug Trail or dirt roads, hikers can make a variety of loop hikes.

▌ *Hunting is permitted in state forests intersected by this trail. Please use caution and wear orange during hunting season.*

Mileage Table   203

NATCHAUG TRAIL

0.0	Goodwin Conservation Education Center (P)
0.3	Jct Blue/Red Interpretive Trail
0.4	Join Air Line State Park Trail
0.6	South jct Blue/Yellow Interpretive Trail / Leave Air Line State Park Trail
0.9	Eleventh Section Rd
1.1	Cannon Rd
1.5	North jct Blue/Yellow Interpretive Trail
2.1	Jct Pine Acres Lake Trail (blue/white)
2.7	Middle Rd
3.1	Nutmeg Ln
3.4	Jct local trail (orange)
3.4	Foundation
3.9	Spur to view (170 ft)
4.3	Marcy Rd
4.6	Morey Rd (P)
5.4	South jct CCC Trail (blue/yellow)
5.7	Unnamed park road (dirt)
6.0	Pipeline
6.5	Old mill dam / Waterfall
6.6	Kingsbury Rd / Begin roadwalk—Forest Rd
6.8	Beaverdam Marsh Area / End road-

	walk—Forest Rd (P)
7.3	Begin roadwalk—Kingsbury Rd
7.5	End roadwalk—Kingsbury Rd
7.6	General Nathaniel Lyon Memorial Park (P)
7.7	Spur to shelter (200 ft)
8.3	North jct CCC Trail (blue/yellow)
9.9	Begin roadwalk
9.9	Join Pilfershire Rd
10.0	Join General Lyon Rd (P)
10.1	Join Ct Rte 198
10.4	Leave Ct Rte 198
10.4	End roadwalk
11.9	Ct Rte 44
14.3	Ashford Rd
15.7	Moon Rd
17.8	Jct Nipmuck Trail (blue)

CCC TRAIL

0.0	South jct Natchaug Trail (blue)
0.3	Unnamed park road (dirt)
1.2	Picnic area
1.5	Unnamed park road (dirt)
2.8	North jct Natchaug Trail (blue)

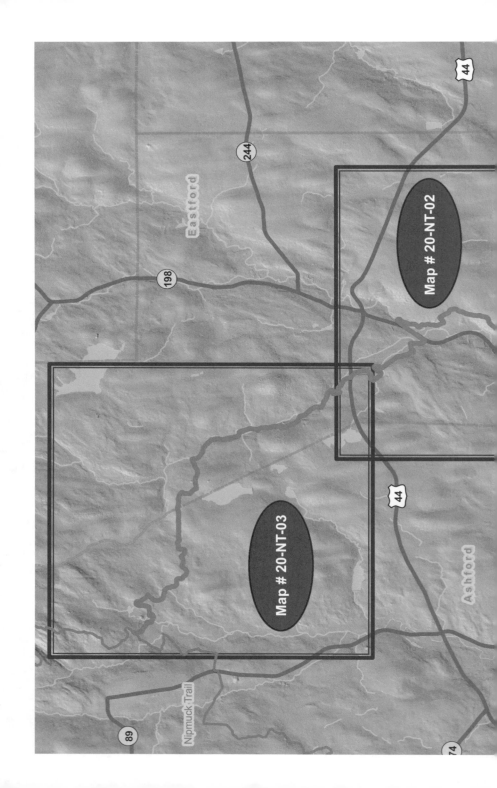

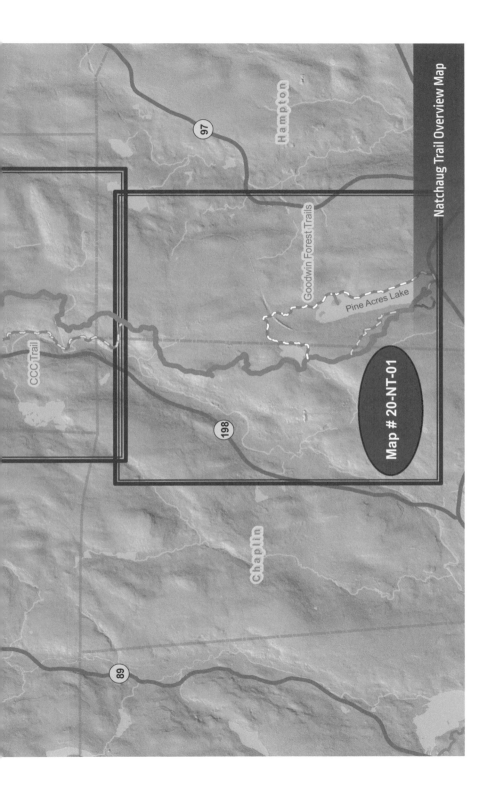

Map # 20-NT-01

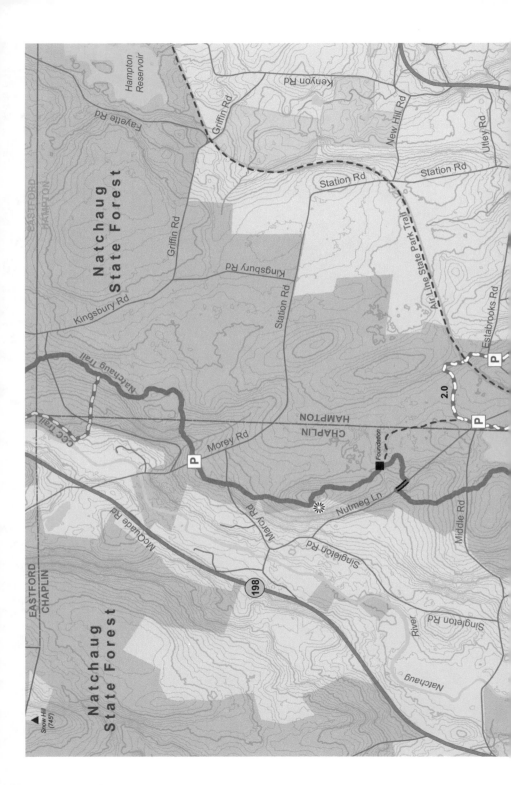

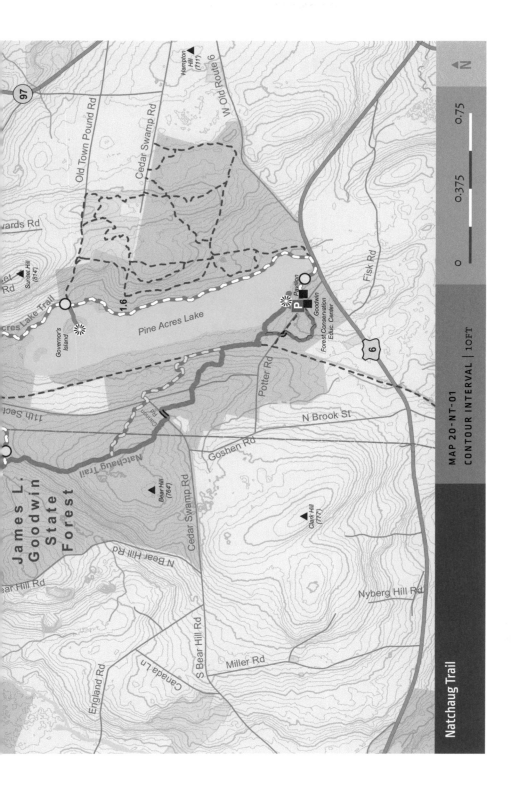

James L.
Goodwin
State
Forest

Pine Acres Lake

Governor's Island

Pavilion

Goodwin
Forest Conservation
Educ. Center

Old Town Pound Rd
Cedar Swamp Rd
W Old Route 6
Hampton Hill (711)
Sunset Hill (814)
Acres Lake Trail
1.6
11th Sect
Canada Rd
Natchaug Trail
Potter Rd
Fisk Rd
N Brook St
Goshen Rd
Bear Hill (764)
Clark Hill (777)
Cedar Swamp Rd
N Bear Hill Rd
Bear Hill Rd
S Bear Hill Rd
Miller Rd
Canada Ln
England Rd
Nyberg Hill Rd
ards Rd
Rd

97

6

N

0   0.375   0.75

MAP 20-NT-01
CONTOUR INTERVAL | 10FT

Natchaug Trail

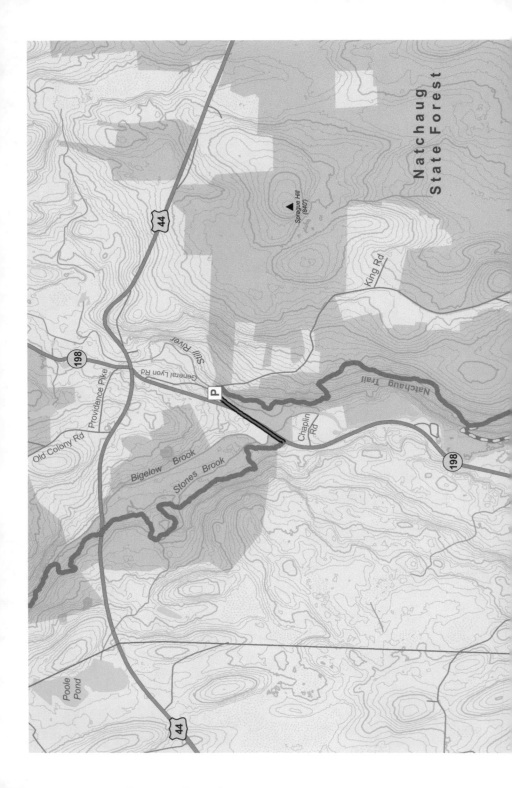

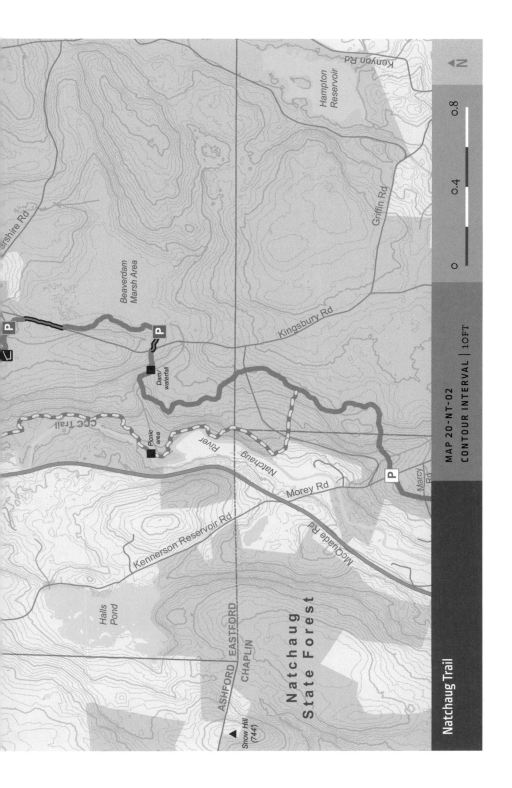

Natchaug Trail

MAP 20-NT-02
CONTOUR INTERVAL | 10FT

N

0   0.4   0.8

Kenyon Rd

Hampton
Reservoir

Griffin Rd

Beaverdam
Marsh Area

Kingsbury Rd

Dam/
waterfall

CCC Trail

Picnic
area

Natchaug River

Morey Rd

Kennerson Reservoir Rd

McQuade Rd

Marcy
Rd

Halls
Pond

ASHFORD EASTFORD
CHAPLIN

Natchaug
State Forest

Snow Hill
(744')

shire Rd

P

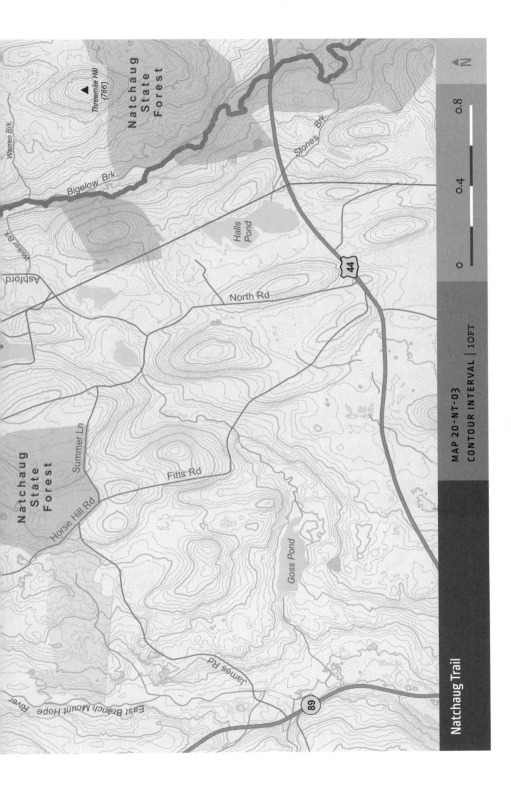

Natchaug Trail

MAP 20-NT-03
CONTOUR INTERVAL | 10FT

Threemile Hill
(786')

Natchaug
State
Forest

Warren Brk.

Bigelow Brk.

Stones Brk.

Halls
Pond

Walker Brk.

Ashford

North Rd

44

Natchaug
State
Forest

Summer Ln

Fitts Rd

Horse Hill Rd

Goss Pond

James Rd

East Branch Mount Hope River

89

N

0   0.4   0.8

Hikers discover elusive ladyslippers on the Nehantic Trail.
Photo courtesy CFPA.

Naugatuck Trail

LENGTH 5.4 miles   **BLAZE COLOR** Blue

The Naugatuck Trail is located within the eastern block of Naugatuck State Forest along an uneven east-west ridge. To the east, the trail winds narrowly through laurel groves along contour lines with the occasional natural trailside rock bench upholstered in moss. Several balds feature seasonal wildflowers. Westward beyond a gorge, there are straighter, flatter sections through open forest with ephemeral ponds. The steepest elevation change is along Egypt Brook near Route 8, marking the eastern slope of the Naugatuck River Valley.

SIDE TRAILS

Beacon Cap Trail

LENGTH 0.3 miles   **BLAZE COLOR** Blue/Yellow

The rougher Beacon Cap Trail branches from the Naugatuck Trail to ascend to Beacon Cap, a glacial, hilltop boulder (elevation 775 feet) in a large open area. It sits on the town line between Bethany and Naugatuck.

Whittemore Trail

LENGTH 0.8 miles   **BLAZE COLOR** Blue/White

The Whittemore Trail leaves the blue-blazed trail and crosses a buried fiber-optic cable and two intermittent brooks before reaching the Route 42 parking area. In combination with the eastern end of the trail it allows for a 3-mile loop hike.

▮ *Hunting is permitted in state forests intersected by this trail. Please use caution and wear orange during hunting season.*

▮ *Beware of confusing side paths crisscrossing the blue-blazed trail.*

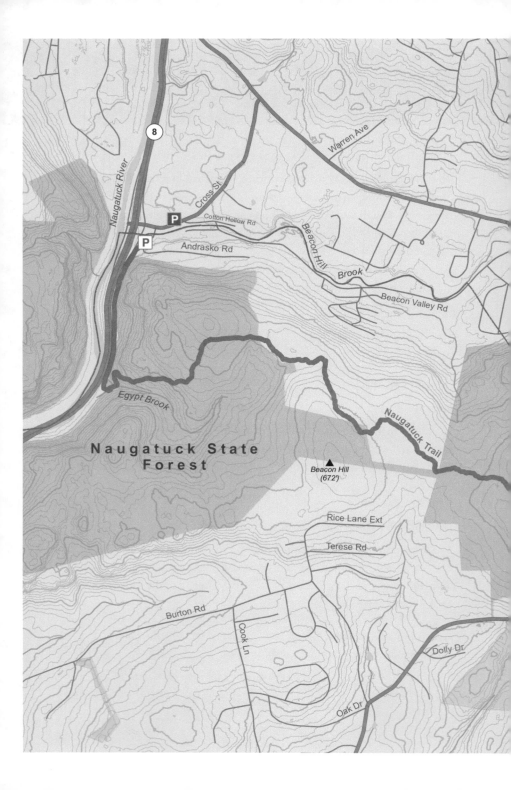

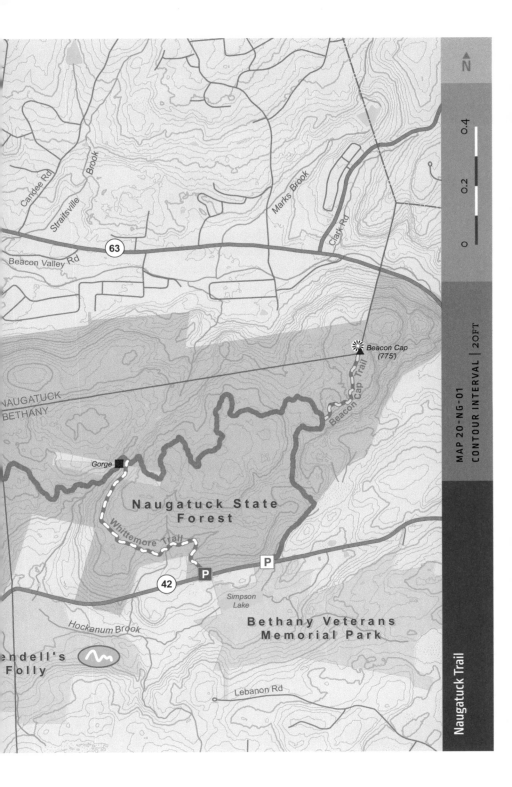

N

0   0.2   0.4

MAP 20-NG-01
CONTOUR INTERVAL | 20FT

Naugatuck Trail

Candee Rd

Brook

Straitsville

Marks Brook

Clark Rd

63

Beacon Valley Rd

Beacon Cap
(775')

Beacon Cap Trail

NAUGATUCK
BETHANY

Gorge

Naugatuck State
Forest

Whittemore Trail

42

P

P

Simpson
Lake

Bethany Veterans
Memorial Park

Hockanum Brook

endell's
Folly

Lebanon Rd

LENGTH 3.4 miles   **BLAZE COLOR** Blue

The Nayantaquit Trail (named after a native tribe that once inhabited the area) is in the western section of Nehantic State Forest. It consists of a single loop bisected by the Crossover Trail with a connector trail leading to the Uncas Pond picnic area. There are many stone walls and stream crossings along the trail, and an old homestead area on Brown Hill. On clear days, the steep ascent to the ledge-rock summit of Nickerson Hill allows distant views of Long Island Sound and beyond.

The Nehantic State Forest has been actively managed by the Connecticut DEEP since 1993. State foresters have made efforts to create, evaluate, and maintain a wide variety of habitats in this forest complex close to the shoreline. Much of the predominantly white oak and hickory forest has been selectively cut, while certain places have been clear-cut to create openings for woodcock, and other areas burned to maintain an open understory. There are dense stands of pine and hemlock, rocky ledges, and a wonderful wetlands complex that connects several ponds and lakes. Birders consider this forest a "hot spot" for spring migrants. Species you may see or hear along this trail include black-throated blue warbler, pine warbler, ruffed grouse, scarlet tanager, ovenbird, wood thrush, chestnut-sided warbler, redstart, black-billed cuckoo, Cooper's hawk, blue-winged warbler, and wild turkey.

Did you know CFPA is a land trust? CFPA's land conservation program seeks to protect working forests and lands intersected by the Blue-Blazed Hiking Trails. Learn more about properties and recent initiatives on our website.

Crossover Trail

LENGTH 0.6 miles   **BLAZE COLOR** Blue/Yellow

The relatively flat Crossover Trail traverses low-lying areas and passes through some rocky and wet terrain.

Uncas Pond Connector Trail

LENGTH 0.8 miles   **BLAZE COLOR** Blue/Green

This connector trail crosses several hills with rocky terrain before reaching the picnic area at Uncas Pond.

❚ *Hunting is permitted in state forests intersected by this trail. Please use caution and wear orange during hunting season.*

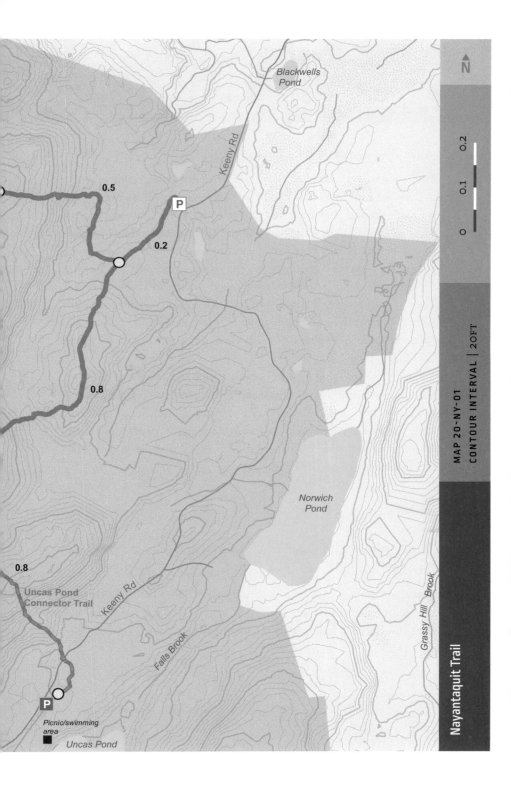

Blackwells
Pond

Keeny Rd

0.5

P

0.2

0.8

Norwich
Pond

0.8

Uncas Pond
Connector Trail

Keeny Rd

Falls Brook

Grassy Hill Brook

P

Picnic/swimming
area

Uncas Pond

N

0   0.1   0.2

MAP 20-NY-01
CONTOUR INTERVAL | 20FT

Nayantaquit Trail

Nehantic Trail

LENGTH 12.7 miles   **BLAZE COLOR** Blue

The Nehantic Trail stretches between Green Fall Pond Recreation Area in Voluntown and Hopeville Pond State Park in Griswold. The trail passes primarily through the 30,000-acre Pachaug State Forest, traveling through white-pine and hardwood forests and occasional open fields. At the summit of Mount Misery (441 feet) expect to see a spectacular, sweeping vista of the forested landscapes encompassing Voluntown and Sterling. Sections of the trail are characterized by gentle hills and exposed ledges. The trail passes several abandoned mill sites situated near brooks. The Nehantic can be linked with the adjoining Narragansett, Quinebaug, and Pachaug Trails, as well as other side trails and woods roads, for longer hiking adventures.

Longer backpacking trips can be achieved by linking the Quinebaug, Pachaug, Nehantic, and Narragansett Trails. Four overnight shelters in the state forest can be used by backpackers on a first-come, first-served basis. The trail also has access to a youth camping area near Headquarters Road. For information on camping and access to Hopeville Pond State Park, visit the Connecticut DEEP website.

SIDE TRAILS

Pachaug-Nehantic Crossover (see Map 20-NE-01)

LENGTH 1.2 miles   **BLAZE COLOR** Blue/Red

This crossover trail links the Nehantic and Pachaug Trails a little more than one mile north of Green Fall Pond. When taken in conjunction with the Laurel Loop, it makes a great circular hike.

Rhododendron Sanctuary Trail (see Map 20-NE-02)

LENGTH 0.2 miles   **BLAZE COLOR** Blue

This wheelchair-accessible path travels a short distance over packed gravel, before continuing on a raised boardwalk through a white cedar swamp, a rare natural community in Connecticut. The boardwalk and nature-observation deck were built in 1998 by CFPA trail volunteers and students from Norwich Free Academy's Outing Club. It provides easy access to the dazzling display of rhododendron blooms in early July and offers an opportunity to observe wildlife in a natural setting.

▌ *Hunting is permitted in state forests intersected by this trail. Please use caution and wear orange during hunting season.*

Mileage Table

NEHANTIC TRAIL

0.0	Green Falls Rd / Jct Pachaug Trail (blue) / Jct Green Fall Pond Trail (blue/orange) (P)
0.3	Green Falls Rd
1.9	Jct Pachaug-Nehantic Connector (blue/red)
2.0	Fish Rd (P)
3.7	Begin roadwalk—Weller Rd
4.3	End roadwalk—Weller Rd / Ct Rte 138 / Ct Rte 165
4.5	Shetucket Tpke
4.8	Begin roadwalk—Ct Rte 49
5.3	End roadwalk—Ct Rte 49 (P)
5.8	Headquarters Rd
6.2	Join Pachaug Trail (blue)
6.3	Begin roadwalk
6.3	Join Cutoff Rd
6.4	Jct Rhododendron Sanctuary Trail (blue)
6.6	Leave Cutoff Rd
6.6	End roadwalk
7.3	Summit, Mount Misery (440 ft)
7.5	Fire Tower Rd
7.9	Leave Pachaug Trail (blue)
8.1	Shelter
8.7	Trail 2 Rd
9.7	Begin roadwalk—Lee Rd
9.8	End roadwalk—Lee Rd
10.2	Breakneck Hill Rd (P)
10.7	Jct Quinebaug Trail (blue)
11.4	Lester Rd
11.9	Roode Rd
12.7	Ct Rte 201
12.8	Hopeville Pond State Park (P)

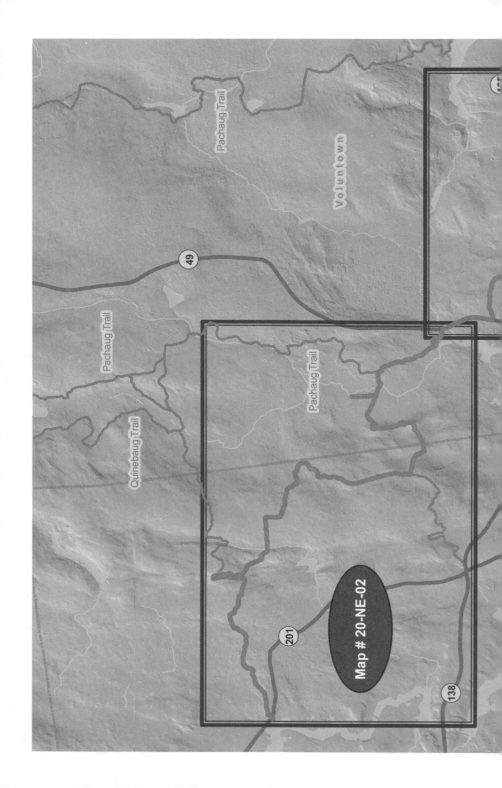

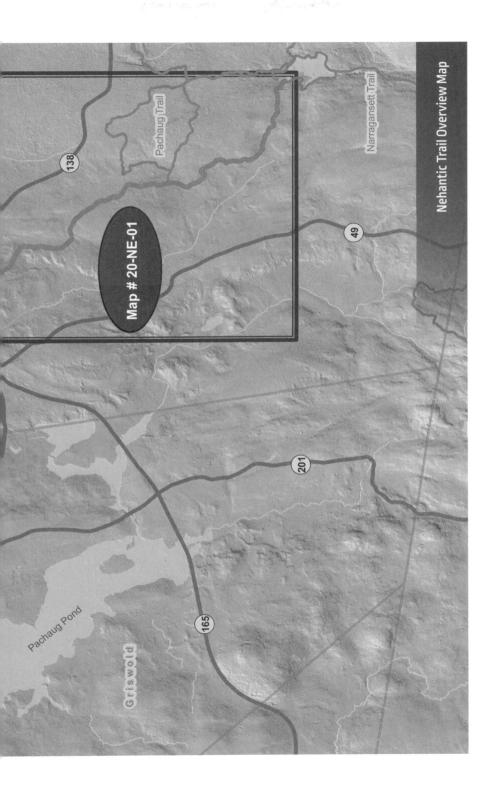

Map # 20-NE-01

Pachaug Trail

Narragansett Trail

138

49

201

165

Pachaug Pond

Griswold

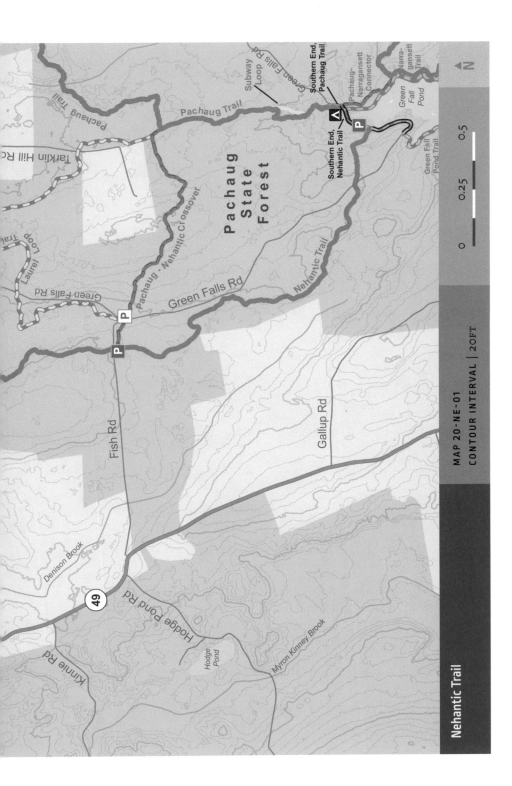

Nehantic Trail

MAP 20-NE-01
CONTOUR INTERVAL | 20FT

0   0.25   0.5

N

Pachaug State Forest

Southern End, Pachaug Trail

Southern End, Nehantic Trail

Pachaug Trail

Subway Loop

Green Falls Rd

Pachaug–Narragansett Connector

Narragansett Trail

Green Fall Pond

Green Fall Pond Trail

Tarklin Hill Rd

Pachaug Trail

Laurel Loop Trail

Green Falls Rd

Pachaug – Nehantic Crossover

Green Falls Rd

Nehantic Trail

Gallup Rd

Fish Rd

Denison Brook

49

Hodge Pond Rd

Hodge Pond

Myron Kinney Brook

Kinnie Rd

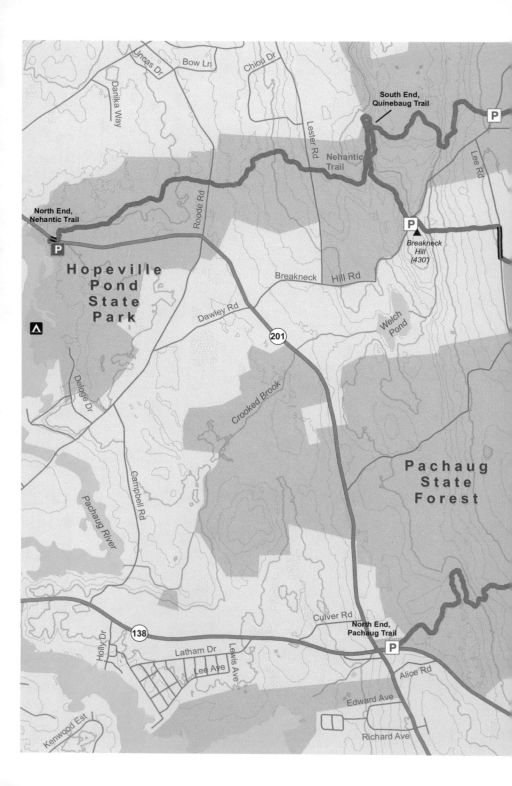

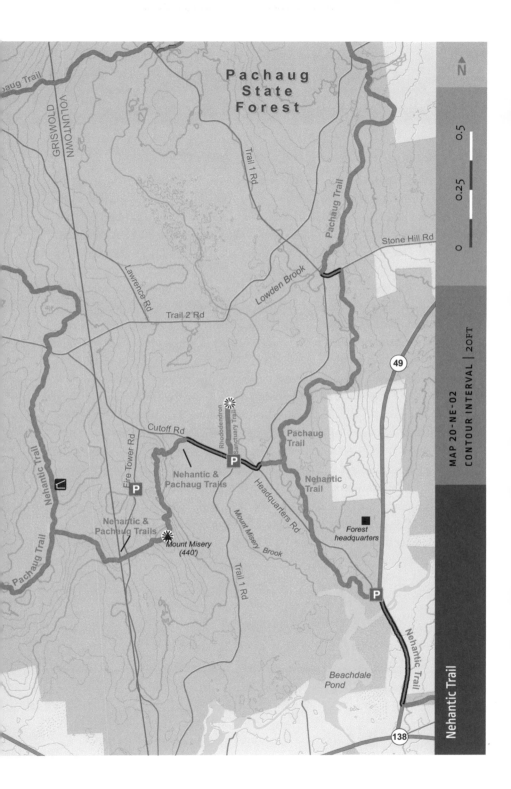

Pachaug
State
Forest

GRISWOLD

VOLUNTOWN

Pachaug Trail

Trail 1 Rd

Pachaug Trail

Stone Hill Rd

Lawrence Rd

Lowden Brook

Trail 2 Rd

Rhododendron

Sanctuary Trail

Cutoff Rd

Nehantic &
Pachaug Trails

Pachaug
Trail

Nehantic
Trail

Fire Tower Rd

Nehantic &
Pachaug Trails

Mount Misery
(440')

Headquarters Rd

Mount Misery Brook

Forest
headquarters

Nehantic Trail

Pachaug Trail

Trail 1 Rd

Beachdale
Pond

Nehantic Trail

N

0   0.25   0.5

0

MAP 20-NE-02
CONTOUR INTERVAL | 20FT

Nehantic Trail

49

138

LENGTH 30 miles   BLAZE COLOR Blue

The Nipmuck Trail extends from Mansfield north to the Massachusetts border. It is shaped roughly like an upside-down fork and has two southern branches: the West Branch starts on Puddin' Lane in Mansfield; the East Branch starts in Mansfield Hollow State Park in North Windham. The northern terminus of the Nipmuck Trail is in the beautiful Bigelow Hollow State Park.

The trail crosses through a number of recreation and conservation areas including Mansfield Hollow State Park, the Natchaug and Nipmuck State Forests, Schoolhouse Brook Park, the Yale Forest, Bigelow Hollow State Park, and other lands owned by towns and land conservation trusts, most notably Joshua's Trust. Highlights on the trail include Wolf Rock (an enormous glacial erratic), the lookout over Mansfield Hollow Lake, Fifty-Foot Cliff, Pixie Falls, Ladies Room Rock, Coye Hill (highest point on the Nipmuck Trail), and the Fenton and Mount Hope Rivers. The Nipmuck Trail crosses open fields, follows along ridges and woods roads, and provides a continuous spine to which numerous other trail systems connect.

In Bigelow Hollow State Park, five additional trails (along with the Nipmuck Trail) are maintained by CFPA, totaling approximately 20 miles. Visit the Connecticut DEEP website for more information on trails and access to Bigelow Hollow State Park and Mansfield Hollow State Park.

SIDE TRAILS

Fenton River Trail (see Map 20-NP-01)

LENGTH 1.0 miles   BLAZE COLOR Blue/White

This alternate trail covers easy terrain and makes a short loop between two iron-truss bridges on the Fenton River.

Bigelow Hollow State Park Trails (see Map 20-NP-05)

East Ridge Trail

LENGTH 3.1 miles   BLAZE COLOR White

The northern end of the East Ridge Trail is located at the Massachusetts
state line marker, a bit south of Breakneck Pond's northern end. This
marker would be the starting point for hikers wishing to travel south on
the East Ridge Trail or Nipmuck Trail. Both trails also meet the Breakneck Pond View Trail at the marker. The East Ridge Trail follows easy
terrain for its 3.3 miles.

Breakneck Pond View Trail

LENGTH 2.2 miles   BLAZE COLOR Blue/Red

This trail is accessed from the East Ridge Trail north of the Bigelow Pond
parking area. Beginning at the southern end of Breakneck Pond, this
trail travels north along the pond's western edge, offering rugged climbs,
excellent views, and access to small islands. The trail's northern terminus
is at the Massachusetts state line marker. This trail can be combined with
the Nipmuck Trail for a longer, circuitous hike around the pond.

229

Ridge Trail

LENGTH 4.5 miles   BLAZE COLOR Blue/Orange

Looking for a challenge? This trail has the steepest sections in Bigelow
Hollow State Park, including a climb from the south to Peter Rabbit Rock
and the east slope of Cat Rocks Ridge, near the north end of the trail.

Mashapaug Pond View Trail

LENGTH 5.0 miles   BLAZE COLOR Blue/White

This loop trail starts at Bigelow Pond parking area, joins the Bigelow
Pond Loop Trail for a short distance, and heads off over moderate and
steep climbs across streams and along ridges. The trail loops back to the
Bigelow Pond Loop Trail.

Hikers enjoy the view after a long climb. Photo courtesy William J. Flood.

Bigelow Pond Loop Trail

LENGTH 1.4 miles   **BLAZE COLOR** Yellow

This loop trail encircles Bigelow Pond. It is one of the easiest trails in the park, except for a short section on the pond's west side where it crosses some large rocks. The trail starts at Bigelow Pond picnic area.

▮ *Hunting is permitted in state forests intersected by this trail. Please use caution and wear orange during hunting season.*

Mileage Table

NIPMUCK TRAIL—EAST BRANCH

0.0	N Windham Rd (P)
2.3	Bassetts Bridge Rd (P)
2.7	Parking (P)
2.7	Mansfield Hollow State Park picnic area
2.8	South jct local trail (yellow) / Spur to parking (P)
2.9	North jct local trail (yellow)
4.0	Ct Rte 89 (P)
4.4	South jct Fenton River Trail (blue/white)
4.5	Iron bridge
5.2	Iron bridge / North jct Fenton River Trail (blue/white)
6.1	Jct local trail (white)
6.3	Spur to lookout at Fifty-Foot Cliff (30 ft)
6.4	Jct Nipmuck Trail (blue) / Jct West Branch Nipmuck Trail (blue)

NIPMUCK TRAIL—WEST BRANCH

0.0	Puddin' Lane (P)
0.4	Jct Jacobs Hill Road Connector (blue/white, 400 ft, P)
1.7	Jct local trail (yellow dots)
1.9	Jct local trail (yellow dots)
1.9	Wolf Rock / View
2.0	Jct local trail (yellow dots)
2.2	Crane Hill Rd (P)
2.4	Browns Rd
3.4	Clover Mill Rd
4.4	Begin roadwalk
	4.4 Join Spring Hill Rd
	4.6 Join Ct Rte 195
	4.6 Leave Ct Rte 195 (P)
4.6	End roadwalk
5.2	Jct Nipmuck Trail (blue) / Jct East Branch Nipmuck Trail (blue)

NIPMUCK TRAIL

Trail mileage re-starts north of the East and West Branches

0.0	Jct West Branch Nipmuck Trail (blue) / Jct East Branch Nipmuck Trail (blue)
0.6	Bousa Rd
0.8	Stoneworks (Chaffeeville Silk Mill)
0.8	Spur to Chaffeeville Rd (blue, 200 ft, P)
2.1	Begin roadwalk
	2.1 Join Grist Mill Rd
	2.2 Join Stone Mill Rd / Gurleyville Grist Mill
	2.2 Leave Stone Mill Rd
2.2	End roadwalk
2.7	Gurleyville Rd (P)
4.7	Begin roadwalk
	4.7 Join Old Turnpike Rd (P)
	5.0 Join US Rte 44
	5.1 Leave US Rte 44
5.1	End roadwalk
6.4	Mason Rd
7.0	Marsh Rd (P)
9.7	Ct Rte 74 (P)
10.9	Perry Hill Rd (P)
13.2	Westford Hill Rd
13.5	Begin roadwalk
	13.5 Join Oakes Rd
	14.2 Join Ct Rte 89
	14.2 Join Iron Mine Ln
	14.4 Leave Iron Mine Ln (P)
14.4	End roadwalk
15.2	Spur to Pixie Falls (red, 150 ft)
15.6	Campsite
15.8	Ladies Room Rock
15.9	Jct Natchaug Trail (blue)
16.5	Eastford Rd (P)
18.1	Boston Hollow Rd (P)
18.9	Spur to lookout (50 ft)
22.3	Begin roadwalk—Barlow Mill Rd
22.4	End roadwalk—Barlow Mill Rd
26.3	Outdoor classroom
26.3	Ct Rte 171
26.5	Jct Nipmuck-Bigelow Hollow Connector (white)
28.0	Jct East Ridge Trail (white)
28.5	Campsite
28.8	Shelter
29.8	Campsite
29.9	Jct East Ridge Trail (white) / Jct Breakneck Pond View Trail (blue/red)
29.9	Northern terminus at state line marker

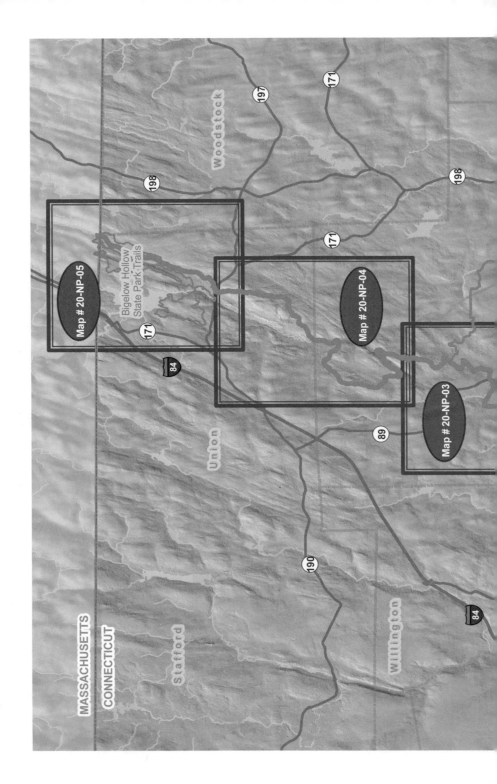

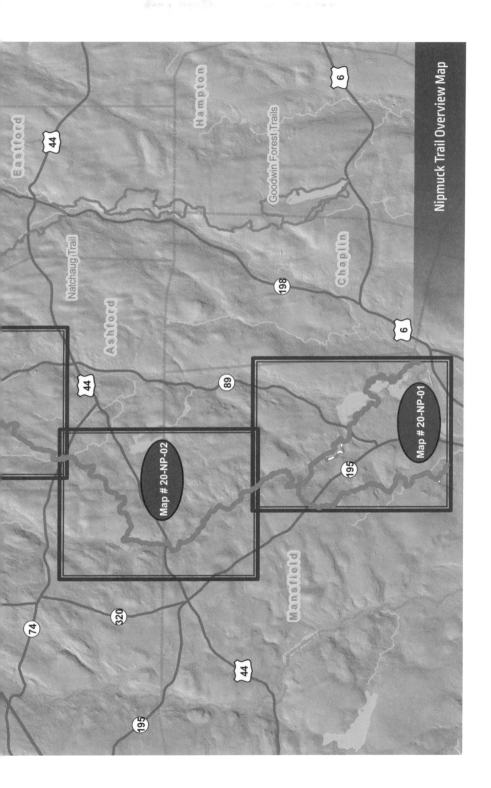

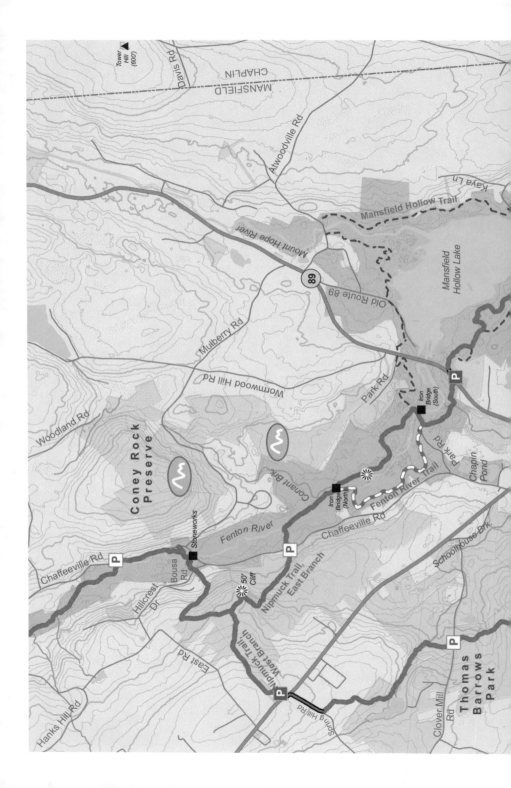

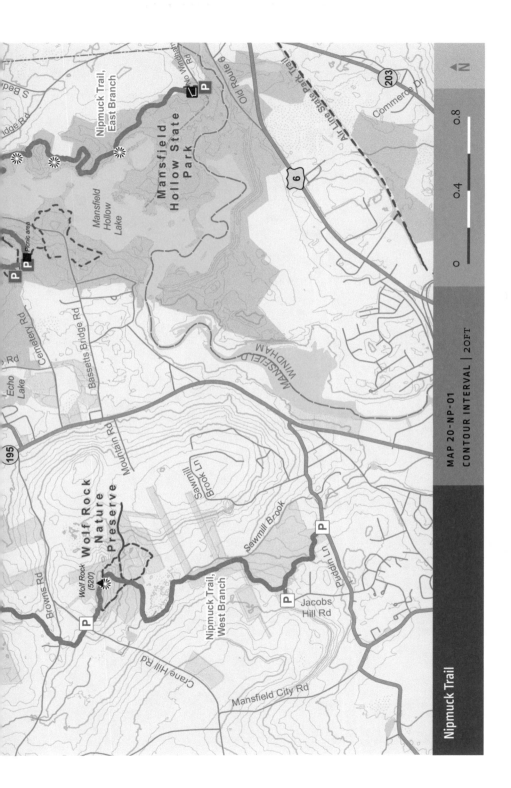

Nipmuck Trail

MAP 20-NP-01
CONTOUR INTERVAL | 20FT

0   0.4   0.8

N

Nipmuck Trail,
East Branch

No Windham Rd

P

Old Route 6

(203)

Commerce Dr

Mansfield
Hollow State
Park

Ar Line State Park Trail

6

MANSFIELD
WINDHAM

Mansfield
Hollow
Lake

Picnic area

P

P

P

Cemetery Rd

Bassetts Bridge Rd

Echo
Rd

Echo
Lake

(195)

Wolf Rock
Nature
Preserve

Mountain Rd

Wolf Rock
(520')

Sawmill
Brook Ln

Sawmill Brook

Browns Rd

P

Nipmuck Trail,
West Branch

P

P

Puddin Ln

Jacobs
Hill Rd

Crane Hill Rd

Mansfield City Rd

S Bed

Idge Rd

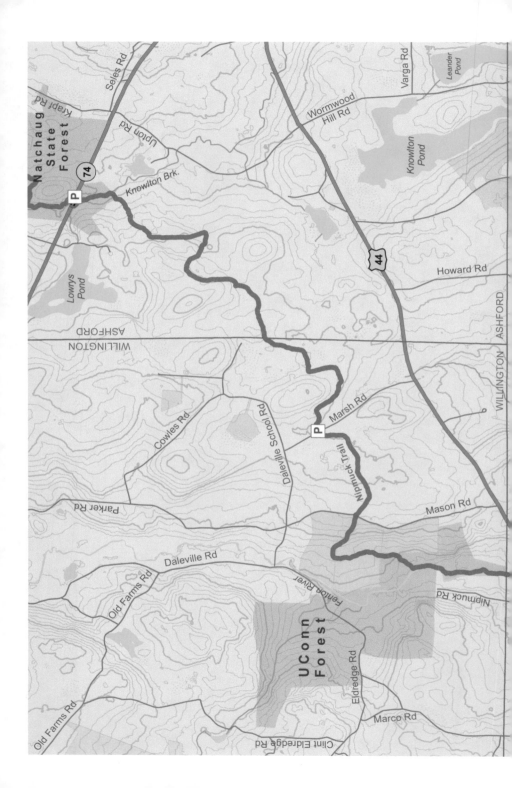

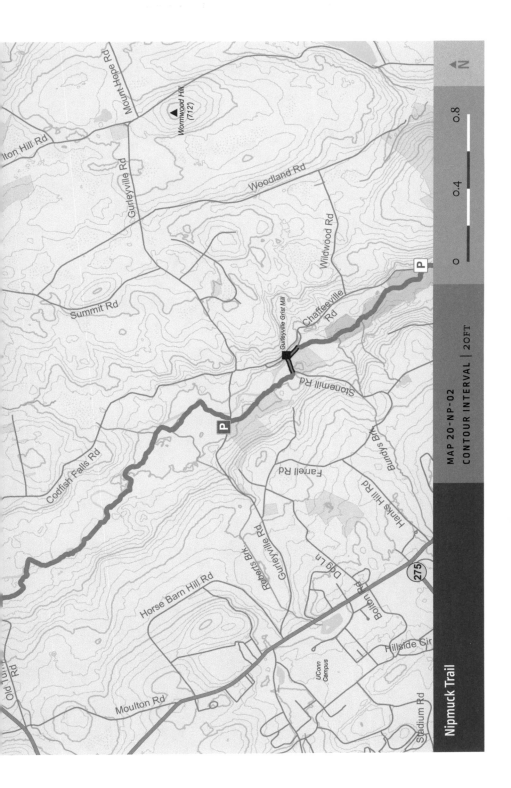

Nipmuck Trail

MAP 20-NP-02
CONTOUR INTERVAL | 20FT

0   0.4   0.8

N

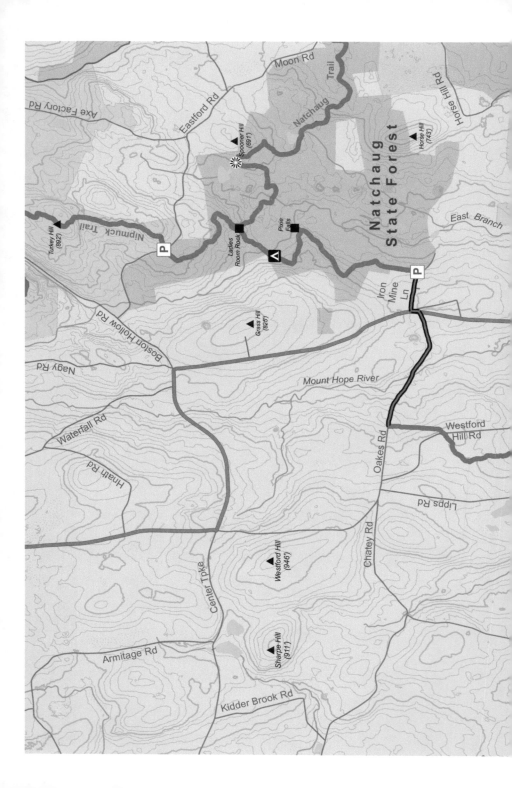

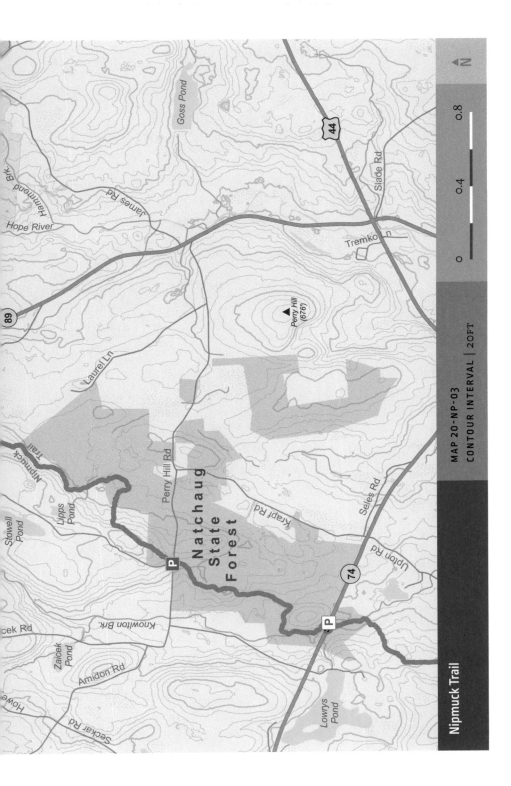

Nipmuck Trail

MAP 20-NP-03
CONTOUR INTERVAL | 20FT

0   0.4   0.8

N

Goss Pond

Hammond Brk.

Hope River

89

James Rd

44

Slade Rd

Tremko Ln

Perry Hill
(676)

Laurel Ln

Perry Hill Rd

Natchaug
State
Forest

Krapf Rd

Seles Rd

Upton Rd

74

Nipmuck Trail

Stowell
Pond

Lipps
Pond

Knowlton Brk.

Zaicek
Pond

cek Rd

Amidon Rd

Howe

Seckar Rd

Lowrys
Pond

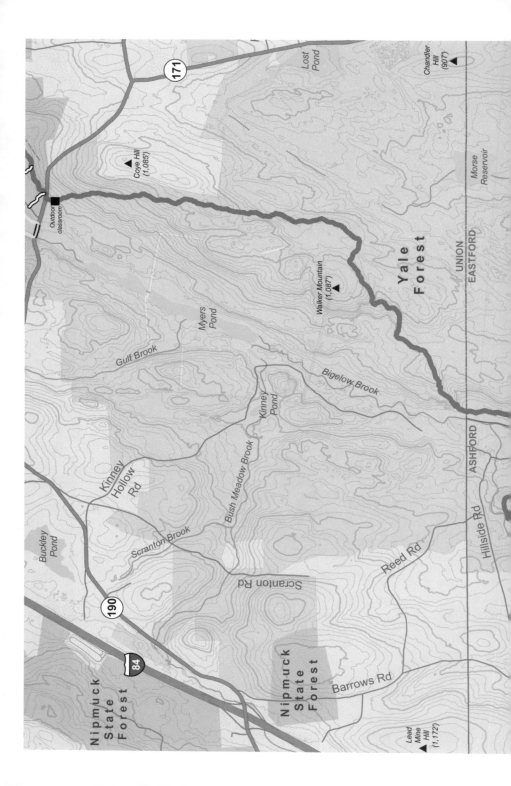

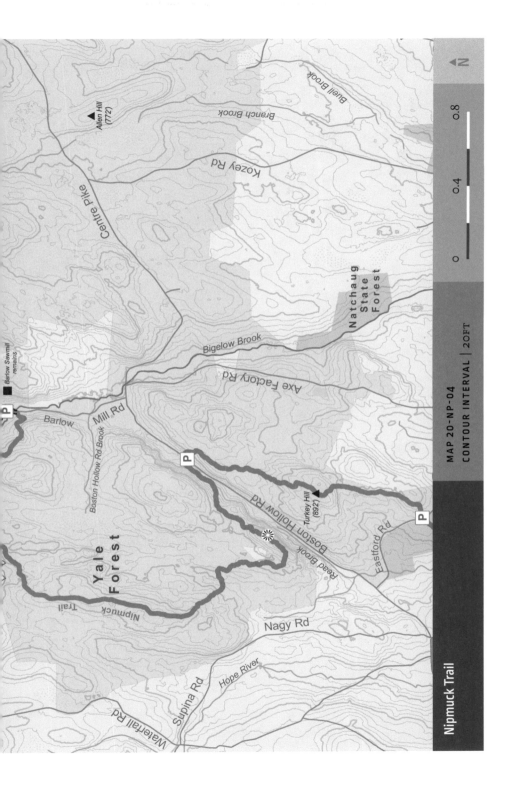

Nipmuck Trail

MAP 20-NP-04
CONTOUR INTERVAL | 20FT

N

0   0.4   0.8

Allen Hill
(772)

Buell Brook

Branch Brook

Kozey Rd

Centre Pike

Natchaug
State
Forest

Barlow Sawmill
remains

Bigelow Brook

Axe Factory Rd

Barlow

Mill Rd

Boston Hollow Rd Brook

Yale
Forest

Boston Hollow Rd

Turkey Hill
(892)

Reed Brook

Eastford Rd

Nipmuck Trail

Nagy Rd

Supina Rd

Hope River

Waterfall Rd

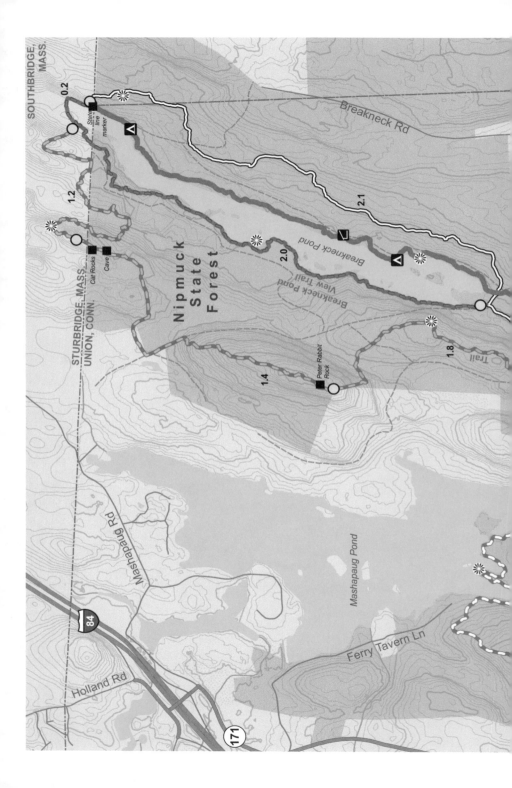

SOUTHBRIDGE, MASS.

0.2

State line
marker

1.2

STURBRIDGE, MASS.
UNION, CONN.

Cat Rocks

Cave

N i p m u c k
S t a t e
F o r e s t

Breakneck Rd

2.1

Breakneck Pond

2.0

Breakneck Pond
View Trail

1.4

Peter Rabbit
Rock

1.8

Trail

Mashapaug Rd

84

Holland Rd

Mashapaug Pond

Ferry Tavern Ln

171

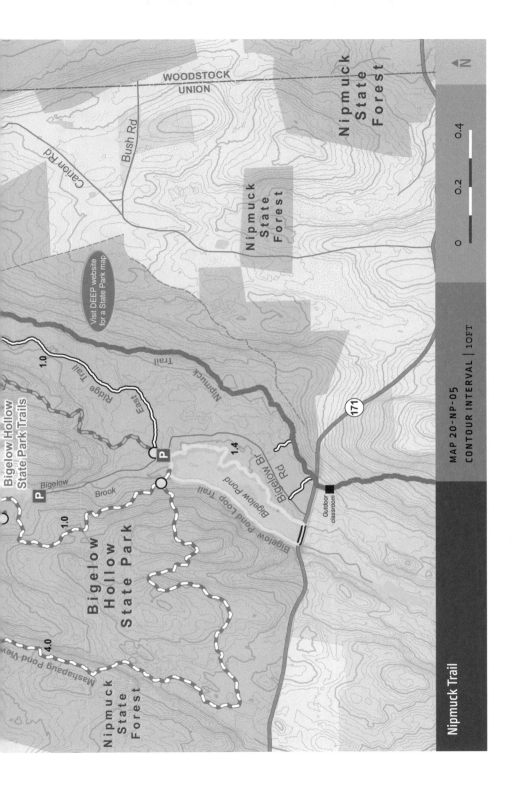

WOODSTOCK
UNION

Nipmuck
State
Forest

Bush Rd

Carlon Rd

Nipmuck
State
Forest

Visit DEEP website
for a State Park map

Bigelow Hollow
State Park Trails

1.0

Ridge Trail

East Trail

Nipmuck Trail

1.4

Bigelow Br.

Bigelow Rd

Bigelow Pond

P

P

Bigelow

Brook

P

Bigelow Pond Loop Trail

1.0

Bigelow
Hollow
State Park

171

Outdoor
classroom

4.0

Mashapaug Pond View

Nipmuck
State
Forest

N

0   0.2   0.4

MAP 20-NP-05
CONTOUR INTERVAL | 10FT

Nipmuck Trail

The woods are alive with incredible wildlife and inspiring beauty.
Photo courtesy Justin Coleman.

Old Furnace Trail

LENGTH 2.2 miles   BLAZE COLOR Blue

The Old Furnace Trail crosses the length of Old Furnace State Park in Killingly. The trek provides a full variety of hiking terrains, including mature and emerging forest, meadows, streams, ponds, ridges, wetlands, ferns, mountain laurels, wildlife, vistas, and more. All in all, this is a delightful, fairly compact trail requiring moderate effort. Scenic highlights include the remains of the Bog Furnace building and Ross Ledge (rumored to have once been a Native American lover's leap).

Colonial industrialists harnessed the running water of Furnace Brook to power iron works during the eighteenth century. During the Revolutionary War, Bog Furnace was a major supplier of iron horseshoes, a commodity greatly needed by the Continental Army.

245

Ross Pond, located at the base of one of the trail access points, has a boat launch and abundant fishing opportunities. Visit the Connecticut DEEP website for additional park information.

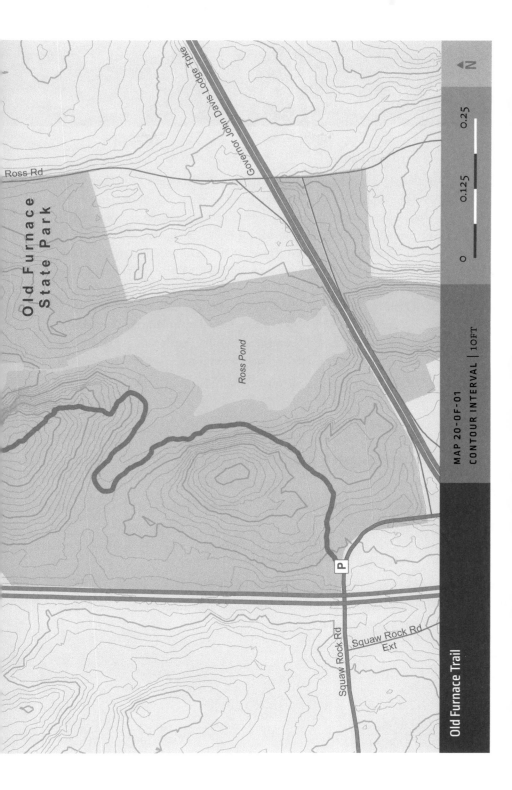

Old Furnace Trail

Old Furnace
State Park

Ross Rd

Governor John Davis Lodge Tpke

Ross Pond

P

Squaw Rock Rd

Squaw Rock Rd
Ext

MAP 20-0F-01

CONTOUR INTERVAL | 10FT

0   0.125   0.25

N

Pachaug Trail

LENGTH 24.8 miles   **BLAZE COLOR** Blue

Primarily a woodland trail, the Pachaug Trail extends from Green Fall Pond in Voluntown to Pachaug Pond in Griswold. It passes ponds, streams, and rock formations, travels through stands of conifers and hardwoods, and features a rhododendron sanctuary. It is almost entirely within Pachaug State Forest. There are side trails, connecting trails, and crossover trails that provide many options for further exploration. The crossover trails connect the Pachaug Trail to the Nehantic, Quinebaug, and Narragansett Trails, allowing for great loop-hiking opportunities.

Longer backpacking trips can be achieved by linking the Quinebaug, Pachaug, Nehantic, and Narragansett Trails. Four overnight shelters in the state forest can be used by backpackers on a first-come, first-served basis.

SIDE TRAILS

Pachaug-Narragansett Connector (see Map 20-PC-01)

LENGTH 0.3 miles   **BLAZE COLOR** Blue/Red

This short connector links the blue-blazed Pachaug and Narragansett Trails.

Subway Loop (see Map 20-PC-01)

LENGTH 0.2 miles   **BLAZE COLOR** Yellow

This trail follows the base of Rabbit Ledge and traverses a gully before rejoining the Pachaug Trail.

Laurel Loop (see Map 20-PC-01)

LENGTH 2.3 miles   BLAZE COLOR Blue/Yellow

The Laurel Loop is a relatively flat hike through open woods and dense laurel thickets. The trail is spectacular in late June when the mountain laurel is in bloom. The trail can be linked with other area trails to make longer loop hikes.

Pachaug-Nehantic Crossover (see Map 20-PC-01)

LENGTH 1.2 miles   BLAZE COLOR Blue/Red

This connector trail links the Nehantic and Pachaug Trails a little more than one mile north of Green Fall Pond. When taken in conjunction with the Laurel Loop, it makes a great circular hike.

Pachaug-Tippecansett Connector (see Map 20-PC-01)

LENGTH 0.6 miles   BLAZE COLOR Blue/Red

This trail links the Pachaug to the Tippecansett Trail in Rhode Island. Use of the connector offers an alternate route to the Pachaug Trail at Beach Pond. Although slightly longer than the Pachaug Trail, it avoids a 0.6-mile walk on Route 165. Note: Rhode Island state law requires hikers to wear blaze orange during hunting season.

Pharisee Rock Trail (see Map 20-PC-03)

LENGTH 1.1 miles   BLAZE COLOR White

This trail follows an old cart path, crosses an old stone dam, passes a wildlife marsh, and finally climbs 200 feet by a moderate gradient. Pharisee Rock summit (560 feet) offers a view of Ekonk Hill to the west.

Pachaug-Quinebaug Crossover 1 (see Map 20-PC-03)

LENGTH 1.0 miles   BLAZE COLOR Yellow

This crossover offers a connection to the blue-blazed Quinebaug Trail.

Blue/White Trail (see Map 20-PC-04)

LENGTH 0.6 miles   BLAZE COLOR Blue/White

This trail provides a connection between the Pachaug Trail and the blue/red-blazed Quinebaug- Pachaug Crossover 2.

Quinebaug-Pachaug Crossover 2 (see Map 20-PC-04)

LENGTH 0.8 miles   BLAZE COLOR Blue/Red

This crossover provides a connection to Phillips Pond picnic area and also links to the Blue/White Trail.

Rhododendron Sanctuary Trail (see Map 20-PC-04)

LENGTH 0.2 miles   BLAZE COLOR Blue

This wheelchair-accessible path travels a short distance over packed gravel before continuing on a raised boardwalk through a white cedar swamp, a rare natural community in Connecticut. The boardwalk and nature-observation deck were built in 1998 by CFPA trail volunteers and students from Norwich Free Academy's Outing Club. It provides easy access to the dazzling display of rhododendron blooms in early July and offers an opportunity to observe wildlife in a natural setting.

▍ *Hunting is permitted in state forests intersected by this trail. Please use caution and wear orange during hunting season.*

Mileage Table

PACHAUG TRAIL

0.0 Begin roadwalk
    0.0 Join Green Fall Pond Rd (P)
    0.1 Jct Pachaug-Narragansett
        Connector (blue/red)
    0.1 Leave Green Fall Pond Rd
0.1 End roadwalk
0.3 South jct Subway Loop Trail (yellow)
0.6 North jct Subway Loop Trail (yellow)
1.1 Jct Laurel Loop Trail (blue/yellow) / Jct
    Pachaug-Nehantic Connector (blue/red)
2.5 Ct Rte 138
3.3 Jct Pachaug-Tippecansett Connector
    (blue/red)
4.0 Begin roadwalk
    4.0 Join Noah Arc Rd
    4.1 Join Ct Rte 165
    4.7 Parking on Ct Rte 165 (P)
    4.7 Jct local trail (yellow, P)
    4.8 Leave Ct Rte 165
4.8 End roadwalk
5.8 View
7.7 Beach Pond boat launch (P) /
    North Shore Rd
9.0 Bassett Mills Rd
9.5 Bassett Mills Rd
9.8 Shetucket Turnpike (P)
10.5 Jct Pachaug State Forest Rd
11.2 Jct Pachaug State Forest Rd
11.9 Pratt Rd
12.9 Pachaug State Forest Rd
13.5 Pachaug State Forest Rd
13.7 Pachaug State Forest Rd
13.9 Pachaug State Forest Rd
14.2 Porter Pond Rd (P)
15.3 Jct Pharisee Rock Trail (white)

15.5 Begin roadwalk
    15.5 Join Cedar Swamp Rd
    16.0 Ct Rte 49 / Join Hell Hollow Rd
    16.6 Leave Hell Hollow Rd
16.6 End roadwalk
17.1 Jct Pachaug-Quinebaug Crossover 1
    (yellow)
17.5 Hell Hollow Rd (P)
18.4 Jct Pachaug-Quinebaug Crossover 2
    (blue/red)
18.9 Jct Blue/White Trail (blue/white)
19.2 Trail 2 Rd / Gardner Rd
20.5 Stone Hill Rd
21.7 Join Nehantic Trail (blue)
21.8 Begin roadwalk
    21.8 Join Cutoff Rd
    22.0 Jct Rhododendron Sanctuary
        Trail (blue, P)
    22.2 Leave Cutoff Rd
22.2 End roadwalk
22.8 Summit, Mount Misery (440 ft)
23.0 Fire Tower Rd
23.4 Leave Nehantic Trail (blue)
24.5 Waterfall
25.1 Ct Rte 138 / Voluntown Rd (P)

LAUREL LOOP TRAIL

0.0 Jct Pachaug Trail (blue) / Join
    Pachaug-Nehantic Crossover (blue/red)
0.0 Leave Pachaug-Nehantic Crossover
    (blue/red)
0.4 Tarklin Hill Rd
1.5 Green Fall Rd
2.3 Green Fall Rd / Jct Pachaug-Nehantic
    Crossover (blue/red) (P)

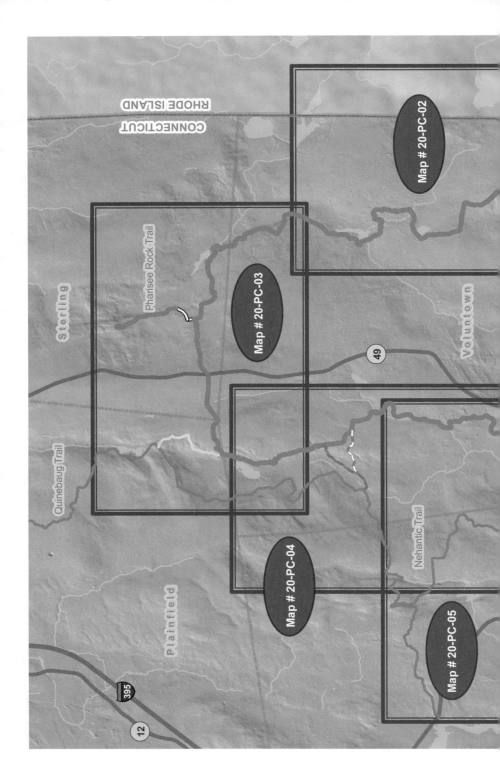

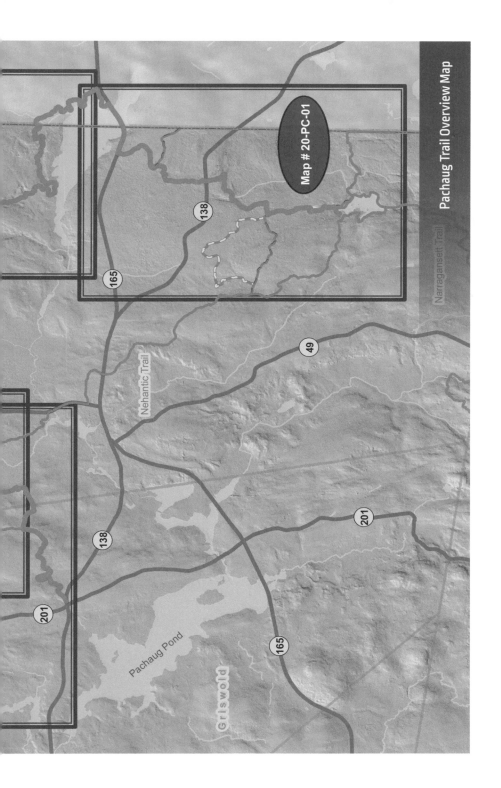

Map # 20-PC-01

Pachaug Trail Overview Map

Narraganseit Trail

Nehantic Trail

Pachaug Pond

Griswold

138

165

49

201

138

201

165

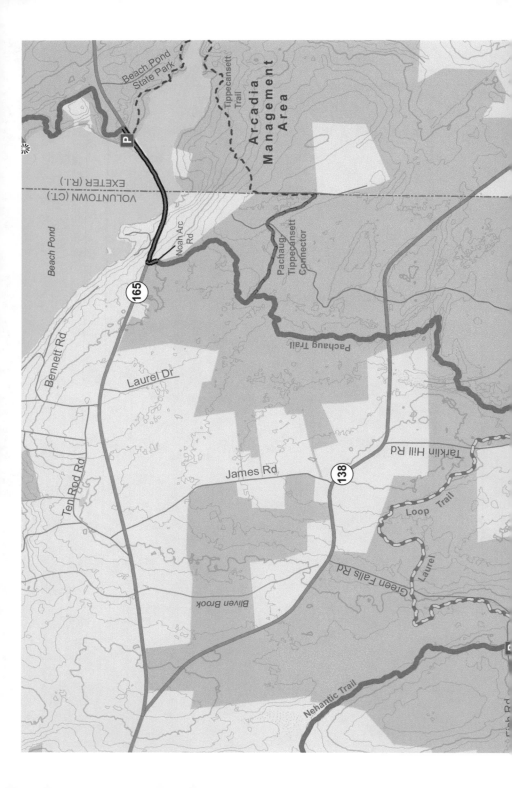

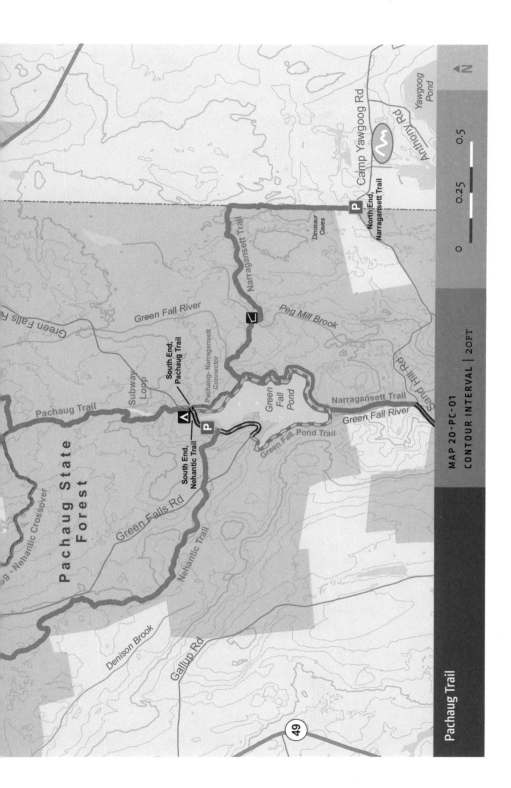

Pachaug Trail

MAP 20-PC-01
CONTOUR INTERVAL | 20FT

0   0.25   0.5

N

Camp Yawgoog Rd

Yawgoog
Pond

Anthony Rd

North End,
Narragansett Trail

Narragansett Trail

Dinosaur
Caves

Peg Mill Brook

Green Fall River

Green Falls R

South End,
Pachaug Trail

Pachaug-Narragansett
Connector

Subway
Loop

Pachaug Trail

Green
Fall
Pond

Narragansett Trail

Green Fall River

Sand Hill Rd

Green Fall Pond Trail

South End,
Nehantic Trail

Pachaug State
Forest

Nehantic Crossover

Green Falls Rd

Nehantic Trail

Denison Brook

Gallup Rd

49

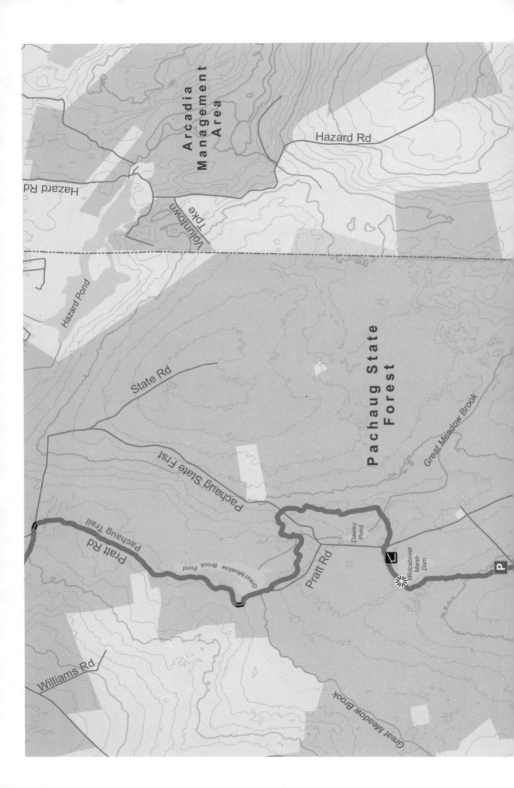

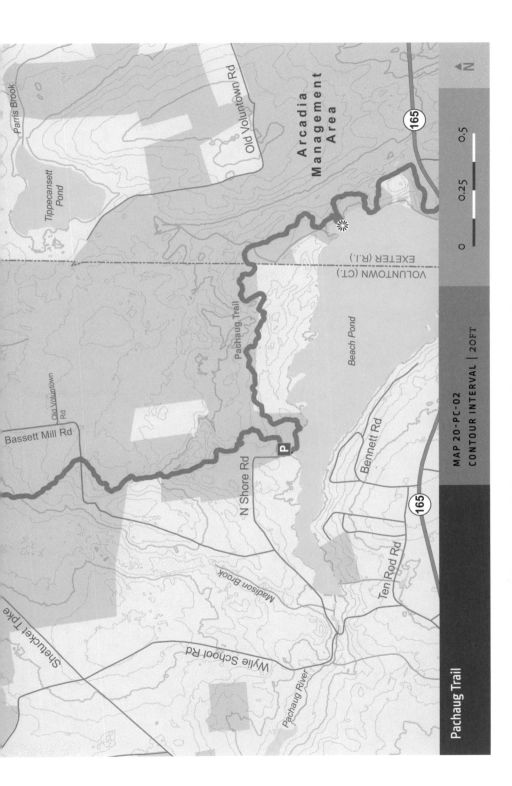

Parris Brook

Tippecansett
Pond

Old Voluntown Rd

A r c a d i a
M a n a g e m e n t
A r e a

165

Old Voluntown
Rd

Bassett Mill Rd

Pachaug Trail

VOLUNTOWN (CT.)
EXETER (R.I.)

Beach Pond

N Shore Rd

P

Bennett Rd

165

Ten Rod Rd

Madison Brook

Wylie School Rd

Shetucket Tpke

Pachaug River

0   0.25   0.5

N

Pachaug Trail

MAP 20-PC-02
CONTOUR INTERVAL | 20FT

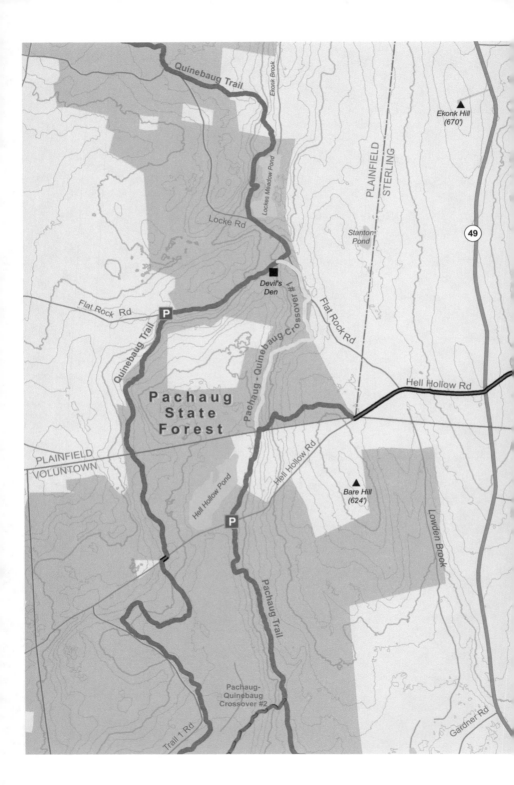

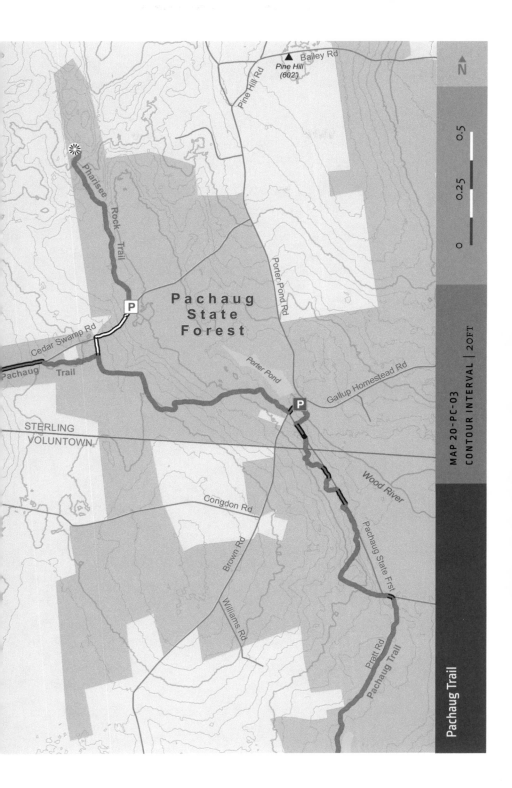

Pachaug Trail

Bailey Rd

Pine Hill (602')

Pine Hill Rd

Pharisee Rock Trail

Porter Pond Rd

P

Pachaug State Forest

Cedar Swamp Rd

Pachaug Trail

Porter Pond

P

Gallup Homestead Rd

STERLING
VOLUNTOWN

Congdon Rd

Wood River

Pachaug State Frst

Brown Rd

Williams Rd

Pratt Rd

Pachaug Trail

N

0   0.25   0.5

MAP 20-PC-03
CONTOUR INTERVAL | 20FT

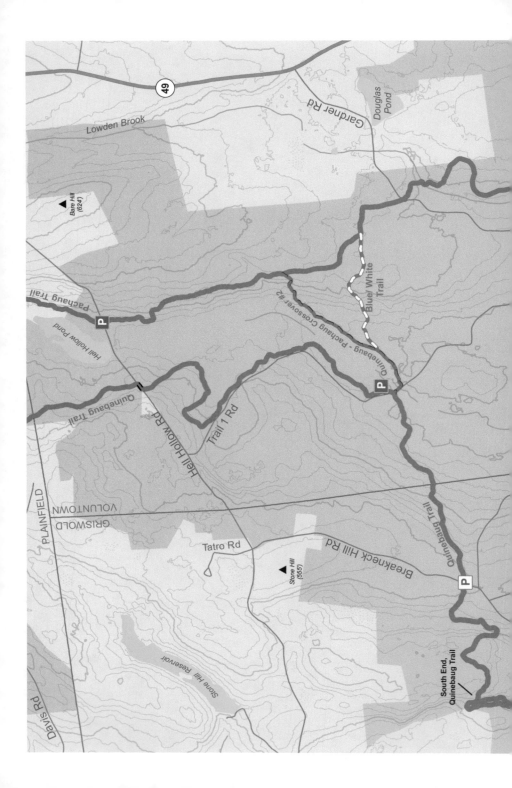

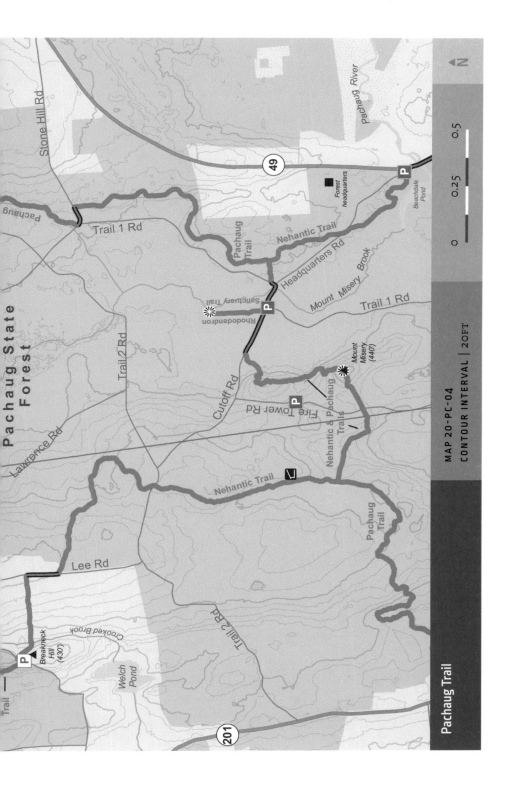

Pachaug State Forest

Stone Hill Rd

Pachaug

Trail 1 Rd

Pachaug Trail

Nehantic Trail

Headquarters Rd

Forest headquarters

49

Beachdale Pond

Mount Misery Brook

Trail 1 Rd

Rhododendron Sanctuary Trail

Cutoff Rd

Trail 2 Rd

Mount Misery (440')

Fire Tower Rd

Nehantic & Pachaug Trails

Lawrence Rd

Nehantic Trail

Pachaug Trail

Lee Rd

Crooked Brook

Breakneck Hill (430')

Welch Pond

Trail 2 Rd

Trail

201

Pachaug River

Pachaug Trail

N

0   0.25   0.5

MAP 20-PC-04
CONTOUR INTERVAL | 20FT

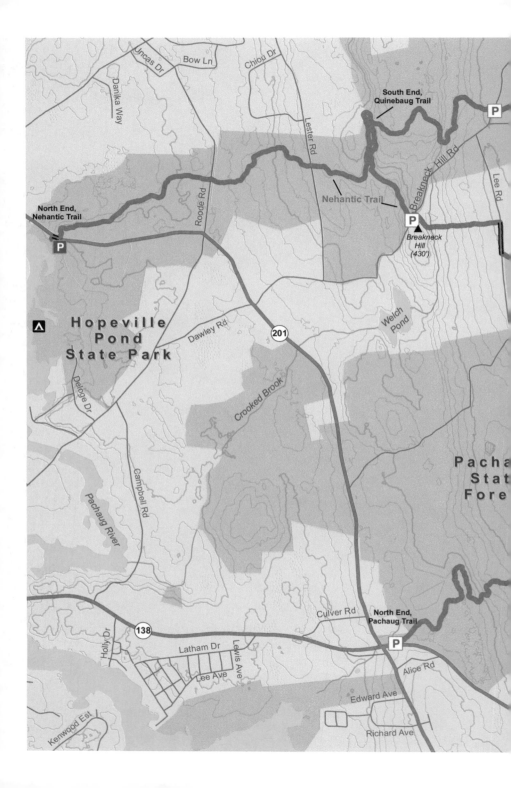

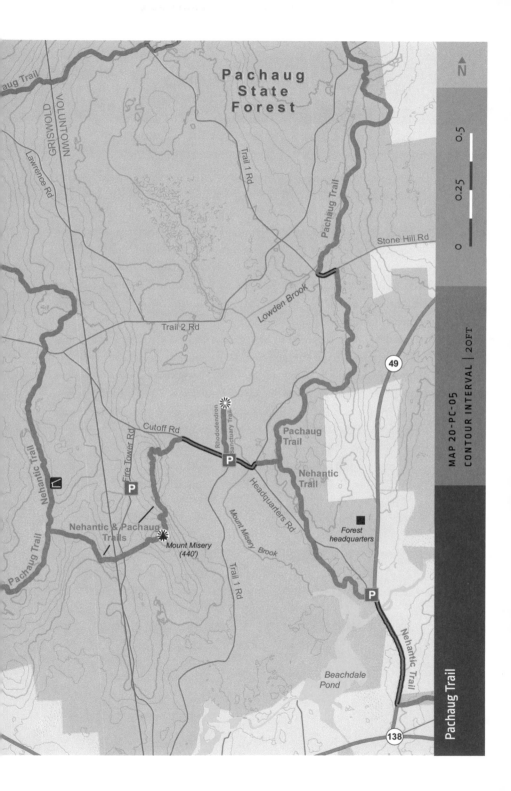

Pachaug
State
Forest

GRISWOLD
VOLUNTOWN

aug Trail

Lawrence Rd

Nehantic Trail

Pachaug Trail

Trail 1 Rd

Pachaug Trail

Stone Hill Rd

Lowden Brook

Trail 2 Rd

49

Cutoff Rd

Fire Tower Rd

Rhododendron
Sanctuary Trail

P

Pachaug
Trail

Nehantic
Trail

P

Headquarters Rd

Mount Misery Brook

Forest
headquarters

Nehantic & Pachaug
Trails

Mount Misery
(440')

Trail 1 Rd

P

Nehantic Trail

Pachaug Trail

Beachdale
Pond

138

0   0.25   0.5

MAP 20-PC-05
CONTOUR INTERVAL | 20FT

Pachaug Trail

Paugussett Trail

LENGTH 13.3 miles   **BLAZE COLOR** Blue

The Paugussett Trail meanders along Boys Halfway River, through Webb Mountain Park and Indian Well State Park, with occasional views of Lake Zoar and the Stevenson Dam along the way. Parts of this trail are challenging, with steep slopes and the occasional rock scramble or boulder climb. Keep a lookout for long-abandoned mill foundations and the entrance to an old silver mine. Numerous side trails in Webb Mountain Park, Indian Well State Park, and the Shelton Lakes Greenway connect with the Paugussett Trail to offer loop opportunities. Camping is allowed at Webb Mountain Park.

Thanks to the work of the Shelton Conservation Commission and Trails Committee, the Paugussett Trail has been restored south to Buddington Road on a corridor of land that was gradually acquired over many years. Constructed by Shelton volunteers, the new trail route from Indian Well State Park to Buddington Road restores an historic trail connection in the city. The trail also provides a critical link to the Shelton Lakes Greenway, offering extensive recreational opportunities.

For more info about Indian Well State Park, visit Connecticut DEEP. Trail maps for Birchbank and Shelton Lakes trail network are available at sheltonconservation.org.

 Show your support for the trails by becoming a CFPA member today. Members receive special discounts and benefits . . . but really it just feels good to be part of something so great. Membership means you care, join today!

Mileage Table

SIDE TRAILS

Tahmore Trail (see Map 20-PT-01)

LENGTH 0.9 miles   **BLAZE COLOR** Blue/Yellow

Tahmore Trail provides access to the Paugussett Trail across Shelton Land Trust property from the Tahmore Place cul-de-sac in Shelton.

Map # 20-PT-02

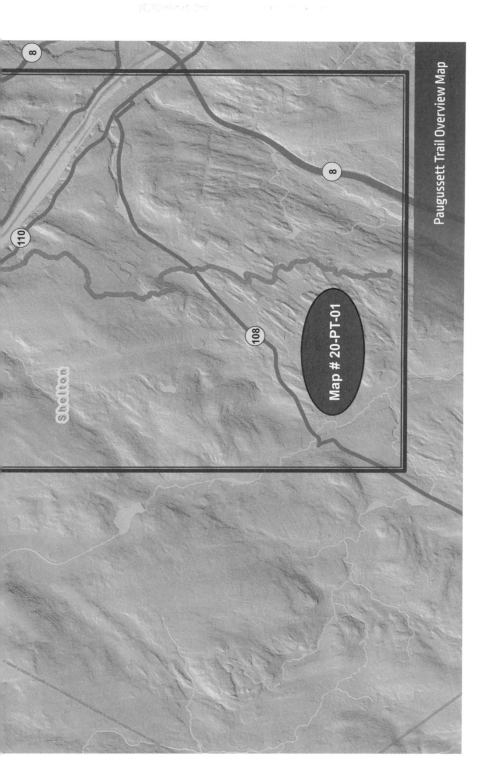

Paugussett Trail Overview Map

Map # 20-PT-01

Shelton

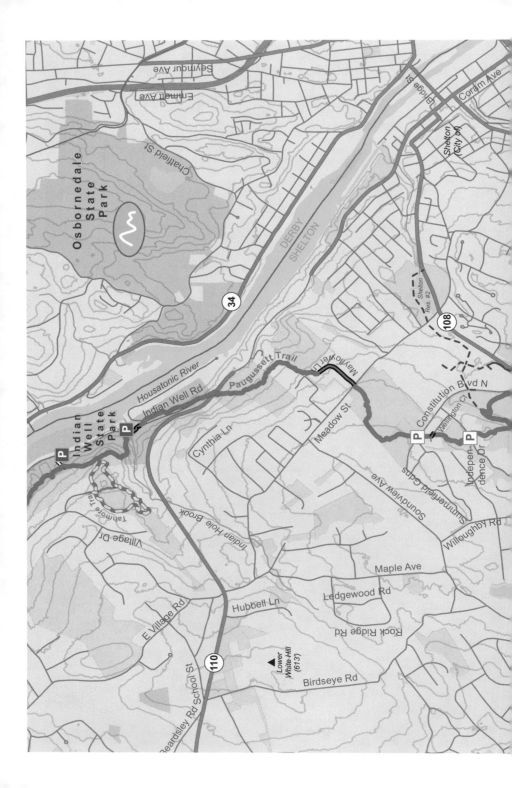

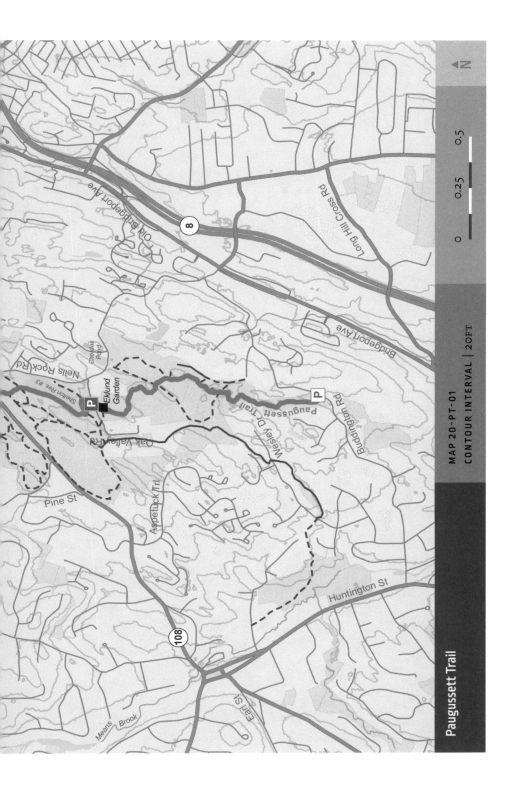

Paugussett Trail

MAP 20-PT-01
CONTOUR INTERVAL | 20FT

0   0.25   0.5

N

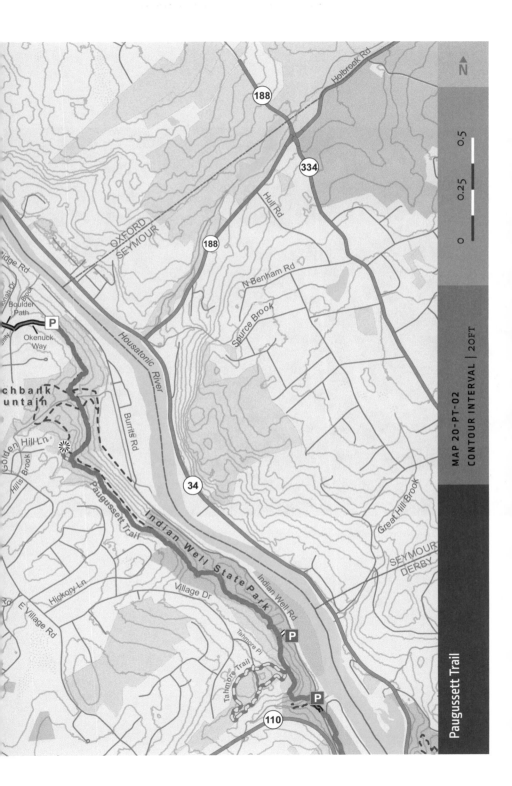

188

334

Holbrook Rd

Hull Rd

0   0.25   0.5

N Benham Rd

Spurce Brook

OXFORD
SEYMOUR

188

idge Rd

Brook

Boulder
Path

P

Okenuck
Way

chbank
untain

Golden Hill Ln

Hills Brook

Housatonic River

Burrits Rd

34

Great Hill Brook

SEYMOUR
DERBY

Paugussett Trail

Indian Well State Park

Indian Well Rd

Hickory Ln

Village Dr

E Village Rd

Rd

Tahmore Pl

Tahmore Trail

P

P

110

MAP 20-PT-02
CONTOUR INTERVAL | 20FT

It's always fun to hike with friends. Photo courtesy CFPA.

Pequot Trail

LENGTH 8.0 miles   **BLAZE COLOR** Blue

The Pequot Trail connects Ledyard with Preston and offers occasional views of the Thames River valley as well as a few gradual climbs, old pastures, and overgrown woods roads. At an elevation of 330 feet, Rose Hill is the highest point on the trail. The trail passes through Preston's Lincoln Park, a recreation area with a jogging track, multiple ball fields, and other facilities, following a part of the park's dog-walking trail to Rose Hill Road. Between Rose Hill Road and the trail's southern terminus, keep your eyes peeled for at least four geocaches and one letterbox. Near the southern trailhead is the Mashantucket Pequot Burial Ground, which is not open to the public and should not be entered. The southern trailhead is within walking distance (by road at this time) of the Mashantucket Pequot Tribal Museum and Research Center, the Mashantucket Pequot Reservation, and the blue-blazed Narragansett Trail.

Near the northern terminus, the trail follows and crisscrosses power lines in a few places. Soaring hawks are often seen above a pair of beaver-inhabited wetland ponds that surround a small rock ridge. Just south of this ridge is a mysterious historical area called Hellgate. Nearby land deeds can be traced back to ownership by the Mohegan sachem, Uncas. Hikers of the Pequot Trail will be surrounded with local history.

❚ *Hunting is permitted in a wildlife management area intersected by this trail. Please use caution and wear orange during hunting season.*

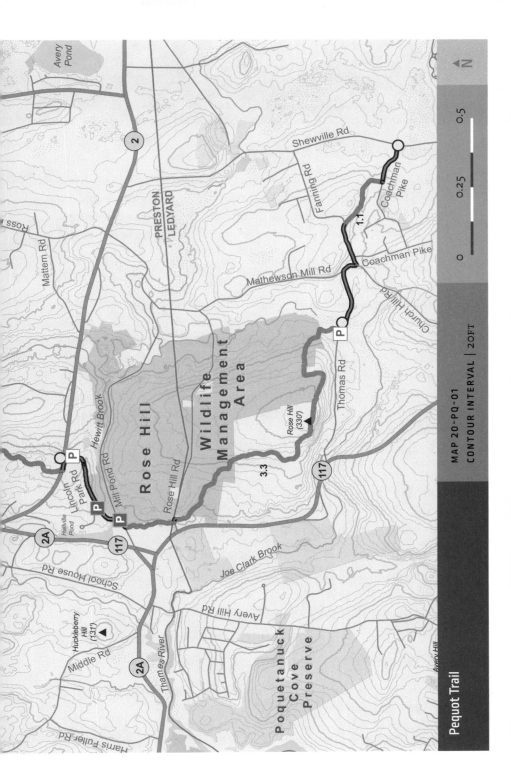

Pequot Trail

MAP 20-PQ-01
CONTOUR INTERVAL | 20FT

0   0.25   0.5

N

Avery
Pond

Ross

Mattern Rd

2

PRESTON
LEDYARD

Shewville Rd.

Fanning Rd

Coachman
Pike

1.1

Coachman Pike

Mathewson Mill Rd

Church Hill Rd

P

Thomas Rd

Rose Hill
(300)

3.3

117

Hewitt Brook

Rose Hill

Wildlife
Management
Area

Lincoln
Park Rd

P

Mill Pond Rd

P

Rose Hill Rd

P

Hallville
Pond

2A

117

School House Rd

Joe Clark Brook

Avery Hill Rd

Huckleberry
Hill
(131')

Middle Rd

2A

Thames River

Poquetanuck
Cove
Preserve

Avery Hill

Harris Fuller Rd

Quinebaug Trail

LENGTH 8.0 miles   **BLAZE COLOR** Blue

Located within Pachaug State Forest, the Quinebaug Trail is a moderate trail that passes over gentle hills, wanders through pine forests, and follows woods roads. The gradual ascents and descents encourage hiking or trail running and make winter snowshoeing a viable option. Excellent bird-watching opportunities abound at Lockes Meadow Pond and the surrounding wetlands. Connecting trails link to both the Pachaug and Nehantic Trails.

Keep an eye out for old stone foundations, the Phillips Pond picnic area, and an unmarked side trail leading to a rock pile known as Devil's Den. Many marked trails intersect the Quinebaug and allow for various loop opportunities. Parts of the Quinebaug Trail coincide with a multiuse trail (marked with red arrows), which is primarily a motorcycle trail.

Longer backpacking trips can be achieved by linking the Quinebaug, Pachaug, Nehantic, and Narragansett Trails. Four overnight shelters in the state forest can be used by backpackers on a first-come, first-served basis.

SIDE TRAILS

Pachaug-Quinebaug Crossover 1

LENGTH 1.0 miles   **BLAZE COLOR** Yellow

This crossover offers a connection to the blue-blazed Pachaug Trail.

Quinebaug-Pachaug Crossover 2

LENGTH 0.8 miles   **BLAZE COLOR** Blue/Red

This crossover provides a connection to the Phillips Pond picnic area.

▍ *Hunting is permitted in state forests intersected by this trail. Please use caution and wear orange during hunting season.*

Occassionally we're able to dedicate a new trail as part of the Blue-Blazed Hiking Trail System. Photo courtesy CFPA.

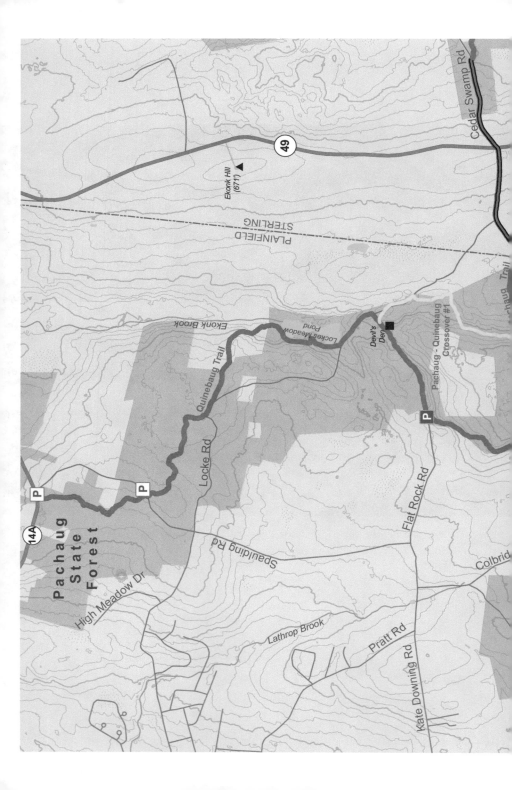

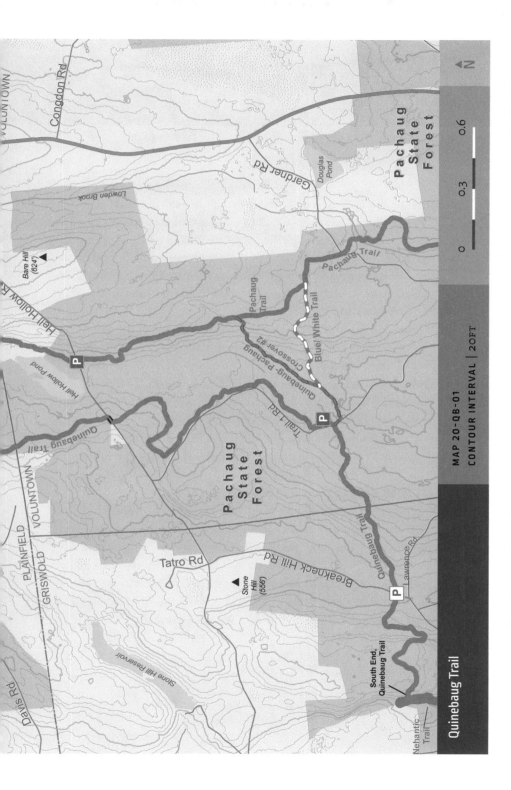

Quinebaug Trail

MAP 20-QB-01
CONTOUR INTERVAL | 20FT

0   0.3   0.6

Quinnipiac Trail

LENGTH 19.2 miles   **BLAZE COLOR** Blue

The Quinnipiac Trail is the oldest in the Connecticut Blue-Blazed Hiking Trail System. Although essentially a wooded trail, it traverses a series of traprock ridges on steep, challenging terrain. The trail passes through Sleeping Giant State Park, Naugatuck State Forest and, at its most northern end, follows the rocky ridgeline of the Prospect-Cheshire border. On this ridge, the trail crosses forested property that has been protected by the Cheshire Land Trust.

The trail offers a succession of commanding views of the central valley, with ascents of York Mountain in Hamden, and Mad Mare's Hill and Mount Stanford in Bethany. It also passes the dramatic chasms of Roaring Brook Falls, Connecticut's highest single-drop waterfall. (The Roaring Brook Falls are located 0.2 miles east of the Quinnipiac Trail, on an orange-blazed Cheshire town trail.)

The Quinnipiac Trail connects to the north end of the blue-blazed Regicides Trail in Hamden, offering additional hiking opportunities.

Quinnipiac Trail in Sleeping Giant State Park

The 5-mile section of the blue-blazed Quinnipiac Trail in Sleeping Giant State Park is crisscrossed by myriad color-coded park trails. The Quinnipiac Trail leaves from the park's east end and follows the length of the Sleeping Giant's "torso," beginning at the feet. This rocky section of trail is the longest and most rugged in the park. All trails in the park are maintained by the Sleeping Giant Park Association. See *Sleeping Giant State Park Trails* below for more detailed trail information.

Sanford Alternate Trail (see Map 20-QP-03)

LENGTH 1.4 miles   BLAZE COLOR Blue/Red

The Sanford Alternate Trail leaves the Quinnipiac Trail near Camp Laurel and heads through Naugatuck State Forest, skirting steep ridges before connecting with the main trail at its north end.

▌ *Hunting is permitted in state forests intersected by this trail. Please use caution and wear orange during hunting season.*

Sleeping Giant State Park Trails (see Map 20-QP-01)

LENGTH 27+ miles   BLAZE COLOR Varied

The Sleeping Giant is a rugged traprock mountain located 8 miles north of New Haven. A prominent landscape feature that is visible for miles, it resembles a slumbering human figure.

281

Sleeping Giant State Park is a popular recreation area containing over 32 miles of hiking trails, including 5 miles of the 23-mile Quinnipiac Trail. The Sleeping Giant Park Association (http://sgpa.org) maintains the extensive trail system within the park. The trails offer distant views from rocky crags, remote quiet woods, pleasant pine groves, and mountain brooks with mossy cascades.

EAST/WEST TRAILS

Six east/west trails traverse the park, with the White Trail and blue-blazed Quinnipiac Trail being the most strenuous.

White Trail

LENGTH 2.8 miles   BLAZE COLOR White

The White Trail forms the south side of the Blue-White circuit of the park's major peaks. The trail is very steep in places and offers good views both to the north and south. One section passes the remains of a tumbledown stone house, while the rocky slabs of the Giant's shoulder offer views to distant horizons, as well as a fine perspective of the great rocky wall of the Giant's massive chin.

Violet Trail

LENGTH 3.2 miles   **BLAZE COLOR** Violet

The Violet Trail travels along Mill River and the edge of the Old Axle Shop Pond, across the lower quarry floor, and over some foundations of old quarry buildings. The trail passes through wooded terrain, offering shade in summer.

Yellow Trail

LENGTH 2.2 miles   **BLAZE COLOR** Yellow

The Yellow Trail makes a good return trip west from the east end of the Violet Trail. This trail also is shady, with outlooks from two rocky spots. Short, steep switchbacks lead down to ancient hemlocks at the Hexagon Trail intersection.

Orange Trail

LENGTH 2.5 miles   **BLAZE COLOR** Orange

The Orange Trail leaves the picnic area road and heads east. It offers views over the Inner Mountain Valley, then joins the Violet, Yellow, Green, and White Trails at its eastern terminus.

Green Trail

LENGTH 1.9 miles   **BLAZE COLOR** Green

The Green Trail passes through the Inner Mountain Valley. Its eastern terminus occurs where the Violet, Yellow, Orange, and White Trails come together.

Five north/south trails connect Mount Carmel Avenue on the south with Tuttle Avenue or Mansion Road on the north, crossing all the east/ west trails. These five red-blazed trails are frequently used as feeders or crossovers to other trails.

Diamond Trail

LENGTH 0.5 miles   BLAZE COLOR Red

The Diamond Trail parallels Mill River and crosses the floor of the abandoned traprock quarry.

Hexagon Trail

LENGTH 1.0 mile   BLAZE COLOR Red

The Hexagon Trail intersects with the blue-blazed Quinnipiac Trail, near the Giant's impressive stone chin.

283

Triangle Trail

LENGTH 1.1 miles   BLAZE COLOR Red

The Triangle Trail offers some steep climbs on both the north and south sides of the Giant; it also intersects the blue-blazed Quinnipiac Trail.

Circle Trail

LENGTH 1.7 miles   BLAZE COLOR Red

The Circle Trail ascends the south slope of the Giant, then goes down the north side along the banks of the brook that drains the Inner Mountain Valley. The trail continues along a delightful stream, descending over mossy rocks and eventually down a series of cascades through a 50-foot deep gorge.

Square Trail

LENGTH 1.5 miles   **BLAZE COLOR** Red

The Square Trail makes an interesting traverse of the Giant just east of the knees. It also intersects the blue-blazed Quinnipiac Trail.

ADDITIONAL PARK TRAILS

Horse Trail

LENGTH 3.0 miles   **BLAZE COLOR** White with horseshoe-shaped blazes

The Horse Trail is designated for horses only for most of the year. In winter, a portion of this trail is open for cross-country skiing. Note: this trail is displayed on the map with a black line and white circles.

Nature Trail

LENGTH 1.5 miles   **BLAZE COLOR** White trees with green circle

The Nature Trail is marked with distinctive white pine trees on green circles. It starts at the bottom of the Tower Path and takes over an hour to complete. The first portion is easy, level walking; the second part of the trail is rougher, steeper, and rocky in places.

Tower Path

LENGTH 1.5 miles   **BLAZE COLOR** Unblazed

This trail winds over easy grades and ascends from the park entrance to the Stone Tower. Note: this trail is displayed on the map with a white and black hash line.

Mileage Table

QUINNIPIAC TRAIL

0.0 Old Hartford Turnpike (P)
1.1 Chestnut Ln
1.3 Jct Yellow Trail
1.3 Jct White Horseshoe Trail
1.4 Jct Orange Trail
1.5 Jct Yellow/Green Connector (green or
yellow Xs depending on direction)
1.9 Jct White Trail
2.0 Jct Green Trail
2.1 Jct Red Square Trail
2.5 Jct Blue/Violet Connector
3.0 Jct Red Circle Trail
3.3 View
3.4 Stone Tower
3.6 East jct Tower Trail (unblazed)
3.6 Red Triangle Trail
3.9 West jct Tower Trail (unblazed)
4.0 Jct Red Hexagon Trail
4.2 Second view on "The Head"
4.6 Join Red Diamond Trail
4.8 Leave Red Diamond Trail
5.0 Mount Carmel Ave
5.2 Begin roadwalk
    5.2 Join Ct Rte 10 / Whitney Ave
    5.2 Join West Woods Rd
    5.5 Join Kimberly Ave
    5.7 Leave Kimberly Ave (P)
5.7 End roadwalk
6.0 Foundation
6.9 Begin roadwalk
    6.9 Join Rocky Top Rd (P)
    7.0 Join Shepard Ave

    7.1 Join Nolan Rd
    7.3 Join Old Coach Hwy
    7.4 Leave Old Coach Hwy (P)
7.4 End roadwalk
7.7 Begin roadwalk—Paradise Ave No. 3
7.9 End roadwalk—Paradise Ave No. 3
8.6 Jct Regicides Trail (blue)
9.8 Brooks Rd (P)
10.4 Old homestead
12.0 Begin roadwalk
    12.0 Join Downs Rd (P)
    12.4 Gaylord Mountain Rd /
        Westwood Cemetery
    12.9 Jct local trail (white)
    12.9 Leave Downs Rd (P)
12.9 End roadwalk
13.2 South jct Sanford Alternate Trail (blue/
red)
13.9 View
14.8 North jct Sanford Alternate Trail (blue/
red)
15.1 Ct Rte 42 (P)
16.5 South jct local trail (red)
16.5 North jct local trail (red)
16.5 Roaring Brook, upper gorge falls
18.4 Begin roadwalk
    18.4 Join Cornwall Ave (P)
    18.8 Join Tress Rd
    18.9 Join Chatfield Rd
    19.2 Ct Rte 68
19.2 End roadwalk

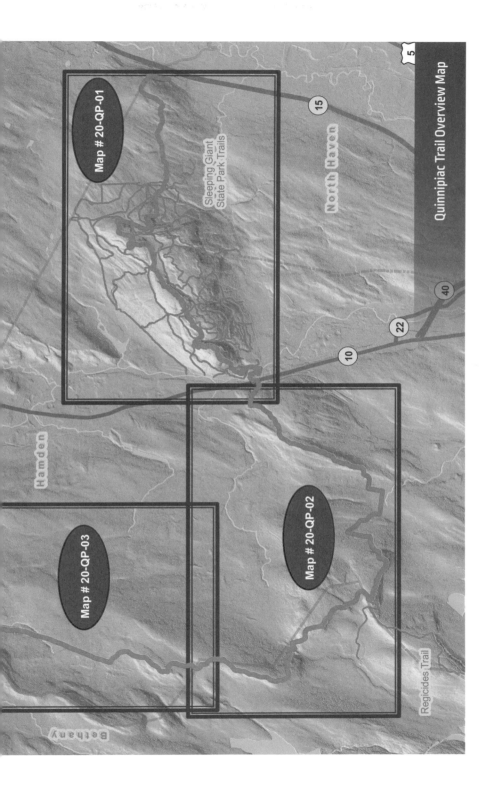

Quinnipiac Trail Overview Map

Map # 20-QP-01

Sleeping Giant
State Park Trails

North Haven

Hamden

Map # 20-QP-03

Map # 20-QP-02

Regicides Trail

Bethany

5

15

10

22

40

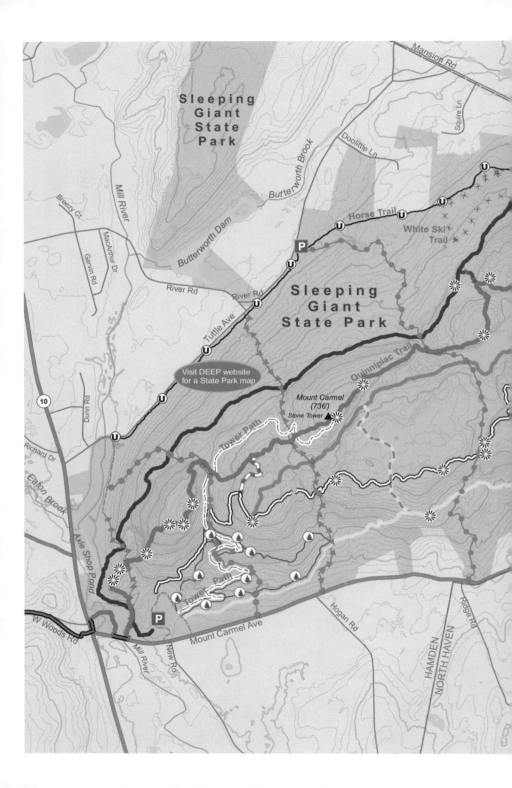

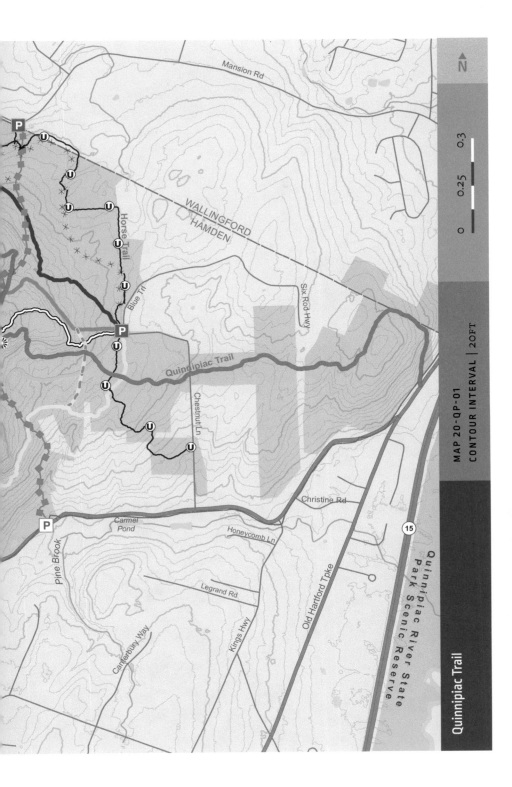

Quinnipiac Trail

MAP 20-QP-01
CONTOUR INTERVAL | 20FT

N

0   0.25   0.3

Quinnipiac River State
Park Scenic Reserve

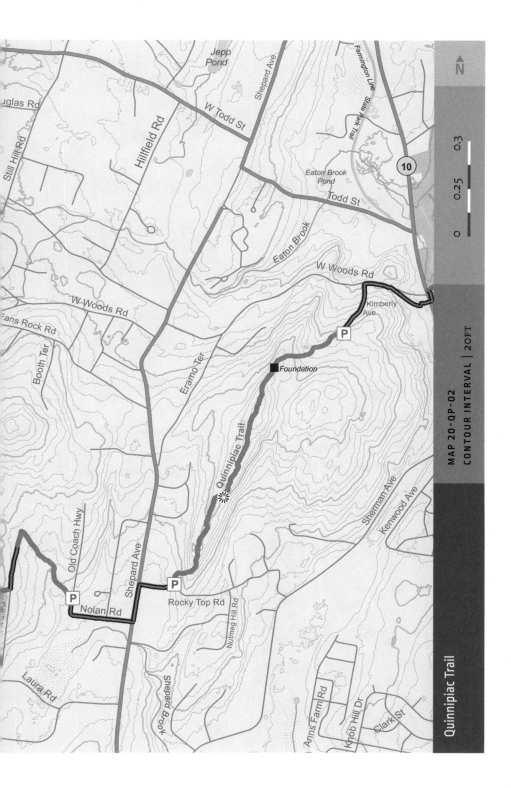

Jepp
Pond

Shepard Ave.

W Todd St

Hillfield Rd

Farmington Line

State Park Trail

Eaton Brook
Pond

10

Todd St

Still Hill Rd

uglas Rd

Eaton Brook

W Woods Rd

Kimberly
Ave.

W Woods Rd

P

ans Rock Rd

Booth Ter

Eramo Ter

Foundation

Quinnipiac Trail

Sherman Ave.

Kenwood Ave.

Old Coach Hwy

Shepard Ave

P

Rocky Top Rd

Nutmeg Hill Rd

P

Nolan Rd

Laura Rd

Shepard Brook

Anns Farm Rd

Knob Hill Dr

Clark St

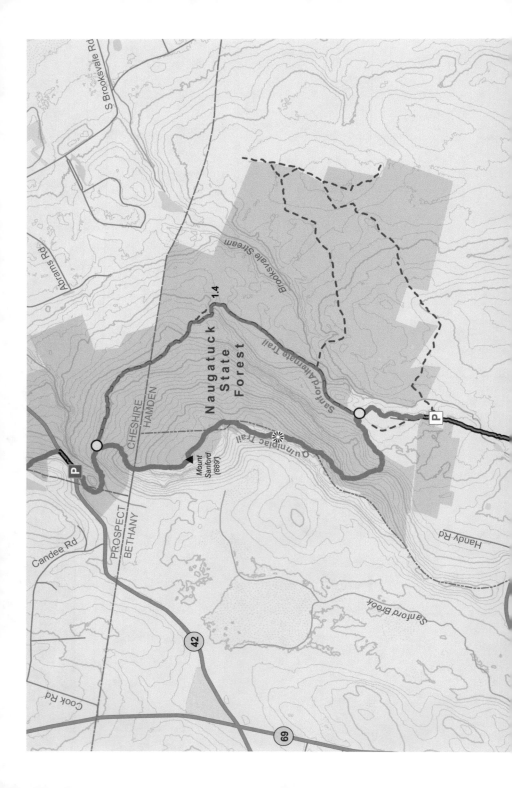

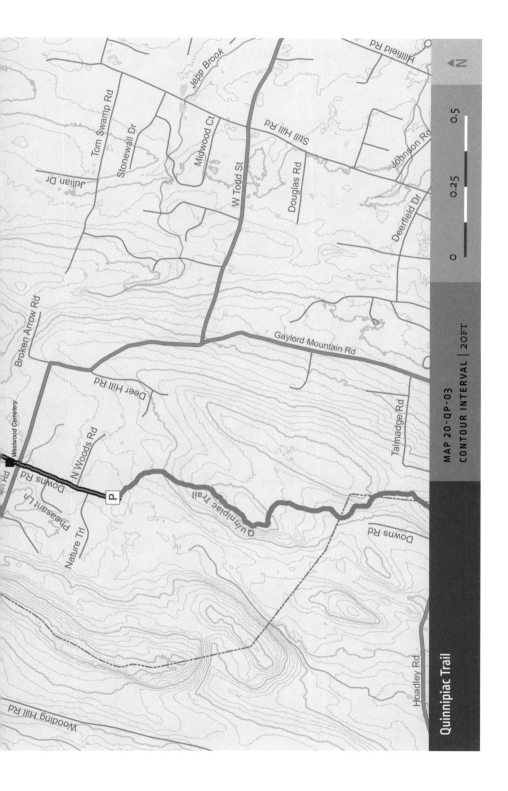

Quinnipiac Trail

MAP 20-QP-03
CONTOUR INTERVAL | 20FT

0   0.25   0.5

N

Jepp Brook

Hillfield Rd

Tom Swamp Rd

Stonewall Dr

Midwood Ct

Still Hill Rd

W Todd St

Johnson Rd

Julian Dr

Douglas Rd

Deerfield Dr

Broken Arrow Rd

Gaylord Mountain Rd

Deer Hill Rd

Talmadge Rd

Westwood Cemetery

N Woods Rd

Downs Rd

Pheasant Ln

Quinnipiac Trail

Nature Trl

Downs Rd

Hoadley Rd

Wooding Hill Rd

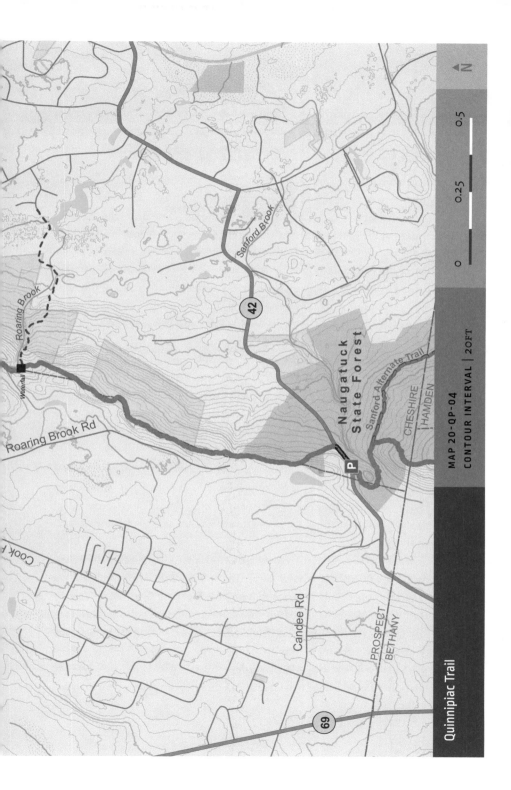

Quinnipiac Trail

MAP 20-QP-04
CONTOUR INTERVAL | 20FT

0   0.25   0.5

N

Roaring Brook

Waterfall

Roaring Brook Rd

Cook F

Sanford Brook

42

Naugatuck
State Forest

Sanford Alternate Trail

CHESHIRE
HAMDEN

Candee Rd

PROSPECT
BETHANY

69

Regicides Trail

LENGTH 7.3 miles   BLAZE COLOR Blue

Located entirely within West Rock Ridge State Park, the Regicides Trail
starts by a stone wall and pavilion at the South Overlook in New Haven,
passes historic Judges Cave, and follows the ridgeline through Hamden,
ending at the Quinnipiac Trail in Bethany. From 375 feet above sea level
at the South Overlook, the traprock ridge rises to more than 600 feet
where the two trails join on the west slope of York Mountain. The trail is
named in honor of William Goffe and Edward Whalley, two of the men
who sentenced King Charles I of England to death. Seeking to avoid
capture by agents of King Charles II, Goffe and Whalley hid at Judges
Cave in 1661 and again in 1664.

The Regicides Trail is considered one of Connecticut's most spectacular cliff walks. Along the western side of the ridge, hikers are rewarded
with extended views of reservoirs and forests in Woodbridge and Bethany. On the eastern side, the trail has a dramatic perspective down the
length of West Rock Ridge, including Farm Brook Reservoir and the
forested slopes of the state park.

At the South Overlook, hikers enjoy a panoramic view of south central
Connecticut including the Sleeping Giant, East Rock Park, New Haven
Harbor, and the shimmering expanse of Long Island Sound. From some
vantage points at South Overlook, the vistas are said to encompass 200
square miles.

The Regicides Trail intersects the Quinnipiac Trail just north of Sanford Notch (Lower Bethany Gap). These trails can be combined for a
variety of longer hike options that include Sleeping Giant State Park in
Hamden or Mount Sanford in Bethany. Numerous trails within West Rock
also connect to the Regicides Trail, making many hiking loops possible.
See the state park map for more details.

The West Rock Ridge Park Association safeguards its preservation,
advocates for additions to the park, and donates time every year to main-

taining park trails. Visit the Connecticut DEEP website for the most-up-to-date information on park access.

SIDE TRAILS

Westville Feeder (see Map 20-RG-01)

LENGTH 0.7 miles   **BLAZE COLOR** Blue/Yellow

Starting at the West River pedestrian bridge at the base of West Rock Ridge, the Westville Feeder provides a direct connection to the Regicides Trail from the Westville section of New Haven. The trail features a peaceful walk along the West River, then ascends steadily up a rocky slope and intersects with the Regicides Trail just south of Judges Cave.

Sanford Feeder (see Map 20-RG-02)

LENGTH 0.6 miles   **BLAZE COLOR** Blue/Red

The Sanford Feeder connects the Regicides Trail with Brooks Road in Bethany, traversing Regional Water Authority land. It follows an abandoned town road over varied terrain, passes former farmsteads, and crosses a wetland before finally ascending West Rock Ridge.

297

Mileage Table

REGICIDES TRAIL

0.0	South Overlook (P)
0.5	Jct Westville Feeder (blue/yellow)
0.6	Begin roadwalk
0.7	Judges Cave
0.7	End roadwalk
0.7	Jct local trail (green)
1.2	Join local trail (green)
1.2	Leave local trail (green)
1.7	Baldwin Dr
1.9	Jct local trail (orange)
1.9	Baldwin Dr
2.0	Spur to view (50 ft)
2.5	Jct local trail (yellow)
2.9	View
3.7	Jct local trail (red) / Join local trail (purple)
3.7	Baldwin Dr pullout / Leave local trail (purple)
4.2	Power line
5.2	Baldwin Dr
5.7	Baldwin Dr
5.8	View of Lake Watrous
6.0	Baldwin Dr
6.3	Jct local trail (red) / View
6.7	Baldwin Dr
7.0	Jct Sanford Feeder (blue/red)
7.3	Jct Quinnipiac Trail (blue) / View

WESTVILLE FEEDER

0.0	Amrhyn Field (P)
0.0	Jct local trail (teal/white)
0.2	Jct local trail (teal)
0.8	Jct Regicides Trail (blue)

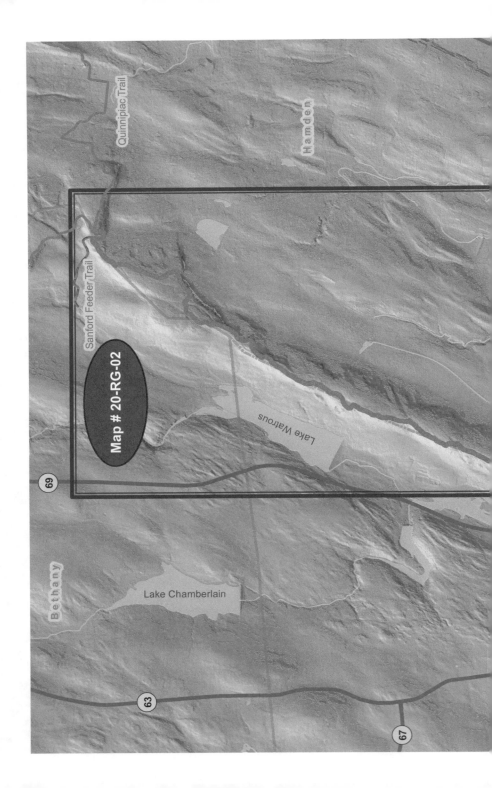

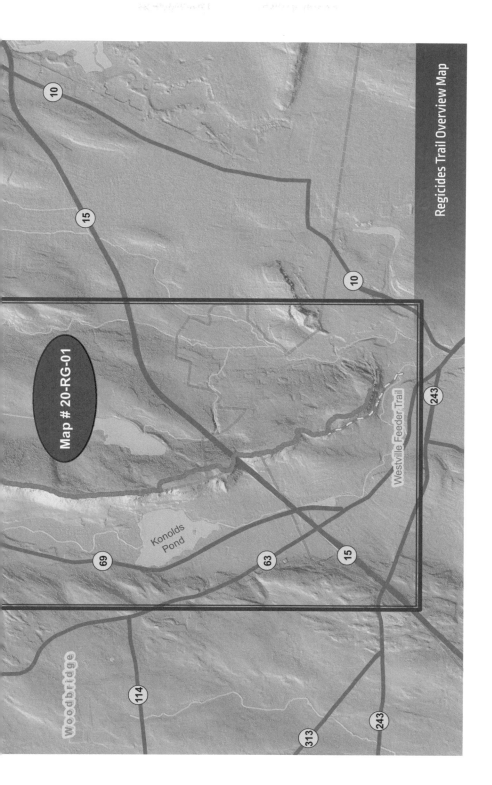

Regicides Trail Overview Map

Map # 20-RG-01

Westville Feeder Trail

Konolds Pond

Woodbridge

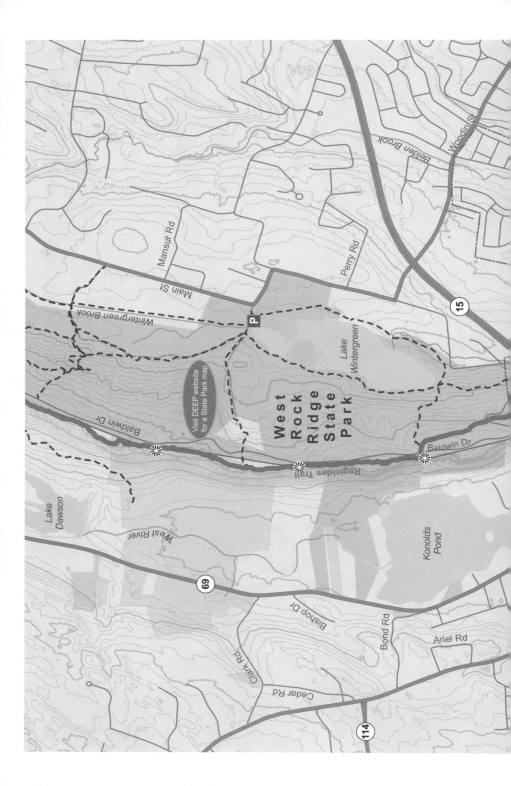

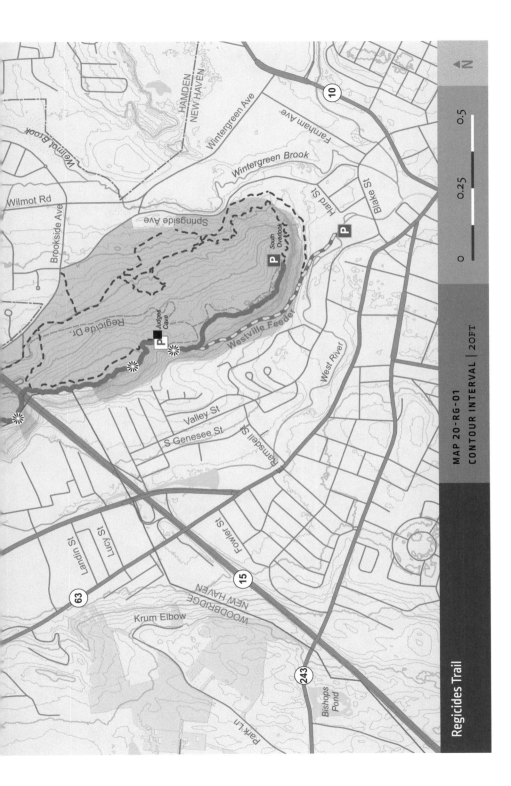

Regicides Trail

MAP 20-RG-01
CONTOUR INTERVAL | 20FT

0   0.25   0.5

N

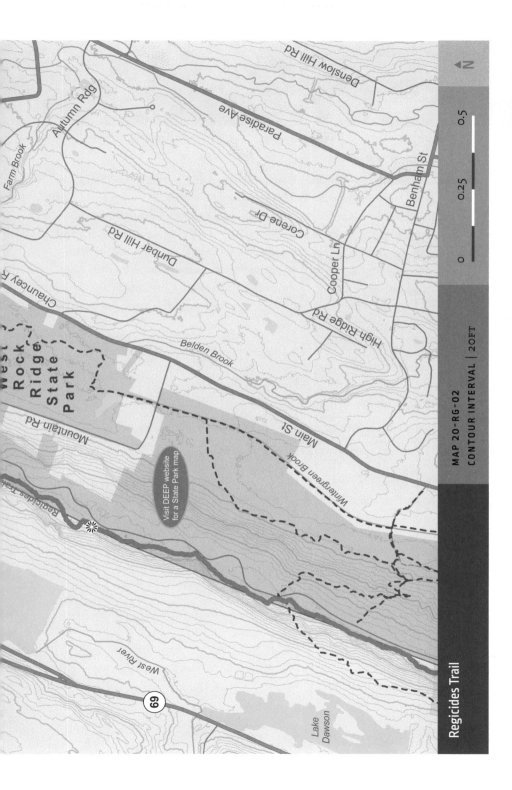

Farm Brook

Autumn Rdg

Chauncey R

West
Rock
Ridge
State
Park

Mountain Rd

Regicides Trail

West River

Lake
Dawson

69

Dunbar Hill Rd

Belden Brook

Visit DEEP website
for a State Park map.

Wintergreen Brook

Main St

High Ridge Rd

Cooper Ln

Corene Dr

Paradise Ave

Denslow Hill Rd

Benham St

N

0   0.25   0.5

MAP 20-RG-02
CONTOUR INTERVAL | 20FT

Regicides Trail

LENGTH 5.0 miles   **BLAZE COLOR** Blue

The Salmon River Trail in Colchester traverses a portion of Salmon River State Forest and loops through Day Pond State Park. Expect to see mixed hardwoods, beautiful views of the Salmon River watershed, and an enormous glacial erratic. Day Pond State Park is wonderful for picnicking and Day Pond itself (regularly stocked with trout) is a great place for fishing and swimming. The trail's Comstock Connector features historic Comstock Bridge, the only covered bridge in eastern Connecticut.

Visit the Connecticut DEEP website for more information about Day Pond State Park.

SIDE TRAILS

Day Pond Brook Spur

LENGTH 0.2 miles   **BLAZE COLOR** Blue/Red

This short spur takes hikers to a waterfall.

▌ *Hunting is permitted in state forests intersected by this trail. Please use caution and wear orange during hunting season.*

Follow the blazes! Volunteers paint the trail markings, or "blazes,"
so hikers won't get lost. Photo courtesy CFPA.

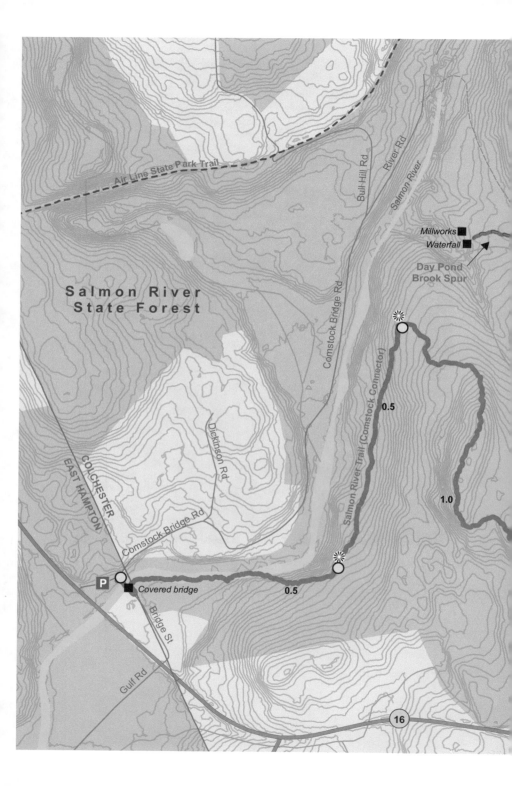

Air Line State Park Trail

Bull Hill Rd

River Rd

Salmon River

Millworks ■
Waterfall ■

Day Pond
Brook Spur

**Salmon River
State Forest**

Comstock Bridge Rd

0.5

Salmon River Trail (Comstock Connector)

1.0

Dickinson Rd

COLCHESTER
EAST HAMPTON

Comstock Bridge Rd

P ○ ■ *Covered bridge*

0.5

Bridge St

Gulf Rd

16

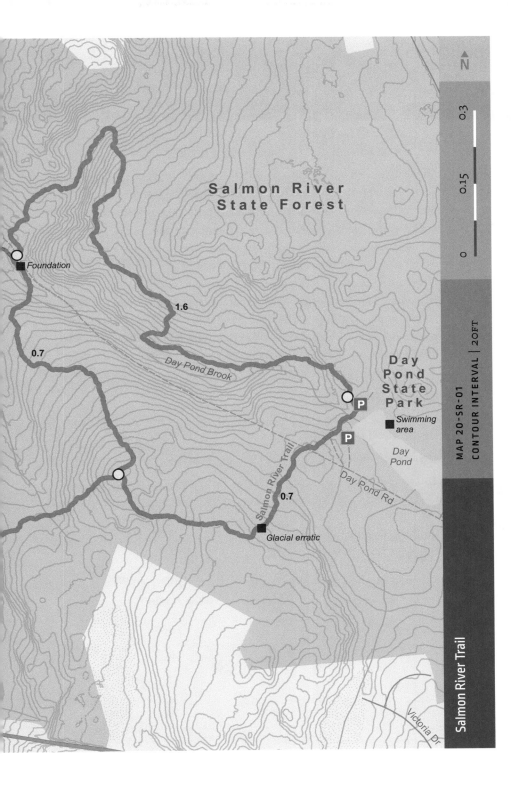

Salmon River
State Forest

Foundation

1.6

0.7

Day Pond Brook

Day
Pond
State
Park

Swimming
area

Day
Pond

Day Pond Rd

Salmon River Trail

0.7

Glacial erratic

Victoria Dr

N

0   0.15   0.3

MAP 20-SR-01
CONTOUR INTERVAL | 20FT

Salmon River Trail

Saugatuck Trail

LENGTH 11.8 miles **BLAZE COLOR** Blue

The Saugatuck Trail is located within the 15,000-acre Centennial Water-shed State Forest and closely parallels its namesake, the Saugatuck Reservoir. The trail offers a variety of terrain—including rock outcroppings, vernal pools, wetlands, and streams—along with spectacular vistas of the reservoir. The trail also connects to the blue-blazed Aspetuck Trail offering longer-distance hiking opportunities.

Because the trail is located within watershed lands, recreational use is regulated by the Connecticut Department of Public Health. Please respect and obey all signs. The Centennial Watershed Forest is managed cooperatively by the Connecticut DEEP, Aquarion Water Company, and The Nature Conservancy. Visit the DEEP website for more information.

SIDE TRAILS

Devil's Den Connector

LENGTH 0.3 miles **BLAZE COLOR** White

This spur trail provides access to Dayton Road parking, Great Ledge, and the Devil's Den trail network maintained by The Nature Conservancy.

Route 53 Connector

LENGTH 0.4 miles **BLAZE COLOR** Blue/Red

This trail heads southwest to Route 53 parking at Stone Pillars and to the Devil's Den trail network maintained by The Nature Conservancy.

Universal Access (UA) Trail Connector

LENGTH 0.1 miles   **BLAZE COLOR** Blue/Red

This trail descends the ridge and connects to a universal access trail and parking area on the Saugatuck Reservoir.

Deer Hill Road Connector

LENGTH 0.3 miles   **BLAZE COLOR** Blue/Red

This short connector trail, through Redding Land Trust property, connects hikers to parking on Deer Hill Road.

▌ *Pets are not permitted on the Saugatuck Trail or on Centennial Watershed State Forest lands.*

▌ *Trail is open to hiking activities only.*

▌ *Hunting is permitted in state forests intersected by this trail. Please use caution and wear orange during hunting season.*

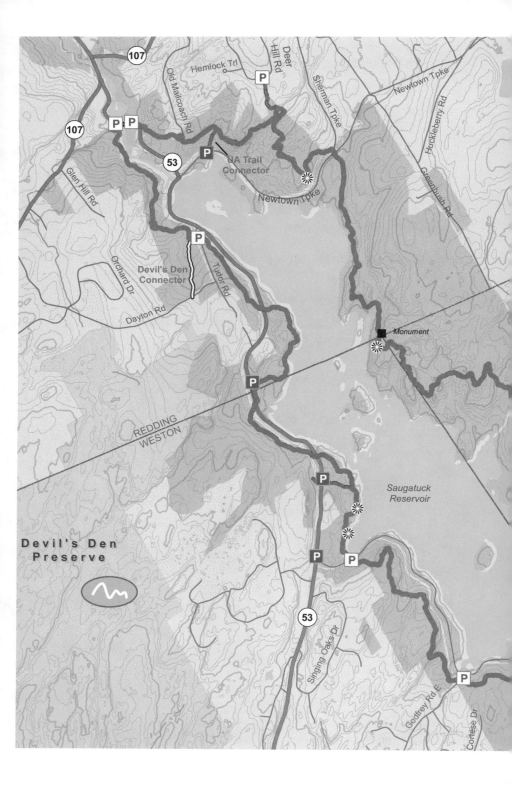

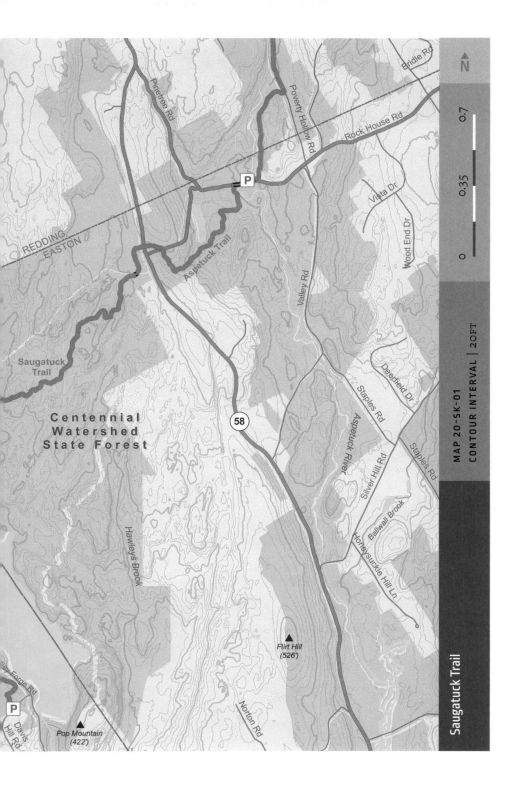

Scovill Loop Trails

LENGTH 2.1 miles   **BLAZE COLOR** Blue

These trails are located within the Hubbard Brook Preserve, which was permanently protected when Connecticut Light and Power (now Eversource) granted a 75-acre conservation restriction to CFPA in 2007. The ensuing partnership between Eversource and CFPA continues to preserve the natural, scenic, and aesthetic character of the property. The preserve offers protected natural habitat for birds, wildlife, and plants. The trails are wooded and generally cover gentle terrain. The beach on the Connecticut River is a great spot for a picnic. These trails are perfect for families with young explorers or for a quiet ramble.

Northern Loop

LENGTH 1.1 miles   **BLAZE COLOR** Blue

The Northern Loop wanders past Moellers Pond, overlooks Hubbard Brook, and leads down to a beach on the Connecticut River.

Southern Loop

LENGTH 0.5 miles   **BLAZE COLOR** Blue

The Southern Loop features an old foundation and mill site, as well as views of the Connecticut River.

Quarry View High Trail

LENGTH 0.4 miles   **BLAZE COLOR** Blue

This trail climbs steeply to an open, rocky ledge with beautiful views of the Connecticut River. Hikers will traverse vestiges of a nineteenth-century quarry operation.

▌ *Trails are open to hiking activities only.*

Trail runners enjoy the trails too. Try a trail run to get your heart pumping and your sweat on. Photo courtesy Miranda Linsky.

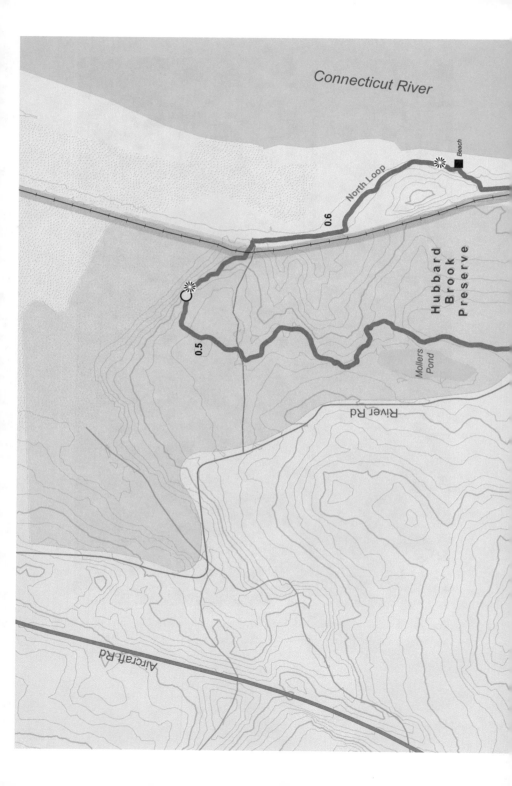

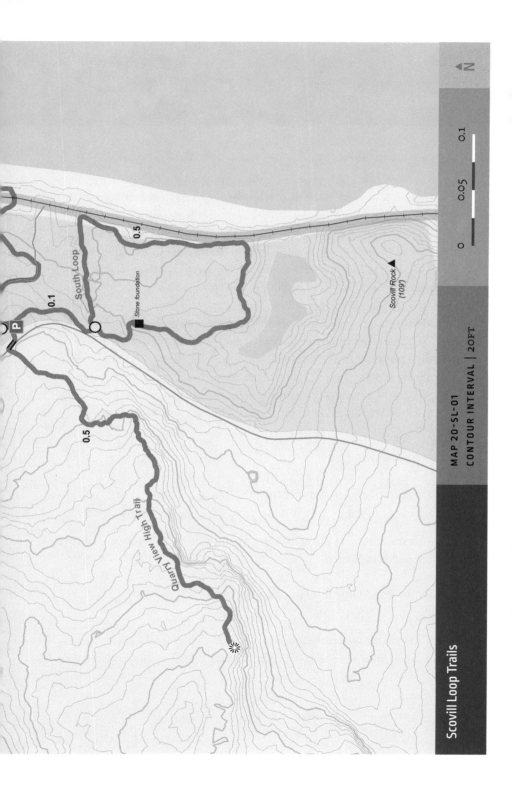

South Loop

Stone foundation

Scovill Rock ▲
(109)

0.5

0.1

0.5

Quarry View High Trail

P

N

0   0.05   0.1

MAP 20-SL-01
CONTOUR INTERVAL │ 20FT

Scovill Loop Trails

Shenipsit Trail

LENGTH 50 miles   **BLAZE COLOR** Blue

The Shenipsit Trail system extends north from the Cobalt area of East Hampton to West Stafford, just shy of the Massachusetts border. The trail traverses the Meshomasic and Shenipsit State Forests primarily on woodland paths and also connects to the trail systems in Gay City State Park in Hebron, Case Mountain Recreation Area in Manchester, and Valley Falls Park in Vernon. Points of interest include a junction with the Hop River Rail Trail in Bolton, and scenic sections on the banks of the Tankerhoosen River in Vernon's Belding and Tankerhoosen Wildlife Management Areas. There are spectacular views of Great Hill Pond and the Connecticut River elsewhere along the trail, and of Hartford from the summit of Case Mountain, along with excellent views to the west, north, and southwest from the fire tower on Soapstone Mountain in Somers. In some places the trail crosses conservation lands protected by the Kongscut Land Trust and the Manchester Land Trust.

316

SIDE TRAILS

Shenipsit/Gay City Connector Trail (see Map 20-SH-03)

LENGTH 1.7 miles   **BLAZE COLOR** Blue/White

This trail connects the main Shenipsit Trail to Gay City State Park and the trail system there.

Risley Pond Loop Trail (see Map 20-SH-04)

LENGTH 2.4 miles   **BLAZE COLOR** Blue

This loop trail's rocky terrain and elevation changes make it a moderately difficult hike. Several spots, such as brook crossings and low stretches, can be unusually wet or muddy following heavy rains. White-tailed deer (as many as six or seven at a time) frequent the trail, wild turkeys have been spotted behind the pond, and the quiet observer can sometimes hear the call of an owl. Mountain laurel along the ridge offers a showy display of flowers toward the end of June and, in the fall, the bright red leaves of the swamp maples are spectacular. Risley Park is owned by the Manchester Land Conservation Trust, Inc. It was donated in 1983 by Gladys R. Hall and Dorothy R. Miller in memory of their father, John S. Risley. The pond is a secondary source of water for the Manchester Water Company.

Valley Falls Loop Trail (see Map 20-SH-05)

LENGTH 3.7 miles   BLAZE COLOR Blue/Yellow

The Valley Falls Loop Trail offers a scenic hike around Valley Falls Park. It follows a section of the Hop River Rail Trail and also intersects other trails. Many smaller loop opportunities exist in the park and in abutting open spaces owned by the Northern Connecticut Land Trust, state of Connecticut, and town of Vernon.

Belding Path (see Map 20-SH-05)

LENGTH 0.5 miles   BLAZE COLOR Yellow

The Belding Path proceeds south from abandoned Snake Hill Road (a dirt road) and the blue/yellow-blazed connector that leads to the Shenipsit Trail. There is limited roadside parking on nearby Reservoir Road.

The land for the Belding Wildlife Management Area was donated to the Connecticut DEEP by Maxwell Belding, who also established a trust for the area's maintenance. Over one hundred species of birds have been seen here. Projects have been initiated to maintain habitats for a wide variety of plants and animals. Environmental education programs are regularly conducted for children.

Soapstone Mountain Bypass Trail (see Map 20-sh-07)

LENGTH 0.5 miles   BLAZE COLOR Yellow

The bypass trail offers an alternate route over Soapstone Mountain.

Gay City State Park Trails (see Map 20-sh-03)

LENGTH 9.2 miles of separate trails BLAZE COLOR Varied

Gay City State Park consists of 1,569 acres in Hebron, Bolton, and Glastonbury and has looping trails totaling almost 10 miles. The blue-blazed Gay City Trail provides access to the longer blue-blazed Shenipsit Trail to the west. Terrain is gently rolling through mature oak and hickory with stream crossings and views of ponds and marshes. There is diverse wildlife, easy walking, and good cross-country skiing. Originally founded by Elijah Andrus and, later, Henry Sumner, the park bears the name of John Gay, the first president of a community of twenty-five families established in 1796. Gay City prospered for years, thanks to several mills powered by the Blackledge River. In 1879, however, Gay City's last mill burned to the ground. The mill ruins, along with the old cellar holes, stone walls, cemetery, and historic roads, are the remaining evidence of the settlers who labored to create this community. In fact, the roads now form the backbone of the modern-day trail system.

The trails are organized into three main routes, marked with different blazes: Gay City Trail (blue), Outer Loop (red), and Pond View Trail (white). There are also connecting trails blazed orange, yellow, and blue-white. A fee is charged from Memorial Day to Labor Day. Visit the Connecticut DEEP website for more detailed information.

Connector Trail

LENGTH 0.8 miles   BLAZE COLOR Yellow

This trail connects the Outer Loop Trail to the Gay City Trail.

Gay City Trail

LENGTH 1.7 miles   **BLAZE COLOR** Blue

This trail roughly bisects the park and follows the historic road from Gay City to Glastonbury. It crosses Birch Mountain Road and connects with the blue/white-blazed Shenipsit/Gay City Connector Trail.

Outer Loop Trail

LENGTH 5.0 miles   **BLAZE COLOR** Red

This loop follows a variety of trails and historic roads. It is an excellent choice for anyone wanting a two- to three-hour hike. The terrain is mostly level with a couple of steep stretches.

Pond Loop Trail

LENGTH 2.5 miles   **BLAZE COLOR** White

This loop trail is the shortest and easiest hike in Gay City State Park. The route passes near the swimming beach and picnic tables.

Split Rock Trail

LENGTH 0.4 miles   **BLAZE COLOR** Red/Yellow

Leaving the Pond Loop Trail, this trail features Split Rock and connects to the park road.

Case Mountain Trails (see Map 20-SH-04)

LENGTH 10+ miles   **BLAZE COLOR** Varied

The Case Mountain Trails traverse 640 acres in the southeastern section of Manchester. The trails and property are owned and maintained by the town of Manchester and the Manchester Conservation Commission in partnership with CFPA. This wooded area contains the summits of Case Mountain (735 ft), Lookout Mountain (744 ft), and Birch Mountain (786 ft). The system consists of more than 10 miles of interconnecting trails that feature rock formations, upland woodlands, and abundant wildlife.

Find your secret spot on the trail and enjoy the magic of the outdoors.
Photo courtesy Justin Benson.

Many of the trails wind their way to Lookout Mountain, which provides panoramic views of the western hills and the Hartford skyline.

Birch Mountain Trail

LENGTH 1.2 miles   **BLAZE COLOR** Blue/Yellow

This is a 3.5-mile loop if combined with a return on the Shenipsit Trail. It passes through hemlock stands, groves of mountain laurel, and glacial rock formations as it ascends to the summits of both Case and Birch Mountains.

Carriage Trail

LENGTH 3.5 miles   **BLAZE COLOR** White

This trail follows the old carriage road that once provided access to the summit of Lookout Mountain. In the 1900s wood was harvested from the mountain for conversion to charcoal for the Case Mills on Spring Street. Watch for remains of charcoal mounds along the trail.

Highland Trail

LENGTH 1.8 miles   **BLAZE COLOR** Pink

This trail offers a longer but more gradual route to the summit of Lookout Mountain. It passes through laurel groves and stands of hemlock.

Lookout Mountain Trail

LENGTH 1.1 miles   **BLAZE COLOR** Yellow

This trail starts at Lookout Mountain summit and heads east from the lookout. It provides a way to reach other trails in the Case Mountain system, starting at the Highland Trail and running along the Shenipsit Trail for a short distance, then crossing the Carriage Trail and Birch Mountain Trail, before ending near the southern end of the Birch Mountain Trail.

▮ *Hunting is permitted in state forests and wildlife management areas intersected by this trail. Please use caution and wear orange during hunting season.*

Mileage Table

SHENIPSIT TRAIL

0.0	Gadpouch Rd (P)
0.4	Great Hill Lookout Spur (white)
1.9	Gadpouch Rd
5.8	Jct Mott Hill Rd Connector (white)
6.9	White Birch Rd
8.6	Begin roadwalk
8.6	Join Dickinson Rd (P)
9.0	Join Mott Hill Rd
9.9	Join Country Club Rd
10.4	Join Wassuc Rd
10.6	Join Toll Gate Rd
11.4	Leave Toll Gate Rd / Join old Rte 2 roadway (P)
11.4	End roadwalk
12.2	Leave old Rte 2 roadway
12.5	View
15.3	View
15.6	Spur to waterfall (blue/white, 300 ft)
16.2	Imperial Dr (P)
16.7	Diamond Lake Rd (P)
17.3	Pheasant Crossing
17.5	Begin roadwalk
17.5	Join Ct Rte 94
17.5	Join Birch Mountain Rd
17.8	Leave Birch Mountain Rd (P)
17.8	End roadwalk
18.4	South jct Shenipsit/Gay City Connector (blue/white)
18.5	Split Boulder at Boulder Jct
19.1	Spur to Pine Ledge overlook (100 ft)
19.2	North jct Shenipsit/Gay City Connector (blue/white)
19.4	Garnet Ledge
19.6	Ruins of old dam
20.9	Jct local trail (red)
21.2	Jct local trail (yellow/gray)
21.5	South jct Birch Mountain Trail (blue/yellow)
21.7	Jct Carriage Path (white)
21.8	Join Lookout Mountain Trail (yellow)
21.9	Leave Lookout Mountain Trail (yellow)
22.3	Jct Carriage Path (white)
22.3	Jct Carriage Path (white)

322

22.4	North jct Birch Mountain Trail (blue/yellow)
22.8	Birch Mountain Rd
23.1	Amanda Dr
23.4	Carter St
23.9	Ct Rte 534
24.8	Begin roadwalk
24.8	Join Ct Rte 85
25.0	Join Williams Rd
25.4	Join US Rte 6/US Rte 44
25.7	Leave US Rte 6/US Rte 44 (P)
25.7	End roadwalk
26.0	View
26.3	Join Hop River State Park Trail
27.7	Jct Valley Falls Loop Trail (blue/yellow)
28.5	Jct Valley Falls Loop Trail (blue/yellow)
28.5	Jct Valley Falls Loop Trail (blue/yellow) / Jct local trail (blue/red) / Leave Hop River State Park Trail
28.7	Jct Valley Falls Loop Trail (blue/yellow) / Valley Falls Park (P)
28.7	Valley Falls Rd
29.2	Bolton Rd
29.3	Jct Belding Path (yellow)
30.3	Jct Shenipsit-Reservoir Rd Connector (blue/yellow, 0.2mi, P)
30.7	Baker Rd
31.8	Begin roadwalk
31.8	Join Reservoir Rd
31.9	Walker Reservoir (P)
32.1	Join Ct Rte 31
32.6	Join Ct Rte 30
32.8	Leave Ct Rte 30 (P)
32.8	End roadwalk
33.4	Begin roadwalk
33.4	Join Gerber Rd
33.6	Join Industrial Park Rd W
33.8	Join Ct Rte 30
33.9	Join Kingsbury Ave
34.4	Join Ct Rte 74
34.6	Leave Ct Rte 74 (P)
34.6	End roadwalk
36.4	Begin roadwalk
36.4	Join Shenipsit Lake Rd (P)

323

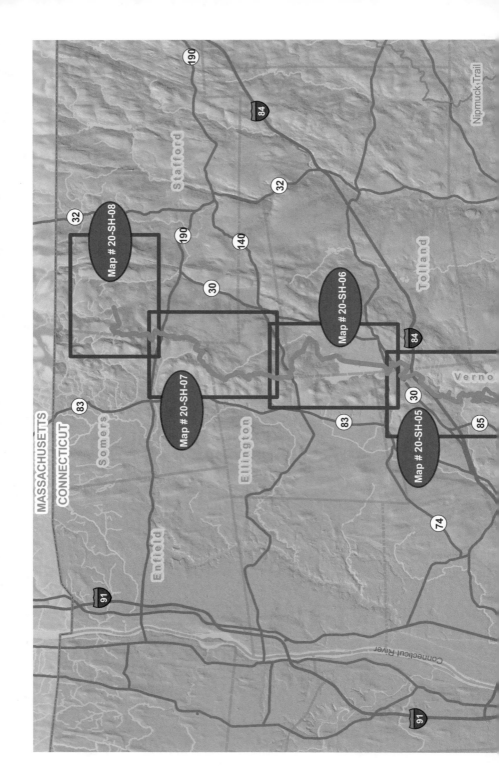

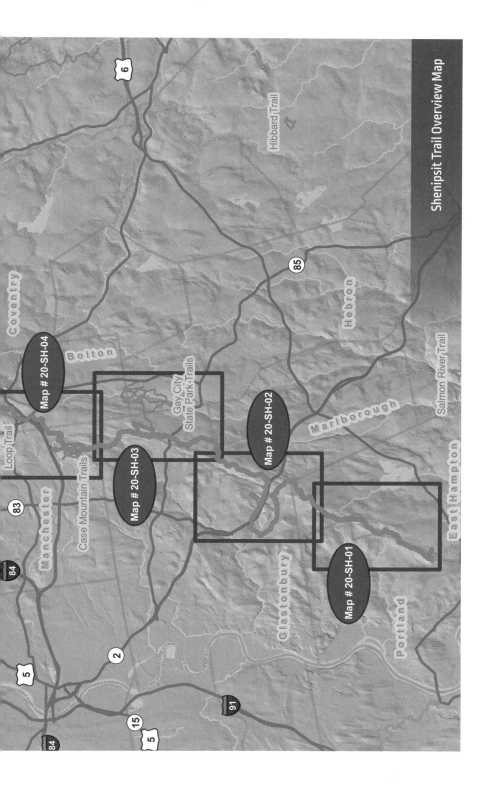

Shenipsit Trail Overview Map

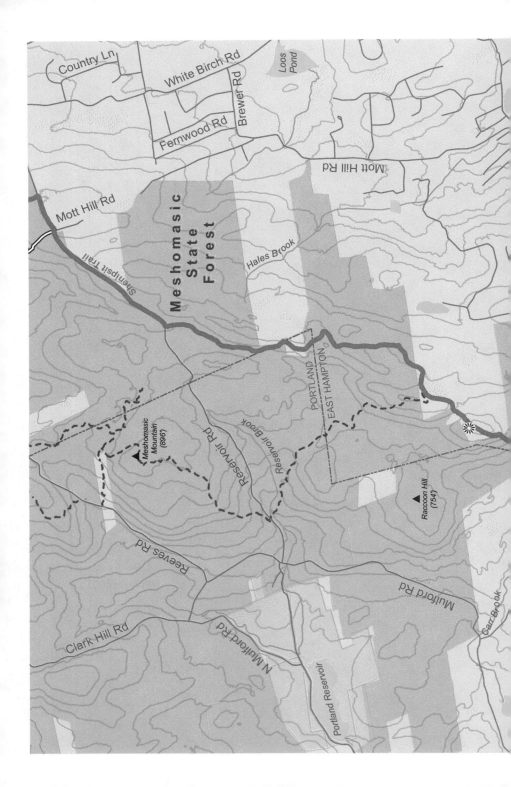

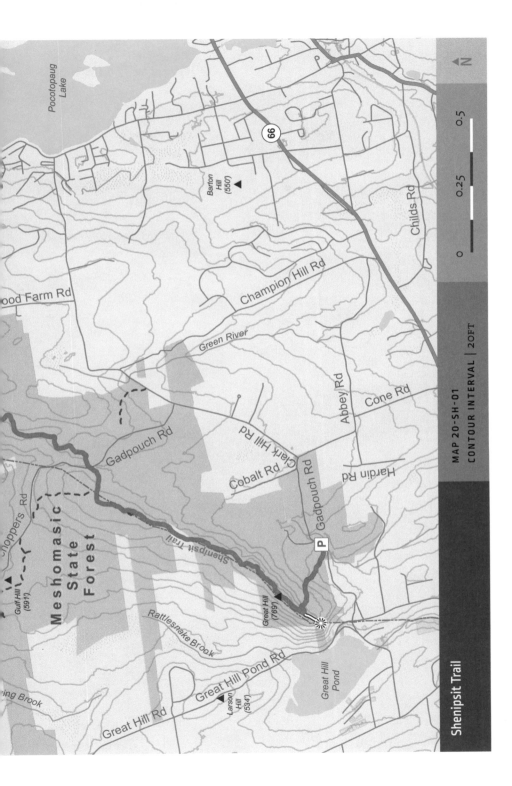

Pocotopaug Lake

ood Farm Rd

Champion Hill Rd

Green River

Barton
Hill
(550) ▲

66

Childs Rd

Gadpouch Rd

Clark Hill Rd

Cobalt Rd

Abbey Rd

Cone Rd

Hardin Rd

Gadpouch Rd

Choppers Rd

Meshomasic
State
Forest

Gulf Hill
(591) ▲

Shenipsit Trail

Rattlesnake Brook

Great Hill
(769) ▲

P

ing Brook

Great Hill Pond Rd

Larson
Hill
(534) ▲

Great Hill Rd

Great Hill
Pond

N ▲

0   0.25   0.5

MAP 20-SH-01
CONTOUR INTERVAL | 20FT

Shenipsit Trail

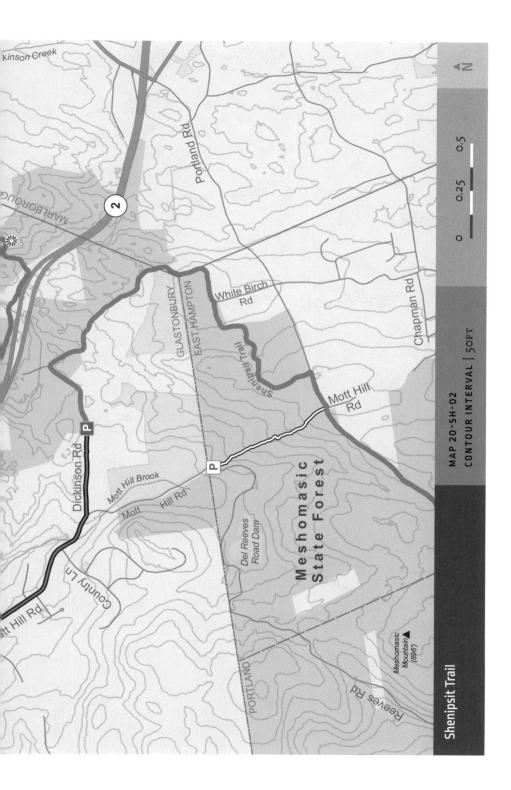

Shenipsit Trail

MAP 20-SH-02
CONTOUR INTERVAL | 50FT

0   0.25   0.5

N

Meshomasic
State Forest

Meshomasic
Mountain ▲
(896)

Del Reeves
Road Dam

PORTLAND

Reeves Rd

Mott Hill
Rd

Chapman Rd

White Birch
Rd

Shenipsit Trail

GLASTONBURY
EAST HAMPTON

Portland Rd

MARLBOROUG

2

Dickinson Rd

Mott Hill Brook

Mott   Hill Rd

Country Ln

ott Hill Rd

kinson Creek

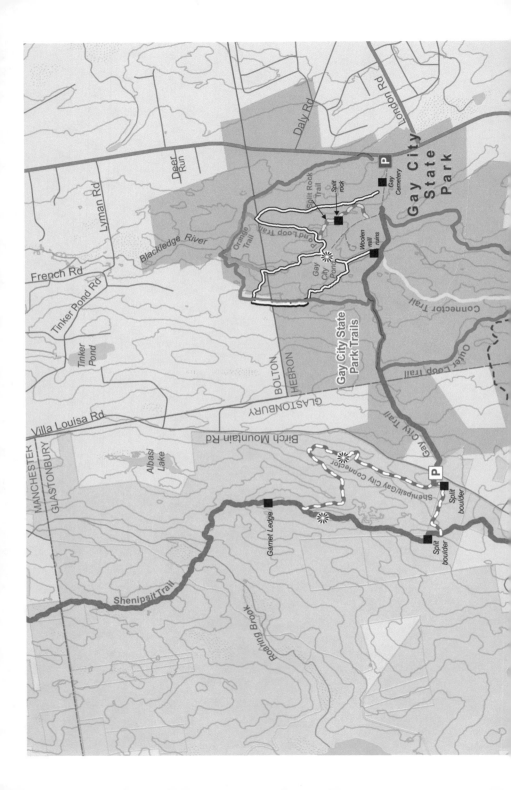

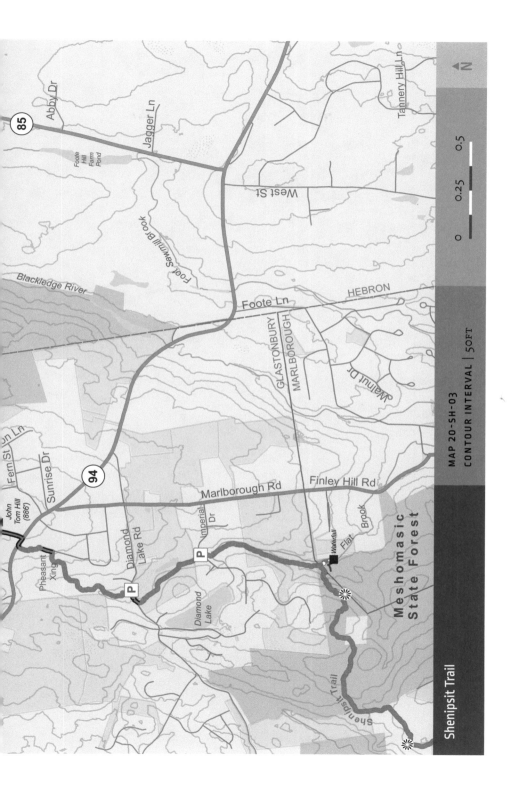

Shenipsit Trail

MAP 20-SH-03
CONTOUR INTERVAL | 50FT

Meshomasic
State Forest

N

0   0.25   0.5

Roads and labels:

85
94

Abby Dr
Jagger Ln
Foote Hill Farm Pond
Foot Sawmill Brook
Blackledge River
West St
Foote Ln
HEBRON
GLASTONBURY
MARLBOROUGH
Walnut Dr
Tannery Hill Ln
Fern St
Sunrise Dr
John Tom Hill (886)
Pheasant Xing
Diamond Lake Rd
Marlborough Rd
Imperial Dr
Finley Hill Rd
Flat Brook
Waterfall
Diamond Lake
Shenipsit Trail

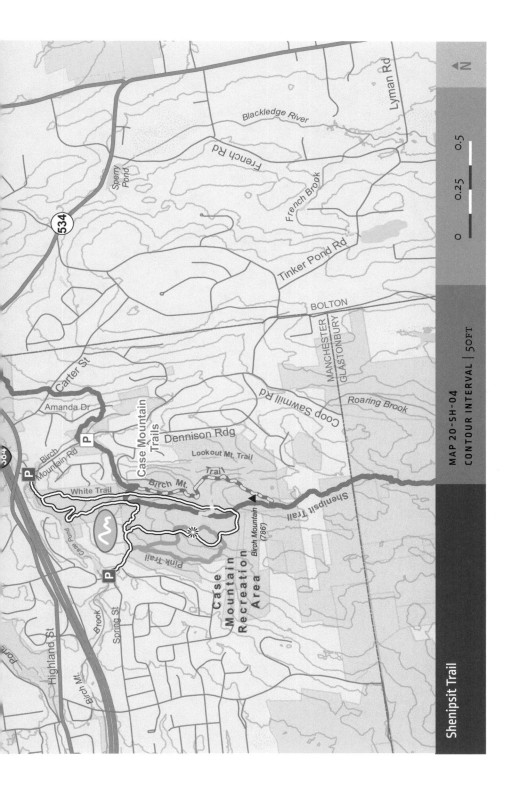

Shenipsit Trail

MAP 20-SH-04
CONTOUR INTERVAL | 50FT

N

0   0.25   0.5

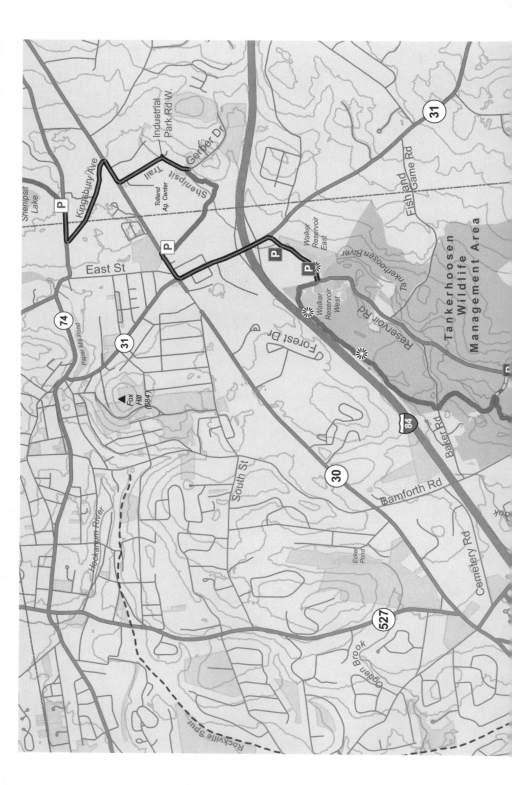

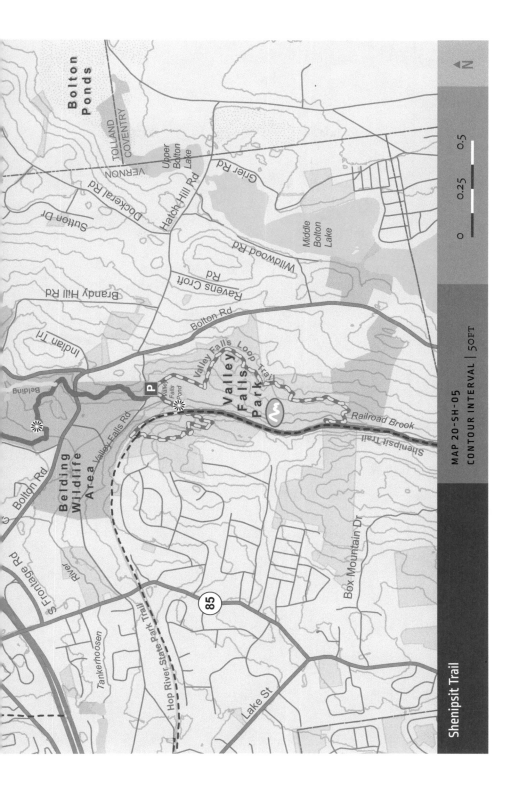

Shenipsit Trail

MAP 20-SH-05
CONTOUR INTERVAL | 50FT

N

0   0.25   0.5

Bolton Ponds

TOLLAND
COVENTRY

VERNON

Upper
Bolton
Lake

Grier Rd

Dockerel Rd

Sutton Dr

Hatch Hill Rd

Middle
Bolton
Lake

Wildwood Rd

Ravens Croft
Rd

Brandy Hill Rd

Bolton Rd

Indian Trl

Belding

Valley Falls Loop Trail

Valley
Falls
Pond

Valley
Falls
Park

Railroad Brook

Shenipsit Trail

Belding
Wildlife
Area

Valley Falls Rd

S Bolton Rd

S Frontage Rd

River

Tankerhoosen

Hop River State Park Trail

85

Lake St

Box Mountain Dr

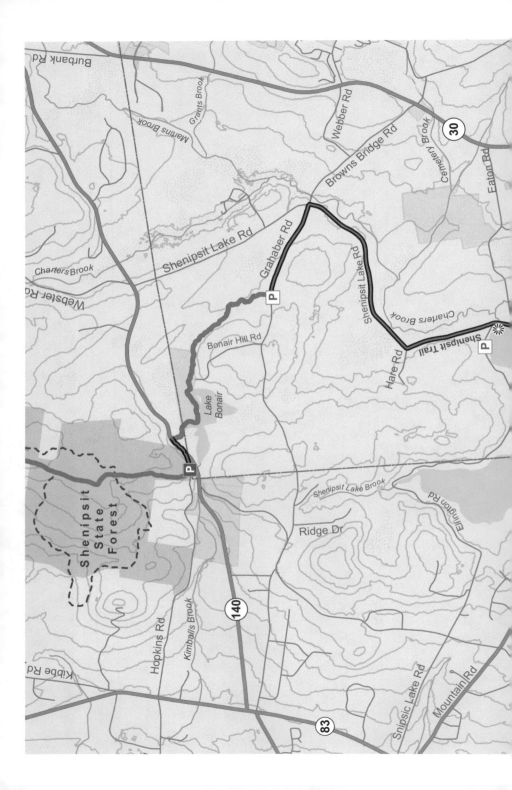

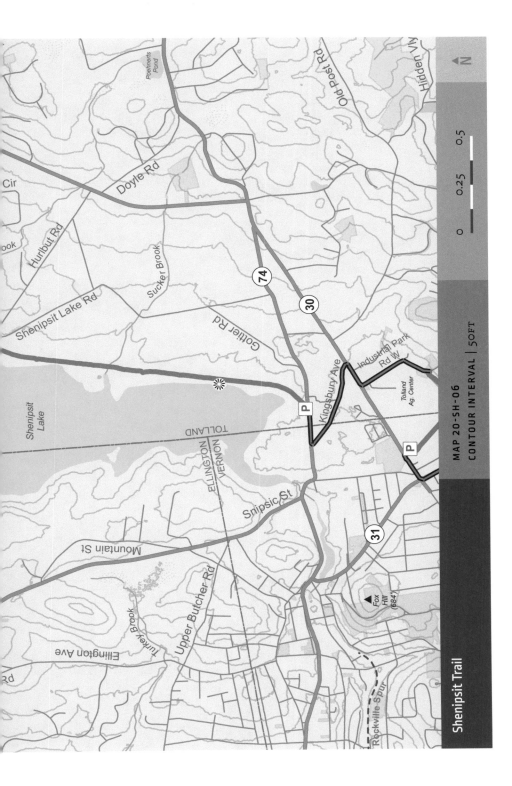

Shenipsit Trail

MAP 20-SH-06
CONTOUR INTERVAL | 50FT

0   0.25   0.5

N

Poehlmerts Pond

Old Post Rd

Hidden Vw

Cir

Doyle Rd

Hurlbut Rd

ook

Sucker Brook

Shenipsit Lake Rd

Gottier Rd

74

30

Shenipsit Lake

Kingsbury Ave

Industrial Park Rd W

Tolland Ag. Center

P

TOLLAND

ELLINGTON
VERNON

Snipsic St

Mountain St

P

Upper Butcher Rd

Turkey Brook

Ellington Ave

Rd

Fox Hill (684')

31

Rockville Spur

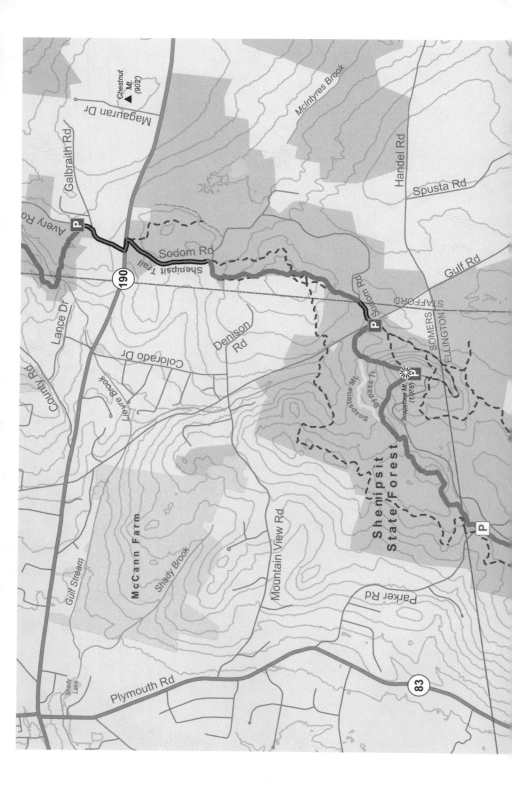

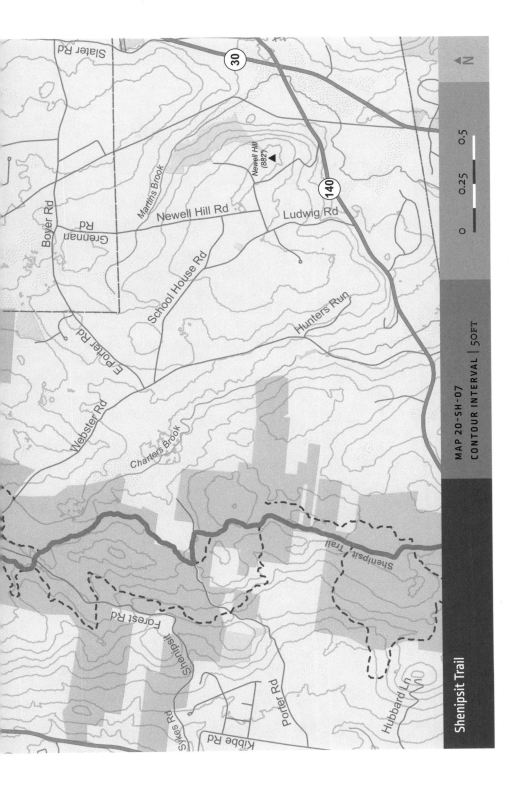

Shenipsit Trail

MAP 20-SH-07
CONTOUR INTERVAL | 50FT

0   0.25   0.5

N

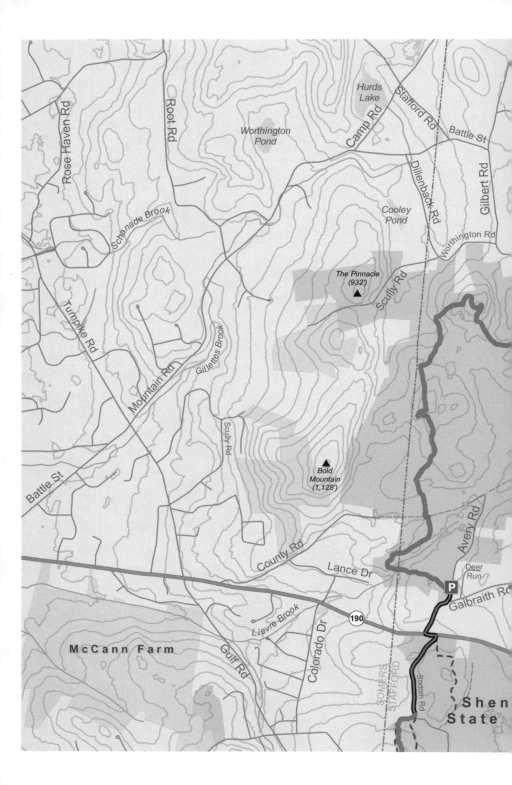

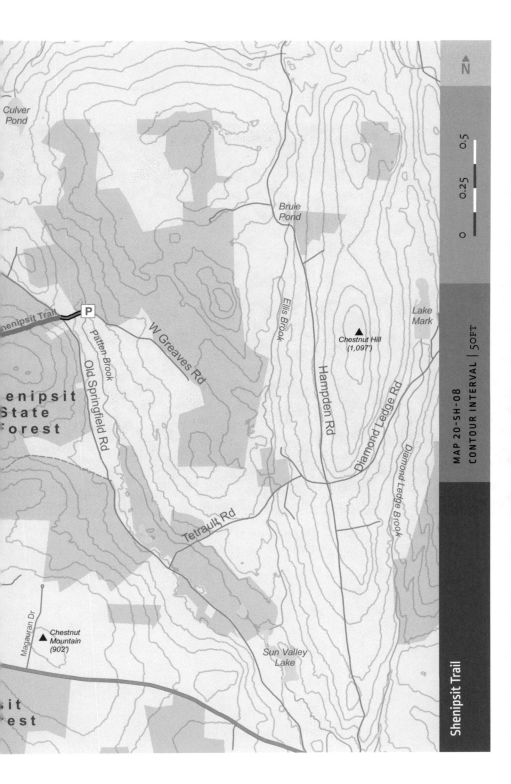

Culver
Pond

Bruie
Pond

Shenipsit Trail

P

Ellis Brook

Lake
Mark

▲
Chestnut Hill
(1,097')

Patten Brook

W Greaves Rd

Old Springfield Rd

Shenipsit
State
Forest

Hampden Rd

Diamond Ledge Rd

Diamond Ledge Brook

Tetrault Rd

Magauran Dr

▲
Chestnut
Mountain
(902')

Sun Valley
Lake

sit
est

N ▲

0   0.25   0.5

MAP 20-SH-08
CONTOUR INTERVAL | 50FT

Shenipsit Trail

Hiking partners can help motivate you to hike a little farther than you might on your own. Photo courtesy Liane Stevens.

Stony Creek Trails

LENGTH 9.9 miles   **BLAZE COLOR** Varied

The Stony Creek Trails traverse the Brooks R. Kelley, Van Wie, and Hoadley Creek Preserves. These preserves combine to form a contiguous 535-acre open space, creating one of the wildest natural areas in Branford. Featuring wetlands as well as ridgelines, this trail system offers many secluded hikes. A portion of the 28-mile Branford Trail, which follows the town's border and is marked with white circles, traverses the Stony Creek region. An internal property is leased by the town of Branford to a company which continues to quarry the world-famous Stony Creek pink granite.

The Stony Creek Trails are connected to Westwoods, a 1,200-acre forestland in Guilford. Westwoods' extensive trail system is maintained by the Guilford Land Conservation Trust. The two systems are connected by a single trail blazed with a green rectangle.

The Stony Creek Trails are maintained cooperatively by the Branford Land Trust and the town of Branford. Trails are open from one hour before sunrise to one hour after sunset. To learn more, visit branfordlandtrust.org.

▌ *At the time of publication, trail locations and blazing for the Stony Creek Trails is in flux. Please visit* CFPA's *interactive map for the latest trail information.*

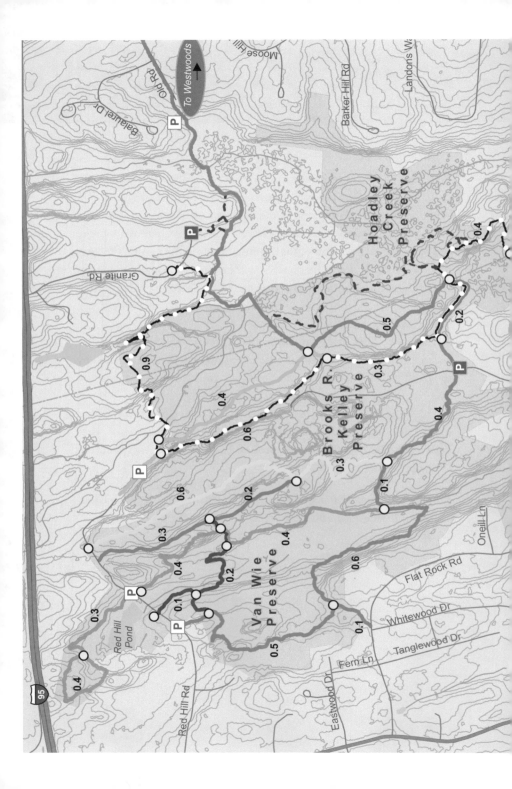

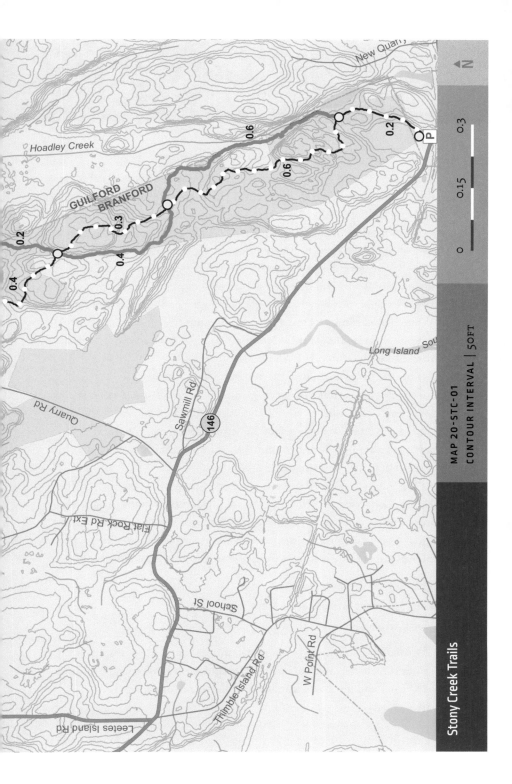

Stony Creek Trails

MAP 20-STC-01
CONTOUR INTERVAL | 50FT

N

0   0.15   0.3
     0.15   0.3

Hoadley Creek

GUILFORD
BRANFORD

New Quarry

0.6

0.6

0.6

0.2

0.2

0.3

0.4

0.2

0.4

P

Long Island Sound

Sawmill Rd

146

Quarry Rd

Flat Rock Rd Ext

School St

W Point Rd

Thimble Island Rd

Leetes Island Rd

LENGTH 13.7 miles   **BLAZE COLOR** Varied

The Nature Conservancy's Sunny Valley Preserve (SVP) consists of more than 1,850 acres of agricultural and natural areas in Bridgewater and New Milford. The Blue Trail is the longest trail in the SVP system. It extends from Bridgewater Town Park on Lake Lillinonah to the south end of the preserve's Iron Ore Hill parcel on Iron Ore Hill Road. Red-blazed trails form loops off the Blue Trail on Iron Ore Hill and on the lake side of Rocky Hill. The yellow-blazed Rocky Hill Trail traverses the rugged slopes of Rocky Hill to link Hemlock Road and Benson Road. White-blazed connector trails provide opportunities for circular walks of various lengths. The Wolf Pit Mountain Trail consists of two loop trails that lead to the summit of Wolf Pit Mountain.

Located in New Milford, the SVP Farm and Nature Trails consist of three color-coded trails of varying difficulty. The main trail is on fairly level terrain ideal for family hiking. It parallels agricultural fields and provides a rare close-up view of an active dairy farm. A half-mile trail traverses a small but rocky mountain, and the third trail follows an old farm path to an interesting red maple swamp.

The Sunny Valley Preserve trails exist through the courtesy of The Nature Conservancy (TNC) and several private landowners. Additional information is available from the TNC website or the preserve office: (860) 355–3716. Hikers using these trails are expected to be respectful of the land and the creatures living there. Additionally, hikers should:

- Stay on the blazed paths.
- Keep dogs leashed at all times.
- Leave no litter.

The following activities are prohibited throughout the trail system: fires, motor vehicles (including snowmobiles and all-terrain vehicles), cutting of live or dead trees, and hunting or collecting of any kind.

Sunny Valley Preserve Trails (see Map 20-sv-01)

Blue Trail

LENGTH 4.2 miles   **BLAZE COLOR** Blue

The preserve's primary trail has three sections. The northernmost section parallels Lake Lillinonah and includes a short walk on a quiet town road. The Silica Mine section, on Rocky Hill, travels through a mixed forest of hemlock, oak and beech. The Ravine section is on Iron Ore Hill, the southernmost part of which is being used for forestry management studies.

The svp Iron Ore Hill Forest Management Area is one of three sites in the state where Connecticut Agricultural Experiment Station foresters are investigating forest regeneration after various harvesting methods have been implemented. Initiated in 1982, the study is designed to determine how each method impacts the quality and quantity of oak tree regeneration. Signs along the trail identify the harvesting methods applied in the test plots. A pamphlet that more fully describes the study is available from Sunny Valley Preserve.

Rocky Hill Trail

LENGTH 1.7 miles   **BLAZE COLOR** Yellow

The Rocky Hill Trail extends southeasterly from Rocky Hill Road across Rocky Hill (elevation 670 feet), then over varying terrain to Christian Street. It begins with an uphill climb to a lookout, then descends through woodlands to a rocky stream and up the other side before entering a meadow that is reverting to woodland. The meadow is active with birds and other wildlife and fragrant in June when trailside roses bloom. Shorter or longer hikes are possible by combining the Rocky Hill Trail with white-blazed connector trails or the Blue Trail.

Silica Mine Hill Trail

LENGTH 1.4 miles   **BLAZE COLOR** Red

This auxiliary trail goes to the shore of Lake Lillinonah and then uphill on an old logging road. It can be combined with the main Blue Trail to create a 1.9-mile circuit hike.

Iron Ore Hill Trail

LENGTH 1.1 miles   **BLAZE COLOR** Red

This side trail bisects numerous stone walls, highlighting the area's agricultural history. It can be combined with the main Blue Trail to create a pleasant circular route with parking located in the middle.

Sunny Valley Preserve Farm and Nature Trails

(see Map 20-sv-02)

This 2.8-mile network of trails traverses agricultural fields, woods, and wetlands. These diverse habitats are home to a wide variety of animals and birds, including many neotropical migrants. Brochures describing the trail system, as well as the numerous species that have been observed on and near the trails, are available at trailheads or from the preserve office.

Yellow Trail

LENGTH 1.3 miles   **BLAZE COLOR** Yellow

The Yellow Trail skirts the perimeter of wooded Round Mountain, traversing edge vegetation that provides important habitat for insects, birds, and small mammals. It's flanked by agricultural fields that provide silage for the preserve's working dairy farm. Nest boxes installed on fence posts around the fields are used by bluebirds, black-capped chickadees, tree swallows, and house wrens, all of which feed on the insects that abound on the farm. Kingbirds, kestrels, and swallows hunt the fields for grasshoppers, while turkey vultures and red-tailed hawks are often seen soaring over the open areas.

White Trail

LENGTH 0.5 miles   **BLAZE COLOR** White

This trail leaves from the northern end of the Yellow Trail, about 200 feet south of the beginning of the loop section. Also called the Over-the-Top Trail, it gradually ascends in a southerly direction to the rocky outcrops at the summit of Round Mountain (elevation 430 feet). The trail passes through oak/maple woodlands that give way to thick stands of mountain laurel on the thinner, rocky soils at the summit where lowbush blueberry crowds the path. The trail descends the mountain's relatively steep south slope to reach its terminus at mile 0.7 of the Yellow Loop Trail. The White Trail can be combined with the Yellow Trail for a hike over more diverse terrain.

Red Trail

LENGTH 1.0 mile BLAZE COLOR Red

The first section of this trail is called Bird Lane because of the multitude of migrant songbirds seen in the fall. State-threatened Cooper's hawks nest and hunt around the preserve's farm and often are flushed from their perches along the laneway. Ravens, which are relatively new residents of Connecticut, have been heard on the hillside above the preserve, croaking their loud, strange calls. The second section is called the Wetland Trail. It goes through a red maple swamp that features a duck blind and an observation platform. This section may be closed during periods of high water.

Wolf Pit Mountain Trail (Clatter Valley Park)

LENGTH 1.2 miles BLAZE COLOR Yellow

The Wolf Pit Mountain Trail follows the hillside's contours to a height of land with seasonal views. The main trail goes into the woods before splitting into a loop that encircles the mountain. A more challenging white-blazed connector trail roughly bisects the primary loop; these two paths can be combined for a 0.7-mile inner loop hike. This option offers a shorter descent, but is steeper and rockier than the main trail. A red-blazed trail offers an alternate route for exploring.

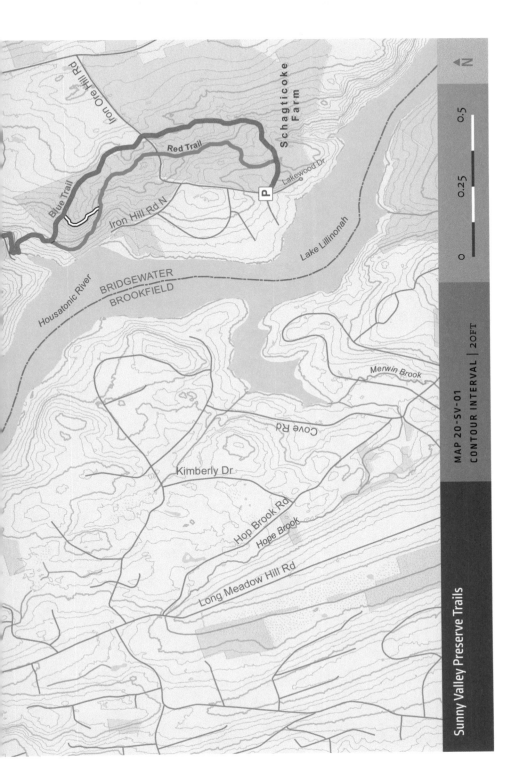

Iron Ore Hill Rd

S c h a g t i c o k e
F a r m

Red Trail

Lakewood Dr

Blue Trail

Iron Hill Rd N

P

Lake Lillinonah

Housatonic River

BRIDGEWATER

BROOKFIELD

Merwin Brook

Cove Rd

Kimberly Dr

Hop Brook Rd

Hope Brook

Long Meadow Hill Rd

N

0   0.25   0.5

MAP 20-SV-01
CONTOUR INTERVAL | 20FT

Sunny Valley Preserve Trails

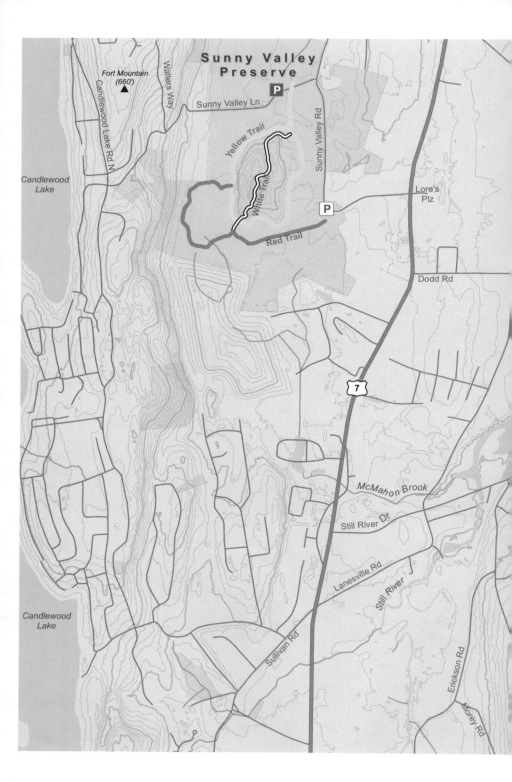

Sunny Valley
Preserve

Fort Mountain
(660')

Walters Way

Candlewood Lake Rd N

Candlewood
Lake

Sunny Valley Ln

Yellow Trail

White Trail

Sunny Valley Rd

Red Trail

Lore's
Plz

Dodd Rd

7

McMahon Brook

Still River Dr

Still River

Lanesville Rd

Candlewood
Lake

Sullivan Rd

Erickson Rd

Morey Rd

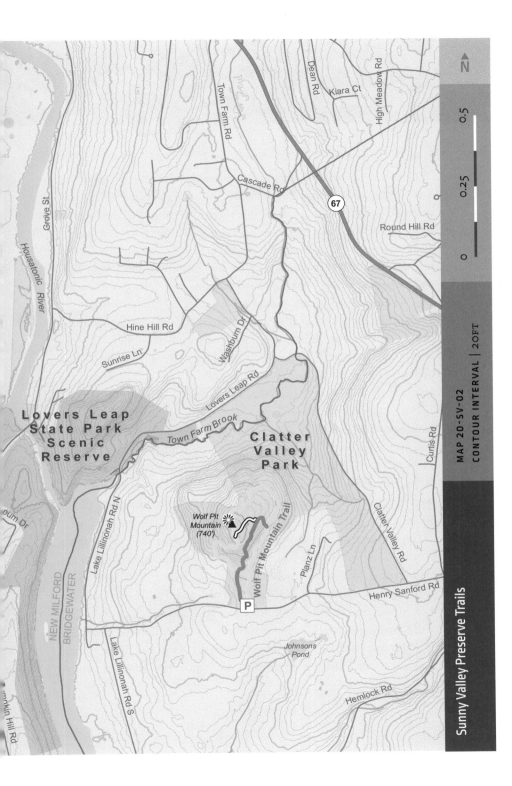

Sunny Valley Preserve Trails

MAP 20-SV-02 CONTOUR INTERVAL | 20FT

N

0   0.25   0.5

Dean Rd

Kiara Ct

High Meadow Rd

Town Farm Rd

Cascade Rd

67

Round Hill Rd

Grove St

Housatonic River

Hine Hill Rd

Washburn Dr

Sunrise Ln

Lovers Leap Rd

Lovers Leap
State Park
Scenic
Reserve

Town Farm Brook

Clatter
Valley
Park

Curtis Rd

num Dr

Lake Lillinonah Rd N

Wolf Pit
Mountain
(740')

Wolf Pit Mountain Trail

Clatter Valley Rd

Planz Ln

NEW MILFORD

BRIDGEWATER

P

Henry Sanford Rd

Lake Lillinonah Rd S

Johnsons
Pond

Hemlock Rd

kin Hill Rd

Tunxis Trail

LENGTH 39.7 miles   **BLAZE COLOR** Blue

The Tunxis Trail is the backbone of a larger system of nineteen trails that totals just over 83 miles of interconnected hiking adventure. The trail system generally traverses the scenic western ridge of the Connecticut River Valley. From its southern trailhead in Southington, the Tunxis Trail runs north to the Massachusetts state line. The trail is interrupted near the Wolcott/Bristol line and resumes in Plymouth. The Tunxis Trail and its myriad adjoining trails offer a range of loop-hiking options and traverse a variety of terrain and landscapes.

The southern portion of the Tunxis Trail is typified by woodland paths that travel along the top and sides of the valley's western wall. The trail offers several outstanding viewpoints, including Julian's Rock and Norton Outlook. The side trails in this southern region vary in length from 0.5 miles to just under 5 miles and travel over diverse terrain.

The middle portion of the Tunxis is primarily in the town of Burlington. Features of the trail system in this region include the challenging Mile of Ledges and the historic Tory Den. Side trails connect to other trail systems in Sessions Woods Wildlife Management Area and Nassahegon State Forest, with opportunities to explore lands protected by the Burlington Land Trust as well. There are ample opportunities for loop hikes, longer-distance hiking, and shorter family rambles.

The northern section of the Tunxis Trail traverses some of the most beautiful woodlands that can be found in Connecticut. Highlights include the Indian Council Caves and Pine Mountain, where 180-degree views provide prime hawk-watching during the spring and fall migrations. The trail crosses and sometimes follows several woods roads and old fire roads, passing along picturesque mountain brooks. Located primarily on Metropolitan District Commission (MDC) lands and Tunxis State Forest, the trail in this region climbs steeply near its northern terminus to meet the Connecticut-Massachusetts state line, then crosses for a short distance into Granville State Forest in Massachusetts.

SIDE TRAILS

Note: Many Tunxis side trails are marked by a blue blaze with an interior "dot" of a contrasting color. In the blaze colors given below, "Blue/Red" means a blue rectangular blaze with a red dot in the middle. These are the only trails in the Blue-Blazed Hiking Trail System marked in this way.

Stonehouse Trail (see Map 20-TU-01)

LENGTH 1.2 miles   BLAZE COLOR Blue/Red

When combined with the Tunxis and Woodtick Trails, this trail makes for a pleasant, relatively short loop hike. Keep your eyes peeled for old foundations along the trail.

Woodtick Trail (see Map 20-TU-01)

LENGTH 1.5 miles   BLAZE COLOR Blue/Black

This trail provides an excellent hike that, when combined with the Tunxis and Stonehouse Trails, is roughly the shape of a lollipop. After a quick ascent to an ancient cemetery, it descends gently to meet the main Tunxis Trail at the north end of New Britain Reservoir. This trail also features the Northeast Burying Ground, where Louisa May Alcott's ancestors are interred.

Compounce Ridge Trail (see Map 20-TU-01)

LENGTH 4.5 miles   BLAZE COLOR Blue/Yellow

Portions of the Compounce Ridge Trail are challenging, with a series of descents and ascents of the western wall of the Connecticut Valley. The trail offers extensive, breath-taking views from Julian's Rock and Norton Outlook. It is met or crossed by the Steep Climb, Bobcat, and Compounce Cascade Trails, then continues north along the ridge to Castle Rock. The trail shares part of its route with the old stagecoach road between Bristol and Waterbury.

Steep Climb Trail (see Map 20-TU-01)

LENGTH 0.5 miles   BLAZE COLOR Blue/Red

This trail provides access to the Compounce Ridge Trail from the south side of Lake Compounce.

Bobcat Trail (see Map 20-TU-01)

LENGTH 0.7 miles   BLAZE COLOR Blue/Purple

This trail connects the Tunxis Trail to the Compounce Ridge Trail and crosses the south branch of Cussgutter Brook.

Compounce Cascade Trail (see Map 20-TU-01)

LENGTH 1.1 miles   BLAZE COLOR Blue/Red

This challenging and rocky trail ascends the western wall of the Connecticut River Valley and goes west and south along Cussgutter Brook, crossing it several times. The cascading brook has many delightful waterfalls.

Blue/White Trail (see Maps 20-TU-02 / 20-TU-03)

LENGTH 9.9 miles   BLAZE COLOR Blue/White

This is the longest of the color-coded routes, the westernmost, and the first to diverge from the main line of the Tunxis Trail in Burlington. It passes through Bristol Water Department lands and connects east to Nassahegon State Forest. The trail features a variety of terrain and beautiful woodlands.

Blue/Yellow Trail (see Maps 20-TU-02 / 20-TU-03)

LENGTH 9.3 miles   BLAZE COLOR Blue/Yellow

This trail features the challenging Mile of Ledges, along with the Sessions Woods Wildlife Management Area. It can be combined with a variety of other trails for longer, more challenging hikes.

Blue/Orange Trail (see Map 20-TU-03)

LENGTH 3.0 miles   **BLAZE COLOR** Blue/Orange

This trail forms a figure eight with the Blue/Yellow Trail. Beginning in the woods north of Sessions Woods Swamp, the trail features Devil's Kitchen (a box canyon), Lamson Corner Cemetery, and multiple stone walls.

Blue/Green Trail (see Map 20-TU-03)

LENGTH 0.7 miles   **BLAZE COLOR** Blue/Green

This trail provides a short link between the Blue/White and the Blue/Yellow Trails. It goes over three minor ledges, crosses a charcoal hearth site, and passes a large glacial erratic.

Red Trail South (see Map 20-TU-03)

LENGTH 1.1 miles   **BLAZE COLOR** Blue/Red

This trail passes Wildcat Mountain in the Nassahegon State Forest and ends at George Washington Turnpike.

Red Trail North (see Map 20-TU-03)

LENGTH 1.3 miles   **BLAZE COLOR** Blue/Red

This trail leaves from the Punch Brook Trail and crosses The Nature Conservancy's Taine Mountain Preserve to reach the ridge that leads to the mountain's 900-foot summit. Situated on gneiss and till, Taine Mountain has unusual strata in its ledges and is scattered with several glacial erratics.

Punch Brook Trail (see Map 20-TU-03)

LENGTH 1.5 miles   **BLAZE COLOR** Blue/Purple

The Punch Brook Trail meanders east and then west, crossing Punch Brook twice. It can be combined with the Blue/Yellow Trail to create a longer loop hike.

Cell service can be limited in the woods, but it's a good precaution to have your phone with you. Photo courtesy Liane Stevens.

Nature Center Connector (see Map 20-TU-03)

LENGTH 2.5 miles   **BLAZE COLOR** Blue/Black

The Nature Center Connector is a long access route from the Harry C. Barnes Nature Center in Bristol to the Blue/Yellow Trail in Sessions Woods Wildlife Management Area. Highlights include a steep rock escarpment nearly 70 feet high, some craggy climbs, and a gentle meander along a small brook.

Tipping Rock Loop (see Map 20-TU-05)

LENGTH 2.0 miles   **BLAZE COLOR** Blue/Yellow

This loop begins and ends on the Tunxis Trail in Nepaug State Forest. It leads to and across several interesting geological formations, including Tipping Rock, whose tipping movement was experienced by hikers as recently as the 1950s.

Valley Overlook Trail (see Map 20-TU-05)

LENGTH 1.2 miles   **BLAZE COLOR** Blue/White

This trail provides access to the otherwise trail-free and roadless western section of the Nepaug State Forest. It is a dead-end spur leading to Rome Spare Outlook, a ledge with an extensive western view of the Nepaug Valley and Yellow Mountain.

Shelter Four Loop (see Map 20-TU-05)

LENGTH 1.0 mile   **BLAZE COLOR** Blue/Green

This trail forms a short loop when combined with the main Tunxis Trail, providing an option for a short but satisfying hike featuring streams and a mature stand of white pines.

▌ *In the northern region, the Tunxis Trail passes by or over a number of gated roads on Connecticut DEEP and MDC lands. Gates are locked in the winter when roads are impassable, usually from mid-December to mid-May. Most of these roads, however, are not open to the public at any time of year. Please respect and abide by all posted signs and regulations.*

359

▌ *Hunting is permitted in state forests intersected by this trail. Please use caution and wear orange during hunting season.*

Mileage Table

TUNXIS TRAIL

0.0	Whitman Rd (P)
1.5	Jct Stonehouse Trail (blue/red)
2.1	Jct Woodtick Trail (blue/black)
3.0	Libby's Lump / Jct Compounce Ridge Trail (blue/yellow)
3.9	Jct Bobcat Trail (blue/purple)

BREAK IN TRAIL Trail mileage continues on Map 20-TU-02 in Plymouth.

3.9	Marsh Rd
4.7	South jct Blue/White Trail (blue/white, 250 ft, P)
5.4	Jct Blue/Yellow Trail (blue/yellow)
5.6	Tory Den
6.5	Jct Greer Rd Connector (blue, 425 ft, P)
8.1	Begin roadwalk
8.1	Join Johnnycake Mountain Rd
8.2	Warren Glen (P)
8.4	Join Old Field Rd
8.5	Leave Old Field Rd (P)
8.5	End roadwalk
9.1	North jct Blue/White Trail (blue/white)
9.9	Rock Rd (P)
10.9	Ct Rte 4 (P)
11.8	Begin roadwalk—Covey Rd

12.0   End roadwalk—Covey Rd

12.2   Jct Hotchkiss Rd Connector (blue, 330 ft, P)

15.6   Begin roadwalk—Southeast Rd

15.9   End roadwalk—Southeast Rd

16.1   Begin roadwalk—US Rte 202

16.3   End roadwalk—US Rte 202 (P)

16.8   Tunxis Trl Rd

17.2   Begin roadwalk

  17.2   Join Satans Kingdom Rd / South jct Tipping Rock Loop (blue/yellow)

  17.6   South jct Shelter Four Trail (blue/green)

  18.4   North jct Shelter Four Trail (blue/green)

  18.6   North jct Tipping Rock Loop (blue/yellow)

  18.7   Leave Satans Kingdom Rd

18.7   End roadwalk

19.0   Begin roadwalk

19.0   Join Satans Kingdom Rd (P)

19.2   Join US Rte 44

19.5   Join Farmington River Tpke

20.0   Leave Farmington River Tpke (P)

20.0   End roadwalk

22.1   Ratlum Rd

22.5   Begin roadwalk—Ratlum Rd

22.7   End roadwalk—Ratlum Rd (P)

23.4   Spur to lookout (blue/red, 480 ft)

25.6   View

26.0   Ratlum Rd (P)

27.0   Ct Rte 219 (P)

28.1   Washington Hill Rd

29.5   Indian Council Caves

30.0   South jct Roaring Brook Campsite Loop (blue)

30.3   Join Pine Mountain Rd (closed to public)

30.8   Leave Pine Mountain Rd (closed to public)

31.4   Summit, Pine Mountain (1,391 ft)

  31.8   Pine Mountain Rd (closed to public)

35.3   Walnut Hill Rd (300 ft, P)

36.3   Balance Rock Rd

37.1   Ct Rte 20 (P)

38.2   Hurricane Brook Rd / South jct Hurricane Brook Bypass Trail (blue/yellow)

38.3   North jct Hurricane Brook Bypass Trail (blue/yellow)

39.5   Spur to state line monument (40 ft)

39.7   Pell Rd / McCarthy Rd (P)

BLUE/YELLOW TRAIL

0.0   Jct Tunxis Trail (blue)

0.3   Dam

0.9   Mile of Ledges

1.5   Begin roadwalk

  1.5   Join Greer Rd (P)

  1.7   Join W Chippens Hill Rd

  1.8   Leave W Chippens Hill Rd (P)

1.8   End roadwalk

2.1   View

2.3   E Chippens Hill Rd

2.4   Jct Nature Center Connector (blue/black)

3.4   Jct Blue/Orange Trail (blue/orange)

4.4   Sessions Woods Ed. Center (P)

4.5   Ct Rte 69

5.2   Jct Blue/Orange Trail (blue/orange)

5.9   Jct Blue/Green Trail (blue/green)

6.7   Jct Blue/Green Trail (blue/orange)

6.8   Begin roadwalk—Stone Rd / Jct Blue/Red South Trail (blue/red)

7.0   End roadwalk—Stone Rd

7.5   George Washington Tpke / South jct Punch Brook Trail (blue/purple)

7.9   Punch Brook Rd

8.8   North jct Punch Brook Trail (blue/purple)

9.0   Jct Blue/White Trail (blue/white)

9.3   Ct Rte 4 (P)

BLUE/WHITE TRAIL

0.0   South jct Tunxis Trail (blue)

0.0   Begin roadwalk—E Plymouth Rd (P)

0.4   End roadwalk—E Plymouth Rd

1.0   Stephen Graves Foundation

1.8   Begin roadwalk—Blueberry Hill Rd (P)

2.8   End roadwalk—Blueberry Hill Rd

5.4   Johnnycake Mountain Rd

6.2   North jct Tunxis Trail (blue)

7.1   Ct Rte 69

8.1   Cornwall Rd

8.2   Jct Blue/Green Trail (blue/green)

8.8   George Washington Tpke
9.9   Jct Blue/Yellow Trail (blue/yellow)

COMPOUNCE RIDGE TRAIL

0.0   Jct Tunxis Trail (blue)
0.6   Jct Steep Climb Trail (blue/red)
1.4   South jct Bobcat Trail (blue/purple)
1.6   South jct Compounce Cascade Trail (blue/red)
1.7   North jct Bobcat Trail (blue/purple)
2.2   North jct Compounce Cascade Trail (blue/red)
4.5   Ct Rte 229 (P)

BLUE/ORANGE TRAIL

0.0   Jct Blue/Yellow Trail (blue/yellow)
0.5   E Chippens Hill Rd
0.7   Ct Rte 69 / Scoville Rd
1.4   Jct Blue/Yellow Trail (blue/yellow)
2.2   Devil's Kitchen
3.0   Jct Blue/Yellow Trail (blue/yellow)

NATURE CENTER CONNECTOR

0.0   Barnes Nature Center / Shrub Rd (P)
0.8   S Main St
1.0   Ct Rte 69
2.4   View
2.5   Jct Blue/Yellow Trail (blue/yellow)

BLUE/RED NORTH TRAIL

0.0   Jct Punch Brook Trail (blue/purple)
0.1   Begin roadwalk—Ryans Way (P)
0.2   End roadwalk—Ryans Way
1.3   End of trail

PUNCH BROOK TRAIL

0.0   South jct Blue/Yellow Trail (blue/yellow)
0.4   Punch Brook Rd
0.7   Jct Blue/Red North Trail (blue/red)
1.5   North jct Blue/Yellow Trail (blue/yellow)

TIPPING ROCK LOOP

0.0   South jct Tunxis Trail (blue)
1.2   Jct Valley Overlook Trail (blue/white)
1.3   Tipping Rock
2.0   North jct Tunxis Trail (blue)

BOBCAT TRAIL

0.0   Jct Tunxis Trail (blue)
0.4   South jct Compounce Ridge Trail (blue/yellow)
0.7   North jct Compounce Ridge Trail (blue/yellow)

COMPOUNCE CASCADE TRAIL

0.0   Lake Ave
0.2   South jct Compounce Ridge Trail (blue/yellow)
1.1   North jct Compounce Ridge Trail (blue/yellow)

WOODTICK TRAIL

0.0   Woodtick Rd (P)
0.9   Jct Stonehouse Trail (blue/red)
1.5   Jct Tunxis Trail (blue)

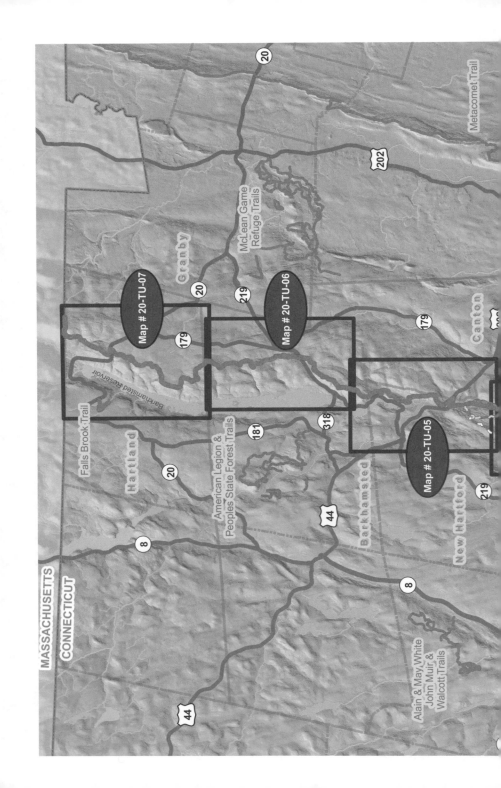

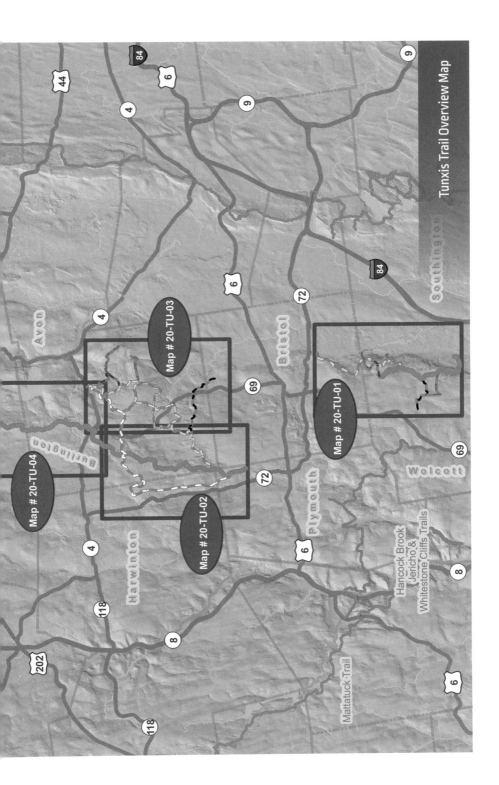

Tunxis Trail Overview Map

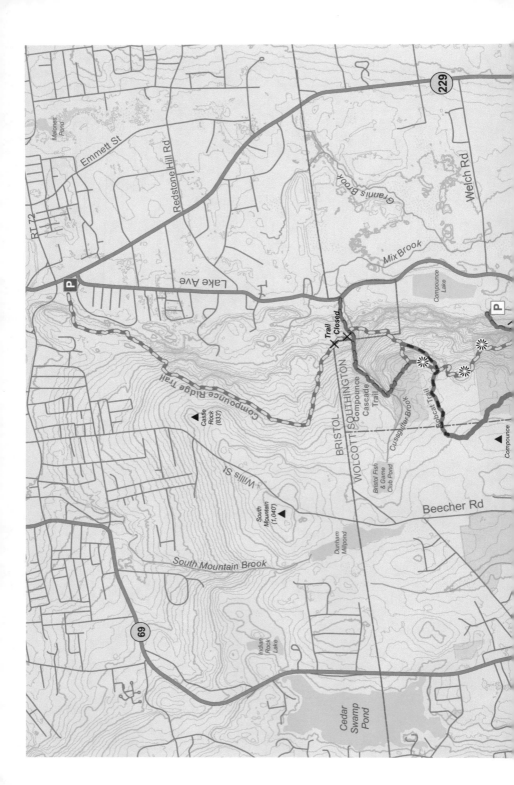

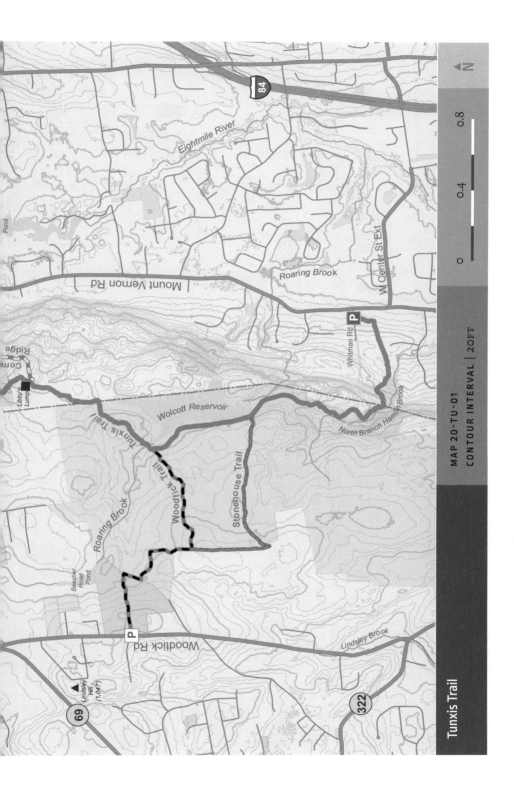

Tunxis Trail

MAP 20-TU-01
CONTOUR INTERVAL | 20FT

N

0   0.4   0.8

Eightmile River

Roaring Brook

Mount Vernon Rd

Com
Ridge

Libby's
Lump

Wolcott Reservoir

Tunxis Trail

Roaring Brook

Woodtick Trail

Stonehouse Trail

North Branch Hamlin Brook

W Center St Ext

Whitman Rd

Beecher
Road
Pond

Woodtick Rd

Lindsley Brook

Lindsley
Hill
(1,047)

Pond

84

69

322

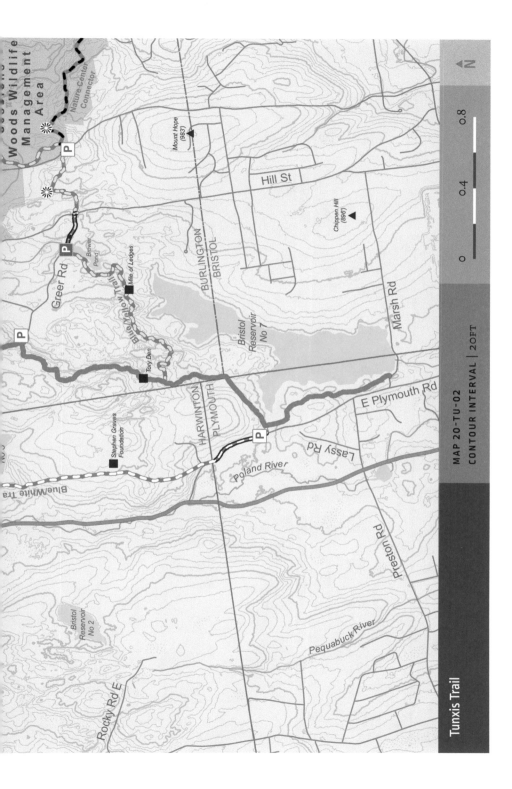

Woods Wildlife
Management
Area

Nature Center
Connector

P

Greer Rd

P

Brewer
Pond

Mile of Ledges

Blue/Yellow Trail

Tory Den

Mount Hope
(983)

BURLINGTON
BRISTOL

Hill St

Chippen Hill
(896)

Bristol
Reservoir
No 7

Marsh Rd

P

E Plymouth Rd

HARWINTON
PLYMOUTH

Stephen Graves
Foundation

Blue/White Tra

Poland River

P

Lassy Rd

Bristol
Reservoir
No 2

Rocky Rd E

Pequabuck River

Preston Rd

N

0   0.4   0.8

Tunxis Trail

MAP 20-TU-02
CONTOUR INTERVAL | 20FT

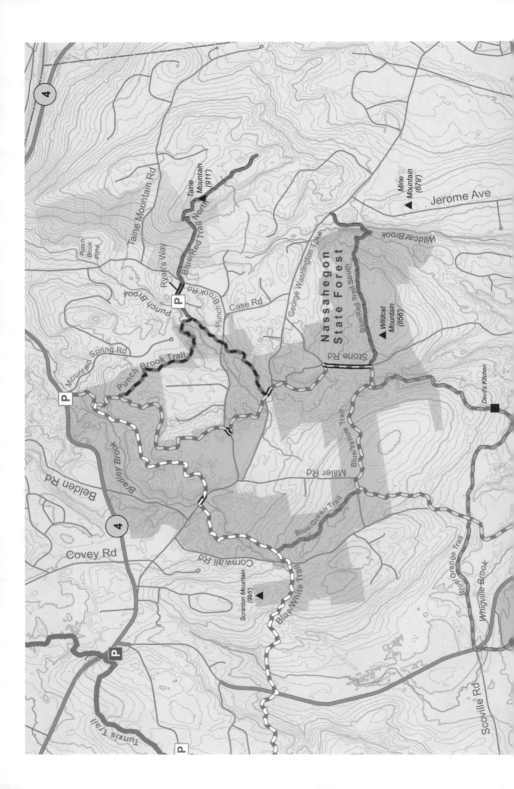

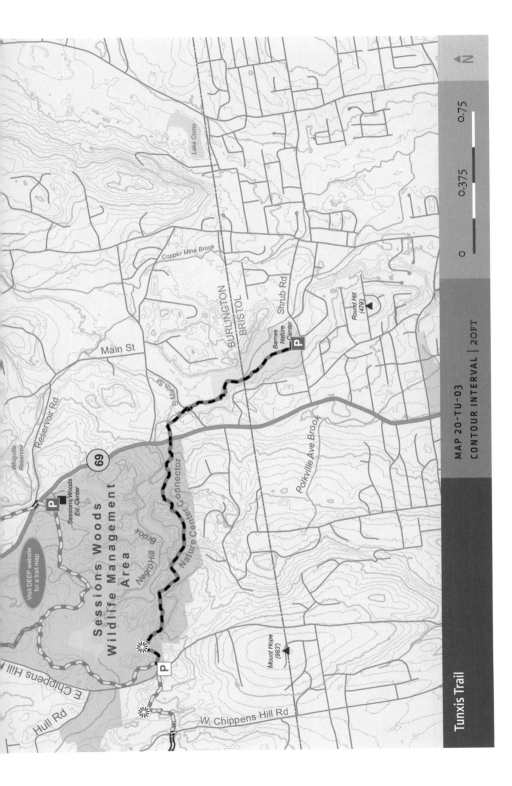

Tunxis Trail

MAP 20-TU-03
CONTOUR INTERVAL | 20FT

N

0   0.375   0.75

Sessions Woods
Wildlife Management
Area

Whigville Reservoir

Reservoir Rd

Sessions Woods
Ed. Center

69

Negro Hill Brook

Nature Center Connector

E Chippens Hill

Hull Rd

W. Chippens Hill Rd

Mount Hope
(937)

Main St

Swamp St

BURLINGTON
BRISTOL

Copper Mine Brook

Lake Como

Barnes
Nature
Center

Shrub Rd

Round Hill
(479)

Polkville Ave Brook

Visit DEEP website
for a trail map

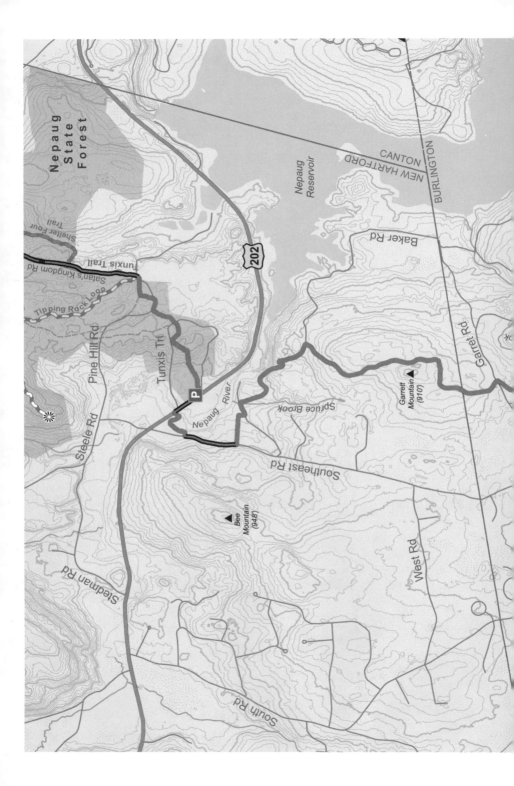

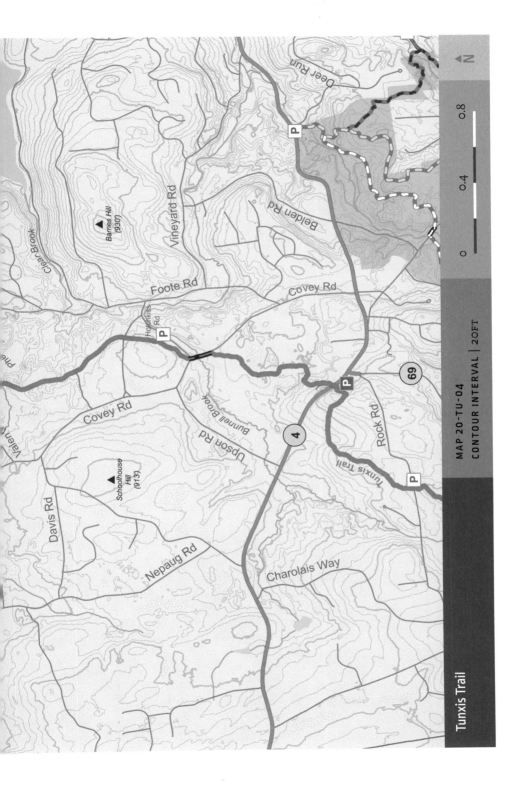

Tunxis Trail

MAP 20-TU-04
CONTOUR INTERVAL | 20FT

N

0   0.4   0.8

Barnes Hill
(930)

Schoolhouse
Hill
(913)

Clear Brook

Vineyard Rd

Foote Rd

Hotchkiss Rd

Covey Rd

Covey Rd

Upson Rd

Bunnell Brook

Davis Rd

Nepaug Rd

Charolais Way

Belden Rd

Deer Run

Rock Rd

Tunxis Trail

4

69

P

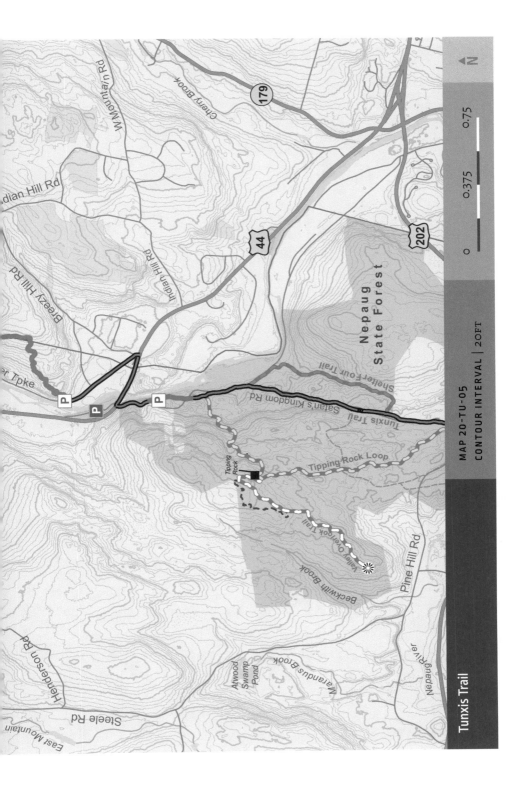

Tunxis Trail

MAP 20-TU-05
CONTOUR INTERVAL | 20FT

0   0.375   0.75

N

179

44

202

Nepaug
State Forest

W Mountain Rd

Cherry Brook

Indian Hill Rd

Breezy Hill Rd

Indian Hill Rd

P

P

P

Shelter Four Trail

Satan's Kingdom Rd

Tunxis Trail

Tipping Rock Loop

Tipping
Rock

Valley Overlook Trail

Beckwith Brook

Pine Hill Rd

Nepaug River

Marandus Brook

Atwood
Swamp
Pond

Steele Rd

Henderson Rd

East Mountain

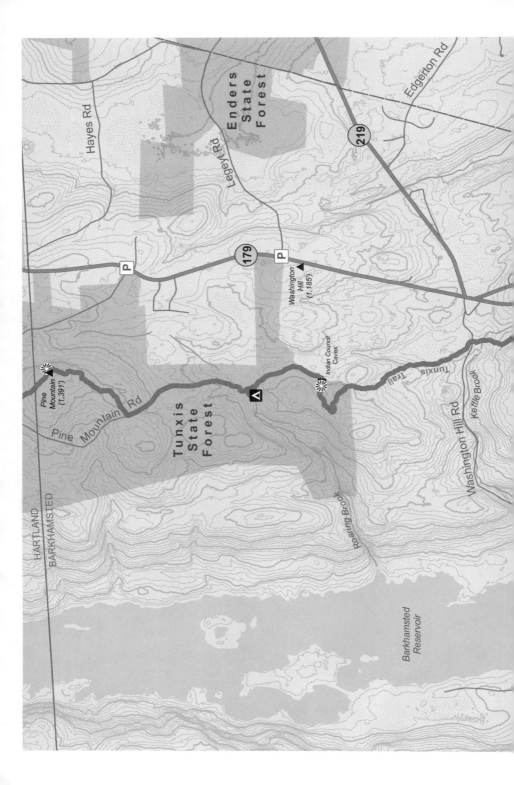

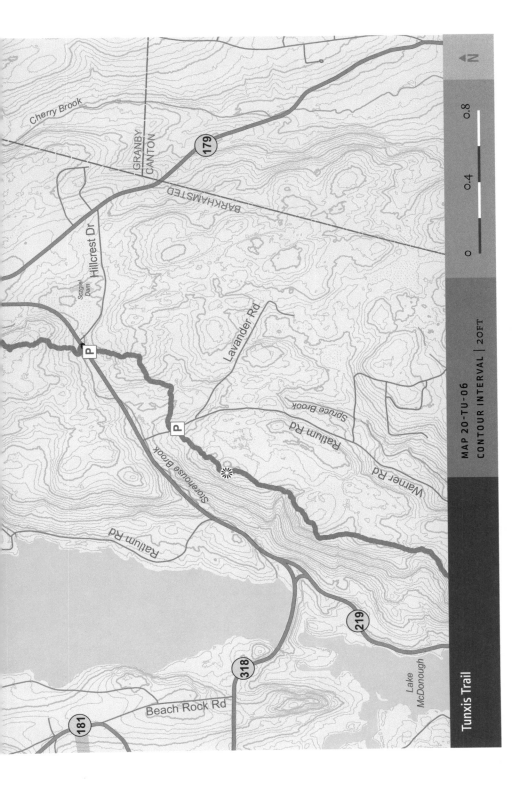

Tunxis Trail

MAP 20-TU-06
CONTOUR INTERVAL | 20FT

0   0.4   0.8

N

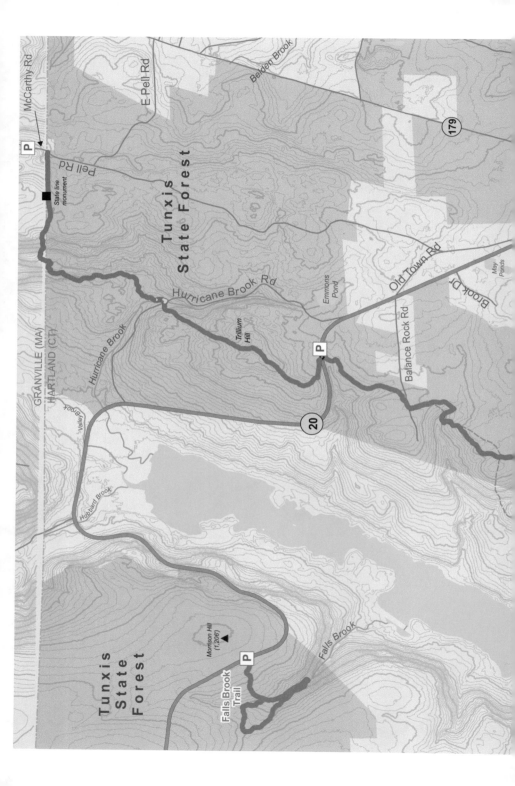

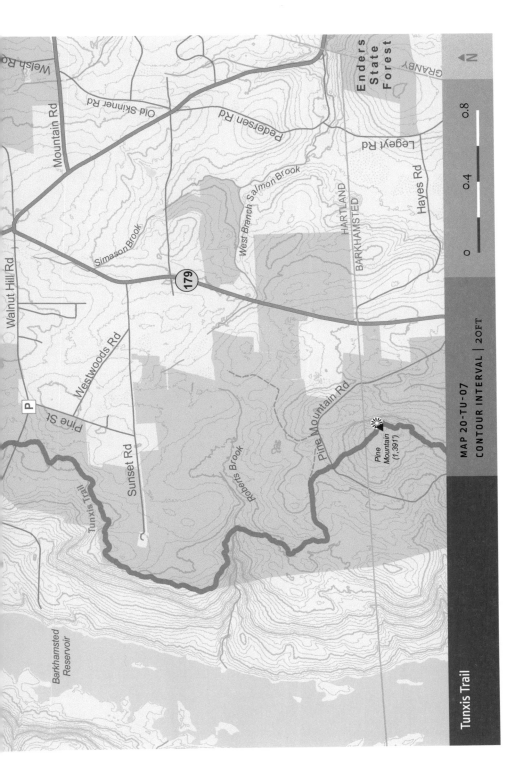

Tunxis Trail

MAP 20-TU-07
CONTOUR INTERVAL | 20FT

0   0.4   0.8

N

Enders
State
Forest

GRANBY

Welsh Rd

Mountain Rd

Old Skinner Rd

Pedersen Rd

Legeyt Rd

Hayes Rd

HARTLAND

BARKHAMSTED

West Branch Salmon Brook

Simason Brook

179

Walnut Hill Rd

P

Westwoods Rd

Pine St

Sunset Rd

Tunxis Trail

Roberts Brook

Pine Mountain Rd

Pine
Mountain
(1,391')

Barkhamsted
Reservoir

Index

379

Connecticut's Parks and Forests Are Waiting ... for You!

Many thanks to the Connecticut Department of Energy and Environmental Protection's Trails Program for its leadership support of Connecticut's Blue-Blazed Trails.

Design and printing of the 20th edition of the *Connecticut Walk Book* funded in part by the members and partners of the Connecticut Forest & Park Association.

Dedicated to
Philip H. Jones, Jr.
1918-2015

Philip Jones was a man in love with life amongst the trees of Connecticut.

As a teenager in the 1930s, he planted trees on the family dairy farm in Shelton to fulfill requirements for his UCONN 4H project. The initial plan was for soil restoration and timber production, but by 1947 friends and neighbors were asking to buy the beautiful conifers for Christmas trees.

While in 4H, he also joined the Connecticut Forest & Park Association and remained active until his passing, 80 years later.

Philip loved to hike through our state's fields and forests. He said, "These walks always renew my spirits!"

As you seek the joy and renewal of your spirits while hiking our blue-blazed trails, think of Phil Jones – a gentle man who loved the forests and hiking paths of Connecticut.

Photo Credit: Robert Pagini

Give to sustain your trails…and bask in the glow of your generosity.

Give a bequest or designate CFPA as one of your IRA, pension, or life insurance beneficiaries.

Make a Planned Gift to CFPA – call today at 860-346-TREE (8733).